LEADING
YOUR PEOPLE
TO SUCCESS

LEADING
YOUR PEOPLE
TO SUCCESS
BY GUIDING CORPORATE CULTURE CHANGE

NICK KITCHIN

THE McGRAW-HILL COMPANIES
London · Burr Ridge IL · New York · St Louis · San Francisco · Auckland
Bogatá · Caracas · Lisbon · Madrid · Mexico · Milan
Montreal · New Delhi · Panama · Paris · San Juan · São Paulo
Singapore · Sydney · Tokyo · Toronto

Leading your people to success: by guiding corporate change
Nick Kitchin

0077098692

Published by McGraw-Hill Professional

Shoppenhangers Road
Maidenhead
Berkshire
SL6 2QL
Telephone: 44 (0) 1628 502 500
Fax: 44 (0) 1628 770 224
Website: www.mcgraw-hill.co.uk

British Library Cataloguing in Publication Data
A catalogue record for this book is available from the British Library

Library of Congress Cataloguing in Publication Data
The Library of Congress data for this book is available from the Library of Congress

Sponsoring Editor: Elizabeth Robinson
Editorial Assistant: Sarah Butler
Business Marketing Manager: Elizabeth McKeever
Senior Production Manager: Max Elvey
Production Editor: Eleanor Hayes

Produced for McGraw-Hill by Gray Publishing, Tunbridge Wells
Printed and bound in the UK by Clays Ltd, St Ives plc
Cover design by Simon Levy Associates

McGraw-Hill books are available at special quantity discounts. Please contact the
Corporate Sales executive at the above address.

Contents

This book is dedicated to Brian Jansen whose presence, principles and beliefs created the very soul of our company culture.

Acknowledgements

I wish to thank the many thousands of people who have directly or indirectly contributed to this book: employees, managers and directors who have taken their company through successful culture change programmes; particularly those organisations that are open enough to take part in the Inside UK Enterprise scheme. These host companies open their doors to business visitors, including direct competitors as well as customers. The idea is to help spread 'best practice', a driving motive that also applies to writing this book. Jennifer Jenkins, and her team at Inside UK Enterprise, played a key role in helping me visit successful culture change companies throughout the UK; companies who subsequently agreed to be case studies for the benefit of other organisation leaders around the world.

For the case study companies, I would like to start with British Airways and their Putting People First Again team who gave me a wonderful day on this programme at Waterside. Barbie Birdseye deserves particular thanks, not only for her considerable help with the British Airways case study, but also for her infectious enthusiasm for the company culture.

Thanks also to Jane Hirst, of Mortgage Express, who is another true culture change champion; so much so that I know you will enjoy reading how she and her team transformed the company en route to winning the UK Quality Award.

At Simon Jersey, my thanks go to Mavis Gradwell, Richard Mullen and Anne Baldwin for creating their inspirational company culture; and also to Mark Fitzmaurice of Dale Carnegie, for his section on developing leaders.

David Stanley of Wates Group deserves a special mention for agreeing to support me, particularly in the early days of my venture.

Two people, Vince Lachowycz and Andy Watts, opened up about the strategy and trust required for annualised hours at Colman's of Norwich. I suspect many leaders, as well as me, will soon be indebted to the Colman's team.

Fred McDonogh, together with his joint union/management team and support from ACAS, masterminded the introduction of self-managed teams at Alcan Foil Europe – Glasgow. The visit I attended turned out to be one of the most heartfelt and open I have experienced, and the self-managed teams obviously appreciated the results of 'Agreement 2000'. Thanks Fred.

Thanks too, to Ruth Spellman, from Investors in People UK, who kindly helped with her support of this case study.

My return visit to Shell Chemicals was a great trip down memory lane for me! Many thanks to you all, as without that experience to demonstrate what is possible, this book may never have been written.

Visiting IBM Greenock felt like a two-day induction programme, as I met too many people to mention everyone individually! I would, however, like to thank two people in particular; Selina Boustred, who co-ordinated the visit and never raised an eye-brow despite my persistent demands for information, and Charlie Morrison who lead the site transformation from manufacturing to service, making the whole case study possible.

From the publishing perspective, Elizabeth Robinson and Sarah Butler at McGraw-Hill did a sterling job; coaching, suggesting improvements to both structure and contents, and generally supporting me through the year-long project. Elizabeth and Sarah, I really enjoyed working with you and thank you for making the book significantly better through your input.

Lastly, but definitely not least, I include a heartfelt thanks to my wife Anne and son James. For James, who put up with me spending many a long day in the office with the door closed, when he would have preferred me to play trains with him; and to Anne for her continued support, faith, and enthusiasm, not to mention proof-reading, as the book began to take shape.

I thank you all for making this book possible.

Preface

In anticipation of your journey through this book I would like to give you some background to its *origins* and *purpose*, so you can understand my own motivation for writing it and better appreciate how some of my personal experiences and those of my colleagues' result in the ability to provide you not only with a *strategy* for, but also a *practical guide* to 'Leading Your People To Success'. Let's start with the origins.

When I joined Shell Chemicals as an engineering graduate back in the early 1980s, little did I realise I would soon be exposed to major cultural changes encouraged by the drive for profitability improvements in the middle of the chemical industry's worst recession for a decade. I remember the Carrington site where I was employed being described by a Shell executive as a 'dog' in the Shell organisation. At that time the 'in' terminology referred to companies as 'dogs', 'cash cows', 'stars' or 'wildcats' depending on which quadrant the company fitted in the growth/share matrix.[1] 'Dogs' were in the worst quadrant as they had a relatively small share of low-growth markets and therefore needed to be turned around to become cash generators, or be disposed of.

Under this threat, the aim was to transform the 'dog' into a 'star'; to turn Carrington into a business with a relatively large share of high-growth markets, in other words to make the site profitable. What transpired was later termed a blueprint for other sites in Shell. A truly inspirational strategy was implemented with military precision and considerable sympathy for the people affected by the change programme. In terms of a *cultural change* this has got to be one of the most radical ever undertaken in British industry.

To give you an idea of the scale, the employees reduced from around 1300 to 600 through a redundancy programme backed up by retraining and outplacement, virtually half the site production plant was decommissioned and demolished, organisational structures changed from matrix to profit centres, a single-union agreement was reached in conjunction with a massive training programme for the remaining multi-skilled technicians, and the site turned round from being a cash drain to one of the most profitable in the Shell group.

At the time I felt really privileged to have experienced this dramatic culture change as well as completing my own personal professional training programme and gaining my initial people-management exposure under the watchful and supportive eyes of far more experienced foremen and managers. It fuelled my interest in the people aspects of managing a business, it showed me what could be done, and with this enthusiasm and experience under my belt I left Shell to study full-time for a Master's degree in Business Administration (MBA) at London Business School.

London Business School introduced me to the latest thoughts of people like Michael Porter[1] on how to analyse businesses and competitive markets. I also had the fortune to be lectured by gurus on strategic management like Gary Hamel.[2] Paul Willman also came up trumps and introduced me to the importance of culture through the book *In Search of Excellence* by Tom Peters and Robert Waterman,[3] which is all about how companies with a strong culture excel.

After London Business School I spent some time starting my own business and management consultancy, as well as joining a couple of companies. One of these firms had a particularly destructive, blame culture that became evident shortly after starting with the firm as an employee. Of course, although tough at the time, this now makes it easier for me to compare a blame culture with the cultural requirements for motivation and success.

Then I had a stroke of luck. Attracted by the descriptions of the company culture, I joined the UK firm Carpenter Ltd. The American parent, Carpenter Co., is a privately owned $1 billion turnover business that very few people have heard of, yet millions of people in the USA, Canada, and Europe are either walking or sitting on Carpenter's products of carpet underlay or the foam/fibre in upholstered furniture. Carpenter Ltd was bought by Carpenter Co. in 1990 and since then has gone through a major transformation with disposals of non-core businesses and a tremendous investment programme. Behind this focus and investment strategy began the cultural transformation towards continuous improvement. I joined the company in 1995 as plant manager and later, general manager, with the brief to help drive the Glossop site continuous improvement and to be a key member of the management team for the company as a whole.

The key reason this book can be written is because of the practical experience the Carpenter team and I have been through in developing the very special continuous improvement culture that reached its peak in 1997, together with recognition of the Glossop site as an Investor in People in the same year. Since then market conditions dictated that we reduce the number of employees, cut overheads and reduce significantly the time and resources available for continuous improvement. We therefore let certain good points drift and had to recapture them again later. In 2000 we were recognised once again as an Investor in People, this time across the whole UK company. This book, particularly the Continuous Improvement section, includes practical examples of cultural change implemented at Carpenter.

In 2001 I established my own consultancy firm called Leading Your People To Success Ltd, which focuses on guiding corporate culture change; hence the book's title.

Since the benefit of cultural change applies in *all* industries, this book also contains case studies about companies in the banking, construction, airline, computer, food, clothing, manufacturing and, of course, petrochemical sectors. All are well-known companies that have already been through cultural change. All tell you their stories for you to learn from. All focus on different aspects of culture change. 'All' includes British Airways, Mortgage Express, and Colman's of Norwich; plus Wates Group, IBM Greenock, Simon Jersey, Alcan Foil Europe – Glasgow, and an update on Carrington. There is also a chapter about Investors in People UK, which has helped over five million people change their working culture through the Investors in People Standard.

Leading Your People To Success is a result of the above experiences.

This book is principally aimed at chief executive officers, managing directors and general managers; people at the top of their company. It also applies to everyone with autonomy in their organisation, everyone who manages their own site, branch, division or department. This includes everyone who influences their own sub-culture, indeed everyone who manages a team of people. The cultural changes discussed apply to public limited, private limited, family-owned, or owner-managed businesses, subsidiaries, and even sites within a larger company. It also extends to the public as well as private sector, service industries in addition to manufacturing, and in certain circumstances even voluntary organisations. It is aimed at leaders.

The *purpose* is to guide you through the cultural change process, to stimulate radical improvements in the way things are performed, and to enable you and your staff to create extra value for your business. Due to the nature of this process, everyone in your organisation is likely to be affected by the changes proposed. Let's look at what this book is really about at grass-roots level.

This book is about motivating your employees. It is about removing frustrations and empowering your people to think for themselves and implement their own ideas. It is about saying 'thank you' for a job well done. It is about supporting your colleagues in a trusting, helpful culture where change is the actively encouraged norm and the word 'blame' does not exist. It is about encouraging your staff to go that extra mile because they want to, not because you've asked them to. It is all about people and how your company can gain a competitive advantage through leading your people to success, where success is measured in terms of motivation as well as profits.

This book is also about communication, vertically as well as horizontally throughout your organisation. It is about giving your people permanently open channels to ask for change, so they can ask for improvements and see these requests implemented as a priority.

It is about establishing values, principles and standards plus well-defined ways of doing things. In short it is a guide to creating a strong sustainable *culture* in which your employees are happy, fulfilled and motivated so they help you drive your business forward because they know and understand where the business is going and they want to share in this success.

Introduction

Change starts when someone sees the next step. William Drayton

If you're a chief executive officer, managing director or general manager and you've been asking yourself 'How can I improve my organisation's performance?' this book is for you. You may be in a manufacturing or service industry, in a publicly or privately owned business, charity or voluntary organisation. This book is for you. If you want to find out how you can change your company culture and move your business on to a higher plane, this is *the* book for you. My aim is to make you feel as though you are holding in your hand right now the main isolator switch to turn on the fantastic progressive firework display seen at the Sydney Olympics, a series of illuminations that built up until you could see the complete structure of the Sydney harbour bridge. It is up to you whether you throw that switch and enjoy the results or simply put the book down and walk away. The contents will undoubtedly challenge you and your team, and together you will go through periods of pain and frustration during the implementation, but you and your people will come out on the other side of this process feeling invigorated, stronger and better prepared to create value for your business.

By the end of the introduction you will know the *scope* of this book and should feel it will be one of the most important you will ever read for your business; more than that, you will know that it is not just significant for your company, but also for your employees.

It doesn't matter whether you lead a manufacturing operation or service business, whether it has local, national or global markets, or even if you've differentiated your business from the competition to date by developing different channels or better technologies than those commercially available to your competition, your competitors are still out there straining forward to beat you in the market-share leapfrog race. Unless you can shoot them in the foot to keep them hopping round in ever-decreasing circles while you continue on your well-defined growth path, this race will always be close; that is until you have one sustainable competitive edge.

This edge used to be availability of funds, but you only have to consider the frenzied explosion of investment in Internet start-ups to see that this no longer applies. Also, unless you are buying better capital equipment ahead of the competition to give yourself a short-term advantage, spending money on the latest commercially available technology is a very expensive way of playing catch-up and normally only brings your strategy closer in line with your competition rather than differentiating it further. The result is likely to be a lower return on capital employed unless you work harder to produce the same returns in the future. There is only one truly sustainable competitive advantage: the quality and motivation of your people. Why? It takes years to develop a really excellent team and the team performance will only be excellent if everyone is highly motivated. It is very true to say 'motivating your people promotes performance'. The reverse also applies. For example, if your people feel sore about the way you treat them, how can you expect them to sincerely offer the best service to your customers? So how do we start to build our competitive advantage?

Transforming any profitable organisation from the 'number two' position to market leader, or to further enhance your profits and market share if you happen to already be in the fortunate position of market leader, takes a combination of leaders, managers, a highly motivated team and of course, some time! The key to this transformation is to establish a strong culture throughout the organisation, which means 'the way we do things' is known and practised daily by everyone. For the purpose of this book I have defined culture as follows:

'The way we do things that affects how our people feel and behave.'

The first and main question has got to be 'How do we achieve this cultural change?' The second is probably 'Where do we start?' The prospect of making the first step may be daunting, but the aim of this book is also to give you many tactics and tools that you can apply in your everyday working life, about how to manage cultural change. I have picked the following simple example about the culture change of a brass band, chosen deliberately even though it is not a business application, to show you how broad the culture change concept is and how widely it can be applied. If you consider the band members to be your own employees you should be able to visualise many parallels in your own organisation. In this scenario, your role would be conductor.

Imagine a championship section brass band preparing for a band contest due to take place in a few months time. The band is made up of really high-calibre musicians who can all play the notes but have their own interpretation of the style, tempo and dynamics. They are conducted by someone who simply asks the band to play the notes over and over again without interpreting the score properly, who accepts when some players turn up late or not at all so the rehearsals don't start on time, and keeps playing the one tune over and over again so the players get bored and frustrated, begin to leave and morale drops. Not surprisingly this band comes towards the bottom of the contest results table.

Then the conductor recognises the need to change and, together with key members of the band, works out a plan of changing 'the way we do things around here'. He also explains to the other band members why changes are required and what the plan consists of. New uniforms are provided, the players are told about time keeping or risk losing their place in the band, rehearsals start on time again with a full complement of players so new chords previously unheard are unlocked from the score, and the conductor introduces and tells the players about the need to follow the dynamics exactly. Suddenly there are almost inaudible pianissimo sections and rousing loud fortissimo chords and the music begins to come alive. So far all we have done is to coach the band in the basic rules of how to play the piece but we have already improved the music's quality.

Then the band enters another contest but this time the conductor takes the score away in between rehearsals and studies it meticulously. He begins to see things he hadn't been aware of before, the structure of the whole piece rather than just the notes on the page. He begins to have a vision of how the piece should sound. He communicates this to the band members who now understand what the conductor is trying to do. He can now 'mentor' the team, take them past just the rules of playing in tune at the right tempo and dynamic. Suddenly the band moves onto a new level of playing; attentive, listening, watching, even breathing at the same time in order to be completely ready to start as the conductor raises his baton to begin the piece. Each player knows what to do, what is expected of him, and trusts that his friends on the opposite side of the band will support his playing. Most of all the conductor encourages and congratulates all the players when a particular section of the contest piece begins to sparkle during rehearsal.

On the contest platform, under the spotlights and with a hushed, expectant audience, the band delivers the best performance of their lives. What a victory! What a dramatic effect the culture change has had!

It all started with the conductor deciding the culture change was necessary. This led on to developing the culture change plan with a small subset of key band members. Then came the team coaching about raising the standards required, the new uniforms that visibly signalled change, and the dismissal of one or two players who refused to practice sufficiently. The result enabled the conductor to mentor the team, and lifted the playing on to a new level. During this process the enthusiasm and dedication of the leaders filtered through to the rest of the band, raising their own commitment and team spirit, with the winning performance as the end result.

So, thinking of your business again and how to achieve this cultural change, we must first answer a few fundamental questions to be sure that a cultural change makes sense.

Why Start 'Leading Your People To Success'?

Continuous investment in your people is critical if they are to feel valued, remain with you, give you their best service and thereby reinvest back into the company your investment in them. No longer is there a job for life, and the best employees will change jobs often to rise to the top of the employment pool. Without doubt the best people produce the top performance, providing they are encouraged and coached rather than controlled by blame and fear; trained and developed rather than buried and left to rot in a bureaucratic administration glue pool; trusted and valued to enhanced levels of responsibility and confidence; and also led and talked with, rather than talked to, so they understand their role in this employment partnership. There shouldn't be whispered discussions behind closed office doors, but open presentations to all employees, whether the news is good or bad.

Another beauty about this cultural change process is that although it takes up much of your time, consider the powerful benefit of having not just one brain trying to lead from the front; with the right culture you could have everyone thinking how to improve the organisation, how to reduce costs, how to make life better; in short – helping you to make the company more successful.

Consider too, that part of this culture change process benchmarks your organisation against the best; not necessarily in your industry because in the proverbial pastures new there is often a different kind of grass, new techniques and new ways of doing things. The book *Who Moved My Cheese?*[1] indicates what happens if you simply sit back, enjoy your current comfort, and refuse to find new opportunities, new customers, new capacity, and ever improved levels of customer service. The corporate graveyard is littered with derelict buildings devoid of people, where the 'leaders' have refused to lead their people to pastures new, let alone to 'success'.

Also there are two key parties interested in your culture change; your shareholders and your employees. Your shareholders, who are looking for a decent and improving return on their investment, and your employees, whose lives, livelihood and career depend on the business's success. The other directly affected groups, your suppliers and customers, are beneficiaries of the culture change rather than drivers. Customers, for example, are attracted because they can rely on you, trust you and enjoy working with you as their supplier; which is why a strong culture that gives excellent customer service together with great employee attitude and behaviour are so critical.

What Do We Mean By 'Leading Your People To Success'?

Put succinctly it is 'Guiding Corporate Culture Change' through the five steps of:

Benchmarking – Planning – Investing – Improving – Reviewing.

This book focuses on what needs to be completed to establish a strong culture, along with practical examples of how to foster this success. Most important of all, it recommends how to integrate all these individual culture-defining elements into an open, friendly, and highly motivational working environment. The book's title, *Leading Your People To Success*, reflects the importance of people in the daily management of your business.

Let's look at where we are heading with *Leading Your People To Success*. Let's create a picture of the future. Let's call it our 'Vision of Success'.

Imagine the following scene of an open plan office, light and airy with everyone within a few metres of windows. Standing up from your desk, located in the middle of the office, you sweep your gaze around the room and can see all your staff. At each end of the office is a series of glass-fronted meeting rooms; there are no offices for individuals. At the entrance is a small, but attractive, informal rest area where people from any part of the company come to drink and swap news – it's amazing how much informal communication goes on there. Large pot plants break up the rigid lines of desks, laptops and portable phones (so you can be contacted at work regardless of location). The wall-mounted TV screen keeps everyone up to date with the latest company news via the intranet, and everyone has his or her own personal e-mail address. Communication is so good that everyone knows what is going on without having to ask.

Everyone is happy, motivated and surprisingly relaxed; there is a good balance between the needs of work and family life. Everyone is staff status and on first name terms.

On the walls where plenty of people pass daily, are the company Mission, Vision, Value and Strategy statements; together with this quarter's objectives and team Key Performance Indicators as decided by each team, not by management.

As the business is now an e-business, even training is done via the Internet and intranet, at the convenience of each individual. You note that efficiency and output are up again; innovation and continuous improvement just seem to keep happening without the need for regular re-launches of 'new' initiatives; there are leaders throughout the company, not just at the top, and excellence is the standard expected, especially for every experience our customers have when they interact with the company. You read the latest customer feedback received via your customer service desk; an e-mail that mentions how pleased this customer is with the latest delivery and the great attitude of the delivery driver. Nothing special, but it's good to see anyway.

You had a meeting earlier on today with someone writing a book about the company, someone who asked if he could speak to some of your staff about what it is like to work for the company. You smile, as you remember their answers: 'Dynamic!' 'Previously you had to give everyone the information [about how the company was performing]. Now you can spend time discussing the information [as everyone knows how the company is performing].' 'Everything keeps changing.' 'I am really proud to work here.'

Perhaps we have got a few things right but we've still got a long way to go. Must get on ... .

How Do We Start 'Leading Your People To Success'?

This book will guide you through the principles, introduce practical ideas, and lay down the interlocking crazy paving of culture to create your 'people path' to success.

We'll start by 'Benchmarking Your Success', using the characteristics of 'poor performance' and 'success' cultures. You can quickly and easily assess where your company lies on the cultural scale now, and identify areas to focus on throughout the rest of the book. There is also a concise, easy to complete questionnaire, which should provoke much thought by identifying themes you may not have considered before. The more questions you can honestly say yes to, the closer your organisation is to a Success Culture.

Throughout the book are 'Case Studies of Success', as I want to excite you and give you ideas for your own organisation to implement. All the case study firms are examples of 'best practice' successful cultural change. All, apart from Investors in People and Shell Chemicals, are also host companies for the Inside UK Enterprise scheme, whose primary aim is to help spread best practice. The case study companies are all international businesses, many are household names, and they come from a specially selected diverse range of service and manufacturing industries to provide a broad spectrum of interest for the readers. Each case study has its own theme, general principles that can be applied elsewhere, and a 'Summary Action List for Your Business'.

In the second section, called 'Planning Future Success', we'll identify the steps required for Leading Your Culture Change. We'll guide you through preparing your Mission, Vision and Values that everyone lives by. Then we'll introduce the Strategic Business Plan, Quarterly Objectives and Key Performance Indicators, show the link between these three, and the importance of communicating these plans to the whole organisation.

Thirdly, 'Investing In Success' introduces the 'Culture Champion' and covers five other areas associated with implementing culture change; raising standards, training, changing attitudes, the 'walk round', and making work fun.

The fourth section, 'Improving Your Success', looks at how to initiate and stimulate continuous improvement. We will uncover the workings of suggestion schemes to help you change from 'we've tried that before but it failed' to a series of open scheme principles. These should result in a significant percentage of your team putting forward and implementing suggestions as visible evidence of their ability to change the working environment. This section will also give you ideas on how to develop a safety culture by continuously reducing your accident levels at work (which is probably most relevant to a manufacturing or other non-office environment).

Finally we shall be 'Reviewing Your Success' to ensure you have truly been leading your people to success. This brings the whole subject of culture change together, including lessons learned from the case studies, and summarises in a one-page figure what constitutes the *Leading Your People To Success* model.

So now we're at the start of a journey into the unknown, a path no longer defined by or based on pure extrapolation, investment, and unit cost reduction. It's a people path to a strong culture. Have you got the courage to proceed along this culture change journey? Can you look your employees in the eye tomorrow and say, 'Let's Do It!'?

I invite you now to start Leading Your People To Success.

Part 1

Benchmarking
Your Success

Chapter 1

Benchmarking Your Current Culture

To know which direction to go in, you have to know where you want to get to; but first you have to know where you are.

You are about to measure your organisation against some of the best in the world. This section will help you assess where your company culture is today, and to benchmark your organisation against those firms operating current 'best practice'.

The benchmarking section is deliberately constructed to include just one figure and one questionnaire for you to complete. You will also doubtless be pleased to know that these two items should take you just a few minutes, as it is your initial view rather than an in-depth analysis that is important at this stage. There are two copies of each figure and questionnaire, one in this section and a further copy in Appendix 1. The second copy allows you, if you wish, to ask these questions of a number of your employees to see if their answers match yours. If they do not, you might like to find out why!

The first step is to benchmark your current culture using Figure 1.1 as the guide. There are two columns with lines drawn between. The left-hand column describes a 'poor performance culture' where the employees are de-motivated and will only do what they have to do, rather than what they are capable of achieving. The right-hand column indicates the cultural characteristics of a company with a 'success culture'; one that positively encourages its employees to perform well with a supporting hand rather than a big stick. Across the top of Figure 1.1 is a scale numbered from 1 to 9. To complete this benchmarking assessment, all

BENCHMARK YOUR CURRENT CULTURE									
Poor Performance Culture	1	2	3	4	5	6	7	8	9	**Success Culture**
Us and them										Equality
Blame/fear culture										Coaching/supportive culture
No leadership										Competent leaders
No vision										Mission, vision and values
No teamwork										Cohesive teams
No time for continuous improvement										Time for continuous improvement is designed into the working day
Focus is on urgent rather than important tasks										Focus is on important rather than urgent tasks
Working to live										Living to work
We have always done it this way. Innovation cannot be started!										Things are always changing and continuously improving. Innovation cannot be suppressed!
Parent/child relationship										Adult to adult trust
'I am not sure we can do that' attitude										'Can-do' attitude
Autocratic control at the top										Responsibility and accountability accepted and thriving at lowest levels in the organisation
Rumours (grapevine) are main communication channel										Excellent, regular, top-down communication with feedback expected/encouraged
Inward focus										Customer focus

Figure 1.1. Benchmark your current culture

you need to do is decide where on the scale your firm is for each pair of statements and then mark this point with a cross.

As an example, for the 'us and them vs equality' scale, if you treat the directors the same as the rest of your employees (Examples might be single status canteen or restaurant; everyone wears the same 'uniform'; directors are in the middle of an open plan office next to their staff; no company cars; no allocated car parking spaces for directors, and so on.) then your score will be 8 or 9. If there is a distinct 'us and them' then your score will be 1 or 2. Mark the relevant score with a cross.

Similarly, for the 'blame/fear culture vs coaching/supportive culture' scale, if there is regular 'finger pointing' in order to blame someone for doing something wrong, where people are scared of making a decision in case it is the wrong decision, your score should be 1 or 2. If, however, people make a mistake but have tried their best and the time is spent finding out how to prevent the same mistake from being made again, without allocating blame to an individual, then your score will be heading towards the 8 or 9 mark again. The rest of the statements should be self-explanatory, but I have put examples in Appendix 1 to help you decide your score for each pair of statements.

The aim is to see how close you consider the culture of your company to be to that of a success culture. Obviously the ratings are subjective, but as a guide any score of 5 or below in any one attribute should raise a 'need to change' flag for you. We will be covering how to help move your company towards the success culture throughout this book.

After scoring your company against 'Benchmark your current culture', you might like to test the concept validity by repeating the process but this time as if you are chief executive officer of, say, McDonalds or Disney. I have picked these two simply because they are global businesses with consumer markets, where your experience as a customer within a McDonalds, or Disney (especially Disneyland, Disney World or Euro Disney) should be a fair reflection of their culture. You may not be able to score every aspect with great knowledge, but those that you are confident about should be up in the 8 or 9 area every time. Are these other companies successful in your eyes? Are the scores for your business similar, or different in specific aspects? Are they doing something that you are not?

Let us next move on to the 'Are you leading your people to success?' benchmark questionnaire. This questionnaire has 11 sections looking at the key facets that underpin the end result, your actual company culture. Each question summarises and encapsulates a whole subject area covered in the following chapters and case studies. This questionnaire therefore gives you a good indication and flavour of what is to come later in the book. It also asks some specific questions about you and your attitude towards your employees; significant questions where the answers make a huge difference to your company's culture. Be honest with yourself when completing this questionnaire, and again you might like to ask your employees what they think. Mentally put McDonalds and Disney through this process too. In general terms, the more answers you can say 'yes' to, the higher your score is likely to be on 'Benchmark your current culture' (Figure 1.1). Again, any questions you have answered 'no' to are worth noting for special attention later in the book.

'Are you leading your people to success?' **benchmark questionnaire**	Yes	No

The aim of this questionnaire is to help you identify if you are already 'leading your people to success', by assessing key components of the cultural jigsaw. If so, you should be able to honestly answer 'yes' to most of these questions. Any 'no' answers will flag possible areas for improvement through cultural change, which we can mentally note as we go through the following chapters and case studies. You may wish to tick your answers for future reference.

1. External benchmarking
   (a) Do you benchmark your business culture against other ❑ ❑
       firms operating 'best practice'?
   (b) Have you assessed your organisation against the European ❑ ❑
       Foundation of Quality Management (EFQM®) Excellence
       Model in the past 12 months?
   (c) Are you recognised as an Investor in People? ❑ ❑
   (d) Is your absenteeism below two per cent? ❑ ❑
   (e) Is your staff turnover less than your industry average? ❑ ❑

2. Strategy
   (a) Have you identified your mission, vision and values ❑ ❑
   (b) Do you have a written strategic business plan that ❑ ❑
       shows a per cent return on capital employed
       (ROCE) and per cent profit before interest and
       tax (PBIT) > per cent cost of capital?

3. Communication
   (a) Do all your employees know the company strategy ❑ ❑
       and their part in it?
   (b) Do you ask your employees their opinions in an annual ❑ ❑
       survey, feed back their responses and act on their
       suggestions?
   (c) Are you visible to your employees by a daily walk-round ❑ ❑
       and by locating your workplace in the middle of open plan
       offices rather than a separate office?

    (d) Do you have volunteers from all levels in the organisation to   ❑   ❑
        broadcast the company strategy, mission, vision and values?

    (e) Do you encourage social interaction during rest   ❑   ❑
        periods by providing suitable facilities?

    (f) Are e-mails used only to pass on important information
        and to ask vital questions where face-to-face or
        telephone conversations are impractical?

    (g) Are you able to focus on the important rather than the   ❑   ❑
        urgent items in your in-tray?

4. Physical environment

    (a) Do you have open plan offices?   ❑   ❑

    (b) Do you provide single status areas for work, rest, eat   ❑   ❑
        and play?

    (c) Is the site/working environment clean?   ❑   ❑

    (d) Is it easy for visitors to find their way to reception?   ❑   ❑

    (e) Is car parking space on a first come first served basis   ❑   ❑
        rather than designated?

5. Goal alignment

    (a) Do you have quarterly objectives and individual   ❑   ❑
        key performance indicators (KPIs)?

    (b) Are all your employees salaried (and/or working   ❑   ❑
        annualised hours)?

6. Continuous improvement

    (a) Do you have a continuous improvement culture that is   ❑   ❑
        alive and well?

    (b) Do you have a suggestion scheme that works?   ❑   ❑

    (c) Have you structured the working week to include   ❑   ❑
        mandatory time for continuous improvement/training
        regardless of other pressures?

    (d) Is your company safety record one you are proud of?   ❑   ❑

7. Employee attitude/behaviour

    (a) Are your employees and any new recruits generally   ❑   ❑
        positive and enthusiastic?

    (b) Do you reward excellent behaviour beyond the call   ❑   ❑
        of duty?

    (c) Is there a general feeling of trust, honesty,   ❑   ❑
        fairness, openness, fun, pride, empowerment, and
        happiness? (Tick no if the answer to any one of
        these is no.)

    (d) Do employees behave properly, respect each other   ❑   ❑
        and company property, and support the team?

    (e) Do your managers and employees actively encourage   ❑   ❑
        safe behaviour?

8. Employee development

   (a) Are your employees trained to be multi-skilled within their core disciplines, and able to work in different departments? ❏ ❏

   (b) Is the training status of each employee published on training matrices? ❏ ❏

   (c) Is significant responsibility and authority thriving at the lowest levels in the organisation? ❏ ❏

   (d) Do you have a rigorous recruitment policy? ❏ ❏

   (e) Do you have 'self-managed' teams? ❏ ❏

   (f) Is your training budget more than 0.5 per cent of your annual turnover? ❏ ❏

9. Customer focus

   (a) Do you have a customer focused, full-time culture champion? ❏ ❏

   (b) Does your organisation focus on excellent customer service and ensuring that each customer contact with your company is an excellent experience? ❏ ❏

   (c) Does each internal department have a customer status with its supplier? ❏ ❏

10. Leadership

   (a) Are you a positive role model for the values of the organisation? ❏ ❏

   (b) Do you consider yourself to be a good leader? ❏ ❏

   (c) Do your employees agree? ❏ ❏

11. Your attitude towards your employees

   (a) Do you consider your employees as an asset (rather than a cost)? ❏ ❏

   (b) Is performance based on output (rather than time at work)? ❏ ❏

   (c) Do you operate an 'open door' policy to make yourself available to your staff? ❏ ❏

   (d) Do you trust your employees and do they trust you? ❏ ❏

   (e) Do you operate a coaching/supportive culture (rather than a blame or fear culture)? ❏ ❏

Part 2

Planning Future Success

'Planning Future Success' covers five areas that together form the bedrock of your cultural change journey to success. We first look at leading your culture change, and then secondly at creating your mission, vision, and values. The third chapter is about preparing the business strategy to realise this vision, followed in the fourth chapter by the role of quarterly objectives and key performance indicators (KPIs) for linking the strategy to its day-to-day practical implementation. Finally, and most importantly, we will suggest ways of communicating your strategy to your employees, as it is only by this process that you can really start leading your people to success.

Within the planning section are the first four case studies of 'best practice' culture change, and you will quickly note that each case study has a main theme that is loosely linked to the preceding chapter. The reason for this connection being loose is the myriad of parallel activities taking place during each firm's culture change, which invariably raises several associated general principles that apply to a wide range of companies and potentially to other chapters too. To help you, the general principles are flagged early on, and each case study concludes with a summary action list for your business.

As this book is your own personal guide, please use the book as intended; as a tool for guiding leaders at the top of the organisation through corporate culture change. I fully expect the fluorescent highlighter and pencilled notes in the margin to be much in evidence shortly!

Chapter 2

Leading Your Culture Change

Effective leaders develop other leaders throughout the organisation.

Now that you have benchmarked your organisation culture, I hope you are already beginning to form ideas for changing your company.

As you read the case studies, you will probably note the similar approach taken to leading each culture change. It is remarkably consistent, and it typically follows the eight-step process I am about to outline so that you, as leader, can lead your own culture change too.

Someone Sees the Need

Some major event in your company life cycle normally triggers a culture change by making someone see the need. Examples include:

▶ The arrival of a new chief executive officer, managing director or autonomous manager, who uncovers the issues and initiates change from the top. To be effective this person will need both the power that comes with the position, and the respect from those around him, to be able to influence others.

▶ The incumbent leader recognises the need, or is encouraged to take action by close subordinates.

▶ Severe financial losses that bring the company/site to the brink of closure.

▶ Benchmarking against the competition or 'best practice' firms, which encourages management to recognise that the company performance can be improved.

▶   An employee survey result that sends seismic shockwaves through senior management.
▶   The simple desire to perform better.

The last one is a relatively rare reason. Normally there is an underlying need to improve the company performance. Often it takes a crisis to 'see the need'.

Plainly it is easier to see this need for change if you look from a fresh viewpoint. Major change normally takes place only when:

▶   The new leader comes from outside the organisation.
▶   That person has experience from other companies, enabling a bench-marked perspective on the need for change.
▶   As a long-standing incumbent, you get outside help.

Change of this kind tends to stimulate improved performance as it encourages another review of the whole organisation and prevents it from bumbling along in its comfort zone rut.

So, bearing in mind all those around you probably still think the garden is rosy, have you seen the need for change? Are you stamping your feet to send warning signals like a rabbit sensing danger? Are you screaming from the rooftops about this impending crisis? Do you perceive a need for cultural change? I hope so. Is change essential? Absolutely!

If you do not change, your customers, competitors, suppliers, and certainly your environment will. Your customers will recruit new flexible suppliers, they will physically move away or change technology to remain competitive, and they will globalise. You will be left, if you are not already left, asking yourself questions like 'What happened to our long-term relationship with our local buyers? They are not making the decisions any more. Our customers' manufacturing has relocated elsewhere around the world so the stability and good prices have gone too. What are we going to do?'

Then there is the e-business revolution; already overturning conventional strategies and norms by trading electronically, and globally, using the power of the World Wide Web. If this is not cause for change I do not know what is!

Old strategies for increasing your efficiency incrementally, or shaving a few percent off the unit costs, are not enough any more. You need to be thinking about factors, not percentages, when you think about reductions in operating costs. You need to be flexible, innovative, excellent at your core business, and above all add value for your customer by offering new services as well as new products. This requires a new way of thinking. Gone are machines and time clocks and industrial engineers. Welcome to the era of people. It is time for change; for cultural change.

Create and Convince a Small, but Key, Team

You are personally convinced that cultural and/or strategic change is vital, long overdue, and 'crisis' is not a strong enough word to use any more! You have begun to create your own vision of what the company will become. Next comes your second test as leader; to convince a small team of influential people around you, with external help if necessary, that your perceived need for change is indeed very real and that your vision is a good one. Your aim is to change their perception; instead of looking at those pretty rose bushes, they are now facing overgrown, uncontrolled briars full of thorns.

The team members will depend on the goal you have in mind. If it is a manufacturing based cultural change, with manufacturing working practice changes only, the team will probably consist of management and union representatives together with an external facilitator. If it is a complete corporate culture change the team is likely to be your top team, with external facilitation as required.

Ideally this small team should consist of volunteers and be given broad guidelines plus the freedom to set their own goals. You will find the productivity of this team is outstanding, just as you would with an advertising account team established to pitch for a new client account, or a problem solving team within a retail outlet. The huge sense of purpose and common goal in this environment makes substantial progress almost inevitable.

Prepare Your Employees for Change

Fairly early in the culture change process, and as soon as you have something worth saying, you must broadcast this need for change. If possible, select groups small enough (around 40–50 people at a time would be my recommendation) to enable initial feedback and questions. You will need to explain first that everyone has been doing a great job, as the last thing you want to do is alienate your employees. However, you must then explain, with examples, why the change is necessary – after all, if everything is fine, why change? You need to create an environment where change is expected so people become receptive to the idea.

You must also share your vision for the future, even if the detailed strategy is not worked out yet. If it is a drive for excellence, say so. If it is to develop self-managed teams or annualised hours, say so. It also really helps people grasp hold of the change, and talk about it, if you give your vision a name (e.g. Alcan Foil Europe – Glasgow's 'Agreement 2000').

Indicate that you have a team who will develop the detailed plan with you. Say too when you will give everyone regular updates. In this way you manage the audience's expectations.

Put yourself in your employees' shoes when you are doing this 'need for change' broadcast, and make sure they know their role in the new world. If you are not sure at this stage, tell them, and tell them when they will know. If you have got bad news to tell, do not shy away from it. If it is a real crisis, make sure everyone knows this, but give him or her a vision to hold on to.

Develop Your Plan

Underneath this culture change umbrella, your role as leader is to help your small team establish and communicate a clear *mission* (why we exist) and *vision* (where we want to go). With external help as required, ask this team to work with you to create the new mission and vision. Ensure that customer service, innovation, and the ability to embrace change are built in to this vision.

Also decide the strategy to achieve this vision. You and your fellow leaders can develop this strategy by brainstorming in a series of off-site meetings (backed up by other research as necessary). There is no great need for a one-man, owner–manager, approach. After all, no man is an island and it is only by getting feedback from a variety of internal and external sources, that a rigorous strategy can be completed; so why try and come up with a strategy on your own? Leading is about having a vision, but it is also about getting your team to buy-in. Involving the team in the strategy forming process will help this buy-in. It also helps develop future leaders throughout your company!

Even change the core values if necessary; values that are engrained into the real soul of the company, values that result in a unique language and way of doing things, values that polarise people's reactions so intensely they either live to work for the company cause or eject themselves out into pastures new. You will find that having your culture founded on values that include trust, with little bureaucracy as a result, will make your organisation more flexible, swifter to embrace change, and more profitable as a result. Indeed innovation really should be one of your core values too. Compare and contrast this flexible scenario with the slumbering giants dependent on rigid controls and autocratic management that get continually bogged down and frustrate their employees with administration.

Later in this section we will introduce the mission, vision, values and strategy. You must believe in these. No, not just believe; be excited and be passionate about them. Because then, and remember it is your future as well as your employees', you will be able to motivate others to come along with you by giving them great sense of purpose too.

Give Progress Updates

Give your total team regular progress updates (again in groups of 40–50) on the mission, vision, values and strategy, and get feedback about their perceptions of progress. These progress updates should be a combination of verbal presentations, backed up with monthly newsletters, letters to each individual, and perhaps even videos or CDs. If the organisation is too big to make this practical, then e-mails at least make the communication consistent and timely. What you decide to do and when will depend on how major these changes are for your employees. The aim, at the end of the day, is to manage your employee expectations and encourage as much two-way communication as practical.

Launch the Plan

Launch the plan to everyone with as much razzmatazz as possible. After all it is everyone's future we are talking about, so let us hear about it loud and clear! Obviously if part of this plan involves redundancy then the mood will be very different, but if you have engineered the future to expand or change people's roles significantly so that their jobs are better quality, add more value, and increase job security, this has got to be something to celebrate.

Your plan will have a name. Your launch will include what is going to happen and when; and it will also disclose details of the strategy to achieve the mission, vision, and values.

It is implementation time!

Reinforce the Culture with a Series of Initiatives and by Living the Values

During the implementation phase, create opportunities to spread and reinforce the mission, vision, values and strategy messages. Making work fun could well be one of these. Seed initiatives such as system, behaviour, and attitude changes to start the wheel rolling in the culture change direction, but do not expect the culture change to be complete in a few months. Assuming the culture change is major, for example, you will probably initiate a huge training, continuous improvement, or safety programme as some of these initiatives. The training, for example, could well last for six months, involve the majority of people in the company, and develop completely new skills and capabilities.

Although systems and behaviours may be changed in months, attitude changes take much longer; of the order of a couple of years or so. Be aware too that the complete cultural wheel turns v-e-r-y slowly, with time frames measured in terms of several years.

This is why the values are so important. They give the fundamental guidelines to employees about what is deemed acceptable behaviour, and what is considered important. Values eliminate the need for rules and promote consistent behaviour, which in turn reinforces the desired culture.

Alcan Foil Europe – Glasgow, for example, employs people within the six-value framework of 'Agreement 2000' (safety, customer driven, teamwork, performance, people focus, and integrity). Alcan keeps reinforcing these values by giving autonomy to the teams in a trust culture. Actions, values and systems that lend support like this, by reinforcing winning, help to get that buy-in and build that growing snowball of momentum for change; one that is large enough to change the landscape and remove any barriers placed in its way. So if you want to lead your people to success, let them know when they are successful!

Just briefly, here are a few words of warning. Kotter and Heskitt[1] say:

> As critics of the strong-culture perspective have said, although the theory posits that a strong culture creates good performance, causality goes the other way too; good long-term performance can cause or reinforce a strong culture. But with much success, that strong culture can easily become somewhat arrogant, inwardly focused, politicised, and bureaucratic. In an increasingly competitive and rapidly changing world, that kind of culture unquestionably undermines economic performance. It can blind top management to the need for new business strate-

gies. It can also make strategic change, even when attempted, diffi-cult or impossible to implement.

As a result it is possible to undermine the many years of work spent reinforcing a positive culture, and very quickly move backwards towards a blame/fear culture. You need to maintain plenty of initiatives to reinforce the positive culture you are trying to create.

You also need to 'live the values' in everything you do every day, because if you do not you cannot expect your employees to either. This is often also called 'walk the talk', or 'do what you say'.

Defining and promoting the company values is one of the most import-ant of your roles; simply because these guide the whole workforce prac-tice, from recruitment right the way through to customer service, in terms of 'this is what we consider to be fundamentally important'. Continually promoting these values will eventually give them an air of mystique, even reverence, and help others know the answers to questions raised in your absence. They eliminate the need for encyclopaedic rulebooks, remove bureaucracy, and enable trust to dominate.

Develop Leaders throughout Your Company

If you are the only leader, how can you expect innovation, entrepreneur-ship and creativity to be bubbling further down your company? Without a leader a team becomes a mere group of people. With a leader, especially one able to communicate a clear vision, the organisation has literally limitless potential providing the relevant resources and opportunities are available.

Part of your role as leader is to encourage, inspire, and actively develop leaders throughout your company to help promote the values, stimulate innovation and, of course, culture change. You can drive this by empower-ing your people, enabling responsibility and accountability to be accepted throughout the company, and creating an environment that actively encourages leaders managed by peer pressure rather than management effort (e.g. Alcan's self-managed teams).

Take time out to get yourself and your senior managers trained to be leaders, so they in turn can coach and train middle managers and super-visors to become leaders too. This training helps develop a common lan-guage, a bond, and of course, trust. Your organisation will be so much stronger for this clarity of vision, drive, and ability to bring your team with you. As Jack Welsh of General Electric said 'Stop managing, start leading.' Turn your managers into leaders if you want an innovative culture. Turn your managers into leaders if you want success.

You can also help develop leaders lower down in your organisation by being a good leader yourself, as a role model. An example of this is to encourage change in the organisation, to keep it flexible and innovative. I do not mean change for change's sake like a bag blowing around in the directionless swirls of windy city streets; I mean adapting and improving all the time, achieving new capabilities and setting new standards, with excellence as your only acceptable benchmark. Lead your people well by pointing them in the right general direction but not telling them which streets to go along when they know the city better than you do. Encourage them to innovate, even if in trying they make mistakes; as it is better to try, but make the occasional mistake, than not to try at all. Encourage a meritocracy, backed up by supportive systems, in which leaders can thrive.

Also develop your leaders by communicating with them and explaining their role. Your communication skills will be tested in this process, as there will be your followers and the inevitable doubters. You will also need excellent communication skills to bring everyone else, as well as your leaders, on board because if you have not got your people with you, irrespective of how great your vision is, you are not leading.

Finally, if you are positive, there is a good chance your other leaders, and their followers, will be too. For example, do your employees look forward to your site visits or do they dread them? Try focusing on their positive achievements rather than picking holes in their performance, and just watch the transformation. You are actively demonstrating trust, and that you value what they are doing. Let us look at it in a different way for a minute. If your boss kicked you for not quite achieving an unachievable goal, even though you had put your whole heart and soul into trying, how would you feel? Consistently make your people feel they are winners, and that is what you will get.

Chapter 3

Creating Your Mission, Vision and Values

If you value your future, decide your values now.

The terms mission, vision and values have already appeared several times, with the briefest of definitions so far. In this chapter we will give you guidelines of how to prepare your own statements, we will define and give examples of each, and also explain why the mission, vision and values statements are fundamental to your company's success.

We will also develop a graphical picture of how the six elements of mission, vision, values, systems, strategy and culture interact over time to show you why regular reviews of all six are important and why Innovation should be one of your values for long-term success.

Let us start with the following definitions, which are simple but very significant:

Mission	Why we exist.
Vision	What we wish to be in the future.
Values	The principles and beliefs on which the business is founded and that determine people's behaviour and business relationships.
Strategy	How we will achieve our vision.
Systems	All systems within our organisation.
Culture	The way we do things that affects how our people feel and behave.

Preparing Your Mission, Vision and Values

Nothing beats professionally coached brainstorming for coming up with ideas for the mission, vision and values. Lynda Gratton[1] neatly summarises this, with an example of brainstorming the vision, as:

The rules of brainstorming are simple: let each member of the team speak, don't interrupt, don't analyse or criticise... just let it be. A team of six will have begun to speak about their vision of the future over a period of approximately two hours. The dreams begin to take form, the hopes find a way of expressing themselves, the team begin to create a field of mutual respect, shared ideas, hopes and dreams. The energy of this collective dreaming is vital to the process – it inspires excitement and fosters support and mutuality. People feel privileged to have their voices heard and they find it moving to hear other dreams of the future.

Each mission and vision statement should be one phrase that is succinct, accurate, unique, memorable, heartfelt and inspiring! For example, *'Transforming Futures'*, which is London Business School's mission statement, or *'Our global quest is to improve the quality of human life by enabling people to do more, feel better and live longer'*, which is the equivalent from GlaxoSmithKline. The vision statements from the same two organisations respectively are *'To be the most important and most respected international business school'*, and *'We want to become the indisputable leader in our industry'*. The best vision I have come across in researching this book is that of Henry Ford,[2] who brought to life the goal of democratising the automobile with this vivid description:

I will build a motor car for the great multitude... It will be so low in price that no man making a good salary will be unable to own one and enjoy with his family the blessing of hours of pleasure in God's great open spaces... When I'm through, everybody will be able to afford one, and everyone will have one. The horse will have disappeared from our highways, the automobile will be taken for granted... [and we will] give a large number of men employment at good wages.

What a brilliant vision! Remember, the mission and vision are there to create meaning and sense of purpose for your employees. This certainly achieves that objective.

You should also aim for no more than six values; again to simply and memorably let your employees know what you consider to be the most important principles for the company to follow every day. Remember too, it is these values that will shape your business of the future. For example, London Business School's values, creating the mnemonic SPIRIT, are: *Scholarship, Professionalism, Innovation, Relevance, Internationalism,* and *Transformation.* GlaxoSmithKline's values are:

We undertake our quest with the enthusiasm of **entrepreneurs**, *excited by the constant search for* **innovation**. *We value* **performance** *achieved with* **integrity**. *We will attain success as a world-class global leader with each and every one of our people contributing with* **passion** *and an unmatched* **sense of urgency**.

Let's explore now in more detail what we should be looking for in each mission, vision, and values statement.

Mission

If we know *why* we are doing something, and believe this is good, we will do almost anything with a greater sense of purpose. This is the underlying reason for preparing and communicating your organisation's one sentence mission statement; so your people can understand the bigger picture and their role in achieving this. It is this understanding of *why we exist* that transforms the job into one with a real purpose; hence the intense meaning and value of the phrase 'I have a mission, not a job'.

To illustrate the difference a mission makes, here is a story I heard years ago. Its principles are as important now as when the story was first told. I will not embellish this story, I will just tell you the salient points. Picture two convicts, each using a sledgehammer to break large rocks into smaller pieces. When asked, 'What are you doing?' the first one replies, 'I am breaking rocks.' The second one, however, says, 'I am helping to build a cathedral.'

Vision

Assuming we now know why we exist, the next key driving force and motivator is to know *what we wish to be in the future* so we can all face in the same direction and start building our future. This is the vision. It should be another big picture, a dream; a future scene that is clear and captures the imagination of your people. It must be unique to your firm, and be painted in bold colourful brush strokes full of oil-based paint and meaning. It needs to stand up to close scrutiny; each brush stroke depicting another small element that together creates the credible whole. And yet it needs to be simple too! It must be easy to understand, easy to communicate, and to withstand duplication without deformation. The same vision must appear in every employee's mind, to gain that coherence and consistent approach every day that brings the desired success for all. It is not easy. It takes time and effort, and many minds to sharpen the focus (in stark contrast to a 'this should satisfy most people' committee approach). It stems from the chief executive and yet pervades the deepest roots of the organisation. It creates that sense of pride, that knowledge that you are working for an excellent and successful firm. It literally carves out in one simple phrase *what we wish to be in the future*.

Collins and Porras[3] found in their research that 'visionary companies often use ... BHAGs [pronounced BEE-hags and shorthand for Big, Hairy, Audacious Goals] – as a powerful way to stimulate progress.' They go on to say:

> *... vision requires a special type of BHAG – a vision-level BHAG that applies to the entire organisation and requires 10–30 years of effort to complete. Setting the BHAG that far into the future requires thinking beyond the current capabilities of the organisation and the current environment. Indeed, inventing such a goal forces an executive team to be visionary, rather than just strategic or tactical.*

I suggest you try this and see what happens!

Values

The values form the very heart and soul of your organisation, the bedrock, *the principles and beliefs on which the business is founded and that determine people's behaviour and business relationships*.

Missions, visions, strategies, systems, and even cultures, may change, but values are practically irrevocable once entrenched. Values in really successful companies are reinforced for generations. They are instilled in employee behaviour, become guidelines for decision-making, and can even reach 'mythical' status. It is a brave chief executive officer that tries to change a successful company's well-established values! The key is to make sure they are the right set of values before they become written in stone.

Assuming your organisation's values are not yet scribed on the proverbial stone tablets, you need to make tough decisions when deciding what is included/excluded from the short list of five or six values. Remember, you personally must espouse these values each and every day, in everything you do and say. If you do not believe in a value, or cannot sustain one in your daily behaviour, do not include it in your set of values.

Take 'Trust' for example, and test yourself against this value. Just how far do you trust your colleagues? Do you share financial information about the company performance with all your employees? Do you trust your employees to organise themselves and make their own decisions; or do they have myriads of rules and regulations dictating what they can and cannot do? For example, do your systems back up this trust ethic – by eliminating bureaucracy, cross-checking, dual signatures, and approval only at the highest level; and replace this with autonomy and freedom to make decisions at the lowest possible levels in the company? Call it empowerment if you like, but really it is freedom to make decisions about how, where, and when you work, which all stem from trust and respect for the individual.

As another example of a value to test, take 'people development'. Your belief in people development needs to be so strong that you do exactly that: through training, continuous improvement, leadership skills and career development; with the systems to back all this up. It means investing in your people at all times, even if other, less important aspects of the business have to take second place. This is a serious commitment, but if you believe it, truly believe it, then include it and make it part of daily life at work, and make sure your appraisals, training, open communication, employee involvement meetings, suggestion schemes, etc. all support the people development philosophy.

The values you agree on should be strong enough and consistent enough to create a culture that polarises job applicants into two camps; those that decide 'This is the company for me' and the others who say, 'I really felt uncomfortable with what they were telling me and I don't want to join'. The idea is not to employ clones, rather to employ people with similar beliefs, principles, attitudes and behaviours. A strong set of values that is reflected in daily business life is therefore a great way to attract the right employees for the future, to reduce your staff turnover, and to reinforce your company culture.

To create your initial set of values you will need to brainstorm with people from throughout the organisation, taking cross sections vertically and in age and length of service. Together, in these brainstorming meetings, you must test these values to ensure they are not just senior management rhetoric. They must pass the following tests:

► Do you all believe in them?
► Are you prepared to uphold them in your daily working life?
► Are you personally prepared to reject the opposite of each value?
► Are you prepared to incur costs in order to uphold your chosen values?
► Are they broad enough to withstand the passage of time?
► Is their meaning crystal clear so all your employees will understand them?

You also need to check what sort of reaction you get from further down the organisation. Does each value strike a chord with your employees or do they look incredulous and laugh at what you have said? If your initial set of values contains what you truly believe to be the most important principles, time will prove the ultimate test of their stability.

The Changing Relationship Between Mission, Vision, Values, Strategy, Systems and Culture Over Time

As a successful company metamorphoses over time, everything changes apart from possibly the values. Consequently you will need to regularly review your mission, vision, strategy, systems and culture. Figure 3.1 shows you why, by plotting a couple of scenarios showing company 'success' against time. It indicates how this success is affected by the changing relationship between mission, vision, values, systems, strategy and culture over time. Each scenario is considerably simplified to make the principles easy to follow, and each scale is deliberately not quantified as it depends too much on the individual company and associated markets.

Let us say you are driving an initial successful business start up (A–B on Figure 3.1). During this time your mission, vision and strategy will all be congruent and will move your company towards that initial vision. You, as both owner-manager and a leader, are likely to naturally select like-minded individuals as recruits during the ensuing growth period. Probably subconsciously the company is already beginning to reinforce its own values and culture.

Your company is still small enough to remain flexible and to adjust its strategy as market conditions change, so the mission and vision do not need to change. At some point, however, your company grows beyond your centralised control, requiring new systems and additional employees, some of whom are managers rather than leaders. Fortunately the systems you have introduced so far are carefully planned to keep the organisation innovative and flexible. The culture becomes better defined, and values begin to be deep-seated.

After a further period of time we then move to two probable scenarios following a major change in market conditions. The first is B–C where you and your management team lead the firm, recognise the changes, adjust the strategy and systems to cope, and as necessary also redefine the mission and vision. You may decide you want to improve the culture,

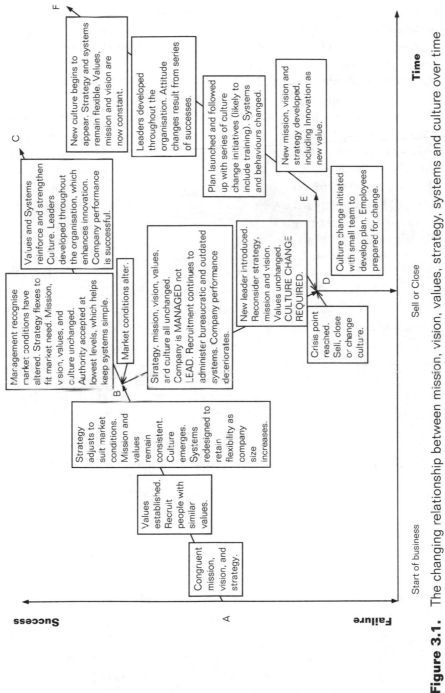

Figure 3.1. The changing relationship between mission, vision, values, strategy, systems and culture over time

although normally this would be unaffected. Your team of leaders continue to perform well by reinforcing the values and consequently strengthening the culture. You develop more leaders throughout the company, and go on to own a very successful business.

The other probable scenario, B–D, is where you and your management team focus internally on squeezing the last bit of profit from the business, so you miss the changing market conditions. Nothing changes internally apart from the systems becoming more bureaucratic as your firm continues to recruit managers rather than leaders. The firm is now being managed, not lead. Suddenly, too late, you and your managers wake up to the fact that the market has changed, performance has dropped off, and the only way forward appears to be to cut costs (mainly people) to maintain short-term profitability.

The situation reaches crisis point when the shareholders start calling for radical change or even closure. A new leader is recruited as chief executive officer, who completely overhauls the strategy, mission, vision, and recognises a culture change is needed to achieve the strategic goals. The basic values are left alone, but now, as part of the culture change, the systems are changed and simplified to reinforce the new culture and the existing values.

As we have already seen in the Leading Your Culture Change chapter, the culture change 'D-E-F' then continues to plan. During the culture change the new chief executive officer introduces a new value, called Innovation, to ensure the company remains flexible. Leaders are developed throughout the company to enhance this flexibility and to promote a strong customer-focused culture. The end result is a better working life for the employees, increased profits for the shareholders, and better customer service.

There are three conclusions from this relationship review:

▶ The only stable element in the company history is the set of values.
▶ The culture may be the *way* things are done, but the values are the reason *why* things are done this way. Values therefore underpin the corporate culture.
▶ Culture is the net *result* of the mission, vision, values, systems and strategy.

Having delved into the dynamics of culture and in particular its links with mission, vision and values, it is time now for us to see these dynamics in action as we visit Mortgage Express for our first case study.

Chapter 4

Mortgage Express
Drives Business and Cultural Change with their Mission, Vision and Values

Introduction

Employees use words like, 'There is a buzz', 'I am proud to work for Mortgage Express', 'I have a mission, not a job', and 'the company is a big family', when describing what it is like to work at Mortgage Express. These statements reflect the really strong, open culture at Mortgage Express today.

Part of Bradford & Bingley plc, Mortgage Express provides specialist lending for the Group. It supplies a quality mortgage service and niche products to Intermediaries as well as selling direct to customers.

In 1991 Mortgage Express committed themselves to the European Foundation for Quality Management (EFQM) Excellence Model, which is owned by the EFQM.[1] To indicate the importance of this model and thus why we should have a case study based on it, and in particular the mission, vision and values contained within it, here are a few facts about the EFQM Excellence Model's background:

> The EFQM is a membership based, not for profit organisation, created in 1988 by 14 leading European businesses, with a mission to be the driving force for sustainable excellence in Europe and a vision of a world in which European organisations excel.

By 2001 the EFQM had over 750 members from most European countries and most sectors of activity. The need for a model is based on the premise that

> *regardless of sector, size, structure or maturity, to be successful, organisations need to establish an appropriate management system. The EFQM Excellence Model is a practical tool to help organisations do this by measuring where they are on the path to excellence; helping them understand the gaps; then stimulating solutions.*

The Mortgage Express commitment to the EFQM Excellence Model led, five years later, to winning the prestigious UK Quality Award. This award is presented by the British Quality Foundation to encourage organisations across the country to strive for business excellence. Only 22 companies in the UK have won this award between its inception in 1994 and 2001, which makes Mortgage Express a very special company; one exhibiting 'best practice' culture change. Mortgage Express is also very much an 'Investor in People', with recognition achieved in 1993, 1996 and 1999.

This case study, which is in four main sections, will first take you along a ten-year journey of interaction with the Excellence Model requirements. It will cover the time period both before and after the award, and focus in particular on the mission, vision and values. Then, secondly, in the EFQM Excellence Model section we will review the model structure in more detail and how Mortgage Express undertakes its 'self assessments'. We will also, in the third and fourth parts, briefly explore two initiatives introduced by the Head of Business Excellence; a service-improvement training programme called Exceeding Expectations, and the Quality Recognition System for individuals providing a service beyond the call of duty.

Woven in to the case study are a number of general principles worth watching out for:

▶ Benchmarking is in operation again, this time against the EFQM Excellence Model.

▶ Regular reinforcement of the desired culture takes many new initiatives – here are several good examples.

▶ Show your employees that you value them, and that you are prepared to stand by your values, by investing in their future even when the pressure is on to cut costs. Look out for the training programmes and the excellent communication.

▶ Work can be fun! Here are some ideas for you.

▶ Managing your culture change requires the right team and regular meetings to drive the culture change process. Look at how the Head of Business Excellence role, as the culture champion, dovetails neatly into the strategic leadership team. Look too at the diversity and impact of this role on the organisation to help you decide who your culture champion should be.

Let us look now at how Mortgage Express has achieved its open, stimulating and fun working environment.

Culture Change

Mortgage Express has been through some major highs and lows since its inception in 1986 as a subsidiary of Trustees Savings Bank (TSB) plc. Throughout the late 1980s, Mortgage Express experienced massive growth and gained around 50,000 customers and £3 billion in mortgage lending. Unfortunately, although excellent at obtaining new customers, the company did not have the systems to collect payments. With this and the turn in the housing market, Mortgage Express ended up closing its doors to new business in 1991 to concentrate on debt collection. The view was to transfer the portfolio, once it was in a reasonable state, back into the TSB Group. It was then losing around £1 million each week.

The drastic change in business emphasis had a major negative impact on staff morale. Staff expected to be made redundant within a period of three years but management recognised that they could not lose all key staff. This led to MORI being invited to survey the staff. The results proved to management that there were key areas to focus on if the business was going to change; key areas being communication and quality of work. As Mortgage Express had to increase their workforce, new staff joining the business received short-term contracts that included loyalty bonuses to ensure they stayed for the duration of their contracts. All staff were also promised major training to make them the most employable people in the industry.

As part of this commitment Mortgage Express introduced the EFQM Excellence Model with the aim of completing a series of internal reviews, achieving a site visit from the British Quality Foundation for the UK Quality Award in 1995, and winning this award in 1996.

As promised the previous year, what followed was a period of intensive quality training for everyone; training so vibrant that a common language became possible throughout the organisation. For the first time, internal staff established the appraisal system to look at *how* you performed your tasks, as well as what you did to gain your achievements. Personal objectives would therefore receive one mark for completing the task and another for behaviour. This kind of scoring meant that someone with an excellent task-achievement score but a poor behaviour score would undergo additional coaching plus training and development to change his or her behaviour.

The following year, with the business starting to reap small profits again, employees completed a second staff opinion questionnaire. This time the questions were written in-house and tailored to particular local issues including working environment and culture, together with training and development. This gave an update on how people were feeling and resulted in the allocation of two hours per month quality time for improvement activities either as a team or on a one-to-one basis. The message was '*It is okay to take time out to improve things*'.

A couple of examples of how teams used this time include:

▶ Customer care teams used to be trained outside normal working hours because they needed to be available to talk to customers. The system changed so they had deputies that allowed training to take place during the normal working day.
▶ A 'green' team was formed to initiate and undertake a series of environmental initiatives.

Around this time, developing the leadership aspect of the Excellence Model encouraged the board to have a facilitated session in which they defined what they wanted from the business and how they wanted people to behave. This led to the team launching 'The Way Ahead', publicised to all staff in an upbeat presentation to the sounds of Tina Turner's 'Simply The Best'. This identified the company *mission*, *vision* and *values*. The *mission*, known internally as 'The Triple Win', is for:

▶ Staff (enabling all employees to achieve their best)
▶ Customers (providing customers with a first class service)
▶ Shareholders (maximising the long-term value for the company's shareholders).

The *vision* is: 'We will be recognised as *the* company for customers with individual mortgage needs. We will do this by providing innovative, value-for-money products and world class service delivered by the best people.'

'The Way Ahead' also established the organisation's *values*, using the acronym TIRQ, which really started the major culture change that makes the company what it is today:

▶ Teamwork (everybody matters and has a valid point of view)
▶ Integrity (we are open, honest and fair in everything we do)
▶ Recognition (we praise achievement and celebrate success)
▶ Quality (we deliver what we promise to all our customers and constantly seek to improve).

Note: you will see shortly that the 2001 mission and vision statements have been rewritten to reflect changed market conditions, but the values as you would expect are exactly the same.

At the end of 1994 the strategy for mortgage products in niche markets was also put into practice, giving the company new direction and the employees fresh energy for the future. This lead, a few months later, to another high profile launch to the employees of a system called MARS (Mortgage Application Review System), using Mars bars and plenty of fun to signal the start of new business. You should now be able to see the way in which management is involving staff at all levels to gain buy-in, both in the preparation, and presentation, of new initiatives. You also now have several examples of the important strategic role played by the Head of Business Excellence, en route to satisfying the EFQM Excellence Model requirements.

In 1996 the company applied for and won the UK Quality Award. 'The reaction throughout the organisation was "electric" after winning this and everyone was on a high.'

Soon after achieving this high point, Mortgage Express entered a period of uncertainty. In May 1997 Lloyds TSB plc sold Mortgage Express to the Bradford & Bingley Building Society. Establishing best practice in the new organisation took most of 1997 and 1998, so the next key culture-shaping event was not until 1999, with a major programme of coaching, training and facilitating of team leaders to improve operational efficiency and communication.

A joint venture in 2000 with the American company Alltel, who have expertise in servicing mortgages, allowed Mortgage Express to concentrate on new business. Mortgage Express reviewed the whole new business process and developed staff to become multi-skilled and to use the whole MARS. The net result now is a broader job scope and potential to increase motivation through ownership of the whole mortgage application, with the added bonus of responsibility being pushed further down the organisation.

However, it is all very good to understand a process, it is another thing entirely to implement this with genuine flair and enthusiasm whilst providing excellent service to your customers; hence the birth of 'Exceeding Expectations', which we will look at shortly.

In 2001 the mission, vision and values review resulted in new mission and vision statements:

The mission is: 'To be the natural choice for innovative mortgage solutions.'

The vision is:

▶ we all take pride in exceeding our customers expectations so that they instinctively recommend us
▶ Mortgage Express is a challenging and rewarding place to work where skilled and knowledgeable staff care enough to make a difference
▶ we work together with our partners to achieve our common goals; and
▶ as a result we deliver exceptional long-term benefit for everyone involved in our business.

EFQM Excellence Model

The EFQM put together a model that could be used in Europe, a model with nine main criteria and 32 sub-criteria that are used by companies in one of three ways:

▶ To carry out self assessments.
▶ For formal submission to EFQM for a feedback report.
▶ To go for a quality award via external assessment and a site visit.

The Excellence Model states that the

> *[four] Excellent results with respect to performance, customers, people and society are achieved through [the five enabler criteria of] leadership driving policy and strategy, people, partnerships and resources, and processes.*

The enabler criteria cover what a company *does* and the results criteria cover what an organisation *achieves*. Many of these criteria impact on the culture of an organisation.

So how does Mortgage Express tackle the requirements of the Excellence Model? Each year the Mortgage Express senior management team starts the process with a self assessment, which is a formal review to see where Mortgage Express stands against each of the 32 sub-criteria. Vast amounts of flipchart paper adorn the training-room walls by the end of each assessment.

During the self assessment, teams of two split the nine main criteria (and associated 32 sub-criteria) into strengths and areas for improvement, and pick three aspects for each. The status against each criterion is then scored using the Excellence Model RADAR approach (Results, Approach, Deployment, Assessment and Review), with the weighted score being the self assessment result. This annual self assessment score is a simple measure of progress against the model criteria.

When Mortgage Express first carried out the self assessment in 1992 they scored 345 (compared to the 600–800 needed to be world class). This score rose steadily each year up to 1996 when they won the UK Quality Award. Mortgage Express carried out a further self assessment in 1997, however did not do another one until 2000 when they found the score had reduced. This was one reason for launching Exceeding Expectations and refreshing the quality review system initiatives, which will be mentioned shortly.

As part of the self assessment, the three improvement opportunities identified against each criterion are linked into the business plans for the coming year. To keep the model live, Mortgage Express holds two management meetings per month; the first to manage the current business and the second to review progress with the Excellence Model activities. Each management team member has team and individual objectives. The idea is to review progress monthly against each objective.

Each year in January Mortgage Express holds a conference, for *everyone*, which covers the company performance and also the plans for the coming year. Covering these topics this way ensures *every* employee knows the strategy, which has the added benefit when setting personal as well as team objectives that these can be aligned to the overall needs of the business.

The Head of Business Excellence for Mortgage Express summed up the cultural aspects of the Excellence Model as:

▶ 'the Excellence Model has provided the basis for the cultural change'
▶ 'it has helped us recognise "where we are at"'
▶ 'it has made us focus on continuous improvement'.

Exceeding Expectations

'Exceeding Expectations' is a great title for a customer service improvement programme! This is another good example of cultural change aimed at achieving the best service from your people. The programme is designed to help everyone in the business focus on how they and their teams can improve their personal skills and service to customers and colleagues.

Mortgage Express staff (one out of every 15 employed) developed a total of nine modules so that each employee could complete a module every month in around 90 minutes. These nine modules look at the key elements in providing excellent service to customers and how to continually monitor and measure achievements. The modules are in a simple booklet format that asks each person relevant questions, with individuals' answers followed up through monthly team meetings led by 'facilitators'. (All managers and team leaders have been trained as facilitators.) Each team agrees actions with target completion dates to facilitate the improvements required.

To show how well this training is received, employee feedback about the exceeding expectations programme includes:

▶ 'great to see everyone involved in the same programme'
▶ 'fun way of getting the message across'
▶ 'interaction between teams has been very good'.

The 'Exceeding Expectations' CD, developed specifically for this high impact launch, contains lively music plus photographs of individual Mortgage Express staff next to feedback from the staff opinion questionnaire and intermediaries satisfaction survey. Feedback is in the format 'You told us you wanted …' and 'Our customers said …', 'So this is why we have launched Exceeding Expectations'. Note how Mortgage Express asked for, and captured, employee and customer feedback from questionnaires on this CD.

So, with the Exceeding Expectations programme, we now have an example of how to ensure everyone is well trained to offer excellent customer service. Also team leaders and managers are developing their own staff. Initiatives like this, that bring home the message to employees about the value every customer can potentially add to your business and the absolute need to give them excellent service, are critical for a company's future success. A culture in which employees feel motivated and are actively encouraged to give exceptional service, will make a major impact on the level of service actually given, the degree of satisfaction felt by the customer, and further promote customer loyalty. Another initiative with customer satisfaction in mind is the Quality Recognition System.

Quality Recognition System

The Quality Recognition System recognises individuals for providing a service beyond the call of duty. The aim is to continuously improve the way Mortgage Express people do things so that they become more efficient and effective; a goal that is achieved when people are supportive, service driven and customised in the way they work. The system is therefore looking at people's behaviour rather than just their ideas.

Behind this scheme is the simple resource to make it work. There are nine Quality Councillors (approximately one person in 25) taken from all levels in the organisation, who meet monthly as the Quality Council to decide which nominees should receive recognition for their outstanding behaviour. The nominee(s) may be an individual or a team.

The nomination criteria are in line with the three promises made to customers:

▶ *Service*: Our staff will always deal with you in a professional and courteous way by providing you with a reliable and efficient service.
▶ *Supportive*: We will provide you with a knowledgeable team to meet your requirements and support all your mortgage needs.
▶ *Customised*: We will provide you with promotional support literature to endorse our customised product range.

These promises are pulled through to the quality nomination form by having three tick boxes for each section. The nominator ticks those boxes that apply.

Service	Supportive	Customised
❏ Customer champion	❏ Supports others and sharing knowledge	❏ Pays special attention to detail
❏ Continuous improvement	❏ Role model behaviours	❏ Clear communicator
❏ 'Can-do' attitude	❏ Displays positive attitude and willingness to help others	❏ Shows unique and innovative style which adds value to customer, staff and company

The system works as follows:

▶ If nomination meets criteria, the nomination is scored by the Quality Council to establish level of award (a leisure voucher to the value of either £25 or £50).

▶ The Quality Council draws out a winner from all that quarter's nominees. The prize is normally in the form of an activity as an 'experience' (e.g. a helicopter flight, or driving an expensive car) to the value of £300.

▶ All successful recognitions are publicised in the monthly company magazine.

A good example of the Quality Recognition System in practice is the nomination for an individual award to a Mortgage Express security guard called Jimmy. The nomination form contains ticks in the three boxes for 'can-do' attitude, role model behaviours, and displays positive attitude and willingness to help others. There is also the following observation:

> *During a night of storms the windows on the second floor started to leak (heavily) on Sunday evening. Whilst doing his rounds of the floor, Jimmy cleared all files and paperwork away from the windows and placed towels/bins on the ledges to minimise the mess. Outside Jimmy's job role, this portrays a level of commitment that others should attempt to meet. Thanks.*

Jimmy received £25 for his service beyond the call of duty.

This scheme typically recognises 50 people (20 per cent of staff) in three months and awards a £300 'experience' every quarter too. The feedback from the employees is that the Quality Recognition System is simple to understand and use. It certainly rewards people's excellent behaviour, which in turn must positively influence the service received by internal and external customers.

To conclude, the Mortgage Express culture captures the imagination and enthusiasm of its staff, creates an atmosphere of fun, and demonstrates daily to its employees that they are truly valued. Through its niche market strategy, and clear mission, vision, and TIRQ values, perhaps it is not surprising Mortgage Express is one big profitable family.

Summary Action List for Your Business

1. Allocate a full-time culture champion, in this case 'Head of Business Excellence', to drive the whole culture change programme.
2. Introduce your people to the EFQM Excellence Model, start benchmarking your organisation against this model and monitor progress monthly.
3. Decide your mission, vision and values.
4. Recognise individuals who have provided a service beyond the call of duty through a quality recognition system that rewards exceptional behaviour.
5. Ensure all your training improves (internal and external) customer service (see the Exceeding Expectations programme).
6. Structure the working day or week so that individuals and teams have time allocated to focus entirely on brainstorming and implementing continuous improvements.
7. Train individuals to be multi-skilled so they are able to work in different departments.
8. Launch new initiatives to support your culture change on a regular and frequent basis. Each launch should be great fun and have as many people as practical involved to help generate buy-in.

Chapter 5

Preparing the Business Strategy

If you keep doing what you are doing, you will keep getting what you are getting.

You can have the best culture in the world, but if the company is not profitable then one day there will not be a company! Remember the crisis point in the previous chapter? One of the fundamental building blocks to support your platform for cultural change is your strategy for *profitable* business.

We shall now explore a fundamental eight-step strategic review process; one that applies regardless of your company size, location, or business sector. This is simply a logical series of steps that make you and your team stand back and *think*. You might, for example, ask yourself questions like:

► What value does my business add to my customers now, and how do we increase this value?
► What are the core strengths and weaknesses of my business, and what can we do to build on these strengths and reduce the weaknesses?
► What differentiates my company from the competition and how can we increase this differentiation?

Analyse Your Existing Business

The first step is to analyse your existing business. A key question is: 'Which parts of the business are genuinely profitable?' If you do not know, start the analysis. Put in the systems to find out. You might, for example, want to know what your return on capital employed (ROCE) is for various elements of the business. You probably already know the ROCE for the whole company. When, however, you start to look at particular processes, or products, market sectors, and customers, the picture may look very different; more like a geographic landscape with huge mountains of profit surrounded by plains of marginal business, with rivers leaching your profits into unplumbed lakes and seas.

This profitability picture can be simplified into two dimensions by identifying the ROCE in each market sector, or by type of product or process. You may already have a series of profit centres, in which case this analysis is relatively easy.

Refer to Figure 5.1, which shows profitability in terms of profit before interest and tax (PBIT) plotted against capital employed. The circle diameter represents the turnover for each market sector. This gives a pictorial image of your business.

What do you need to do to increase the overall company ROCE? Do you divest, or invest in, current loss-making sectors? Can you move some of these market sectors around this graph by increasing turnover at profitable prices, or drag the major loss-maker shown on the graph into a viable, profitable operation? Whether and how you move the various sectors around depends on your strategy. It also depends on your view of competitor, customer, supplier and other operating-environment reactions. Although this graph does not in itself provide the solutions, it can clarify the current situation and make decision-making much simpler.

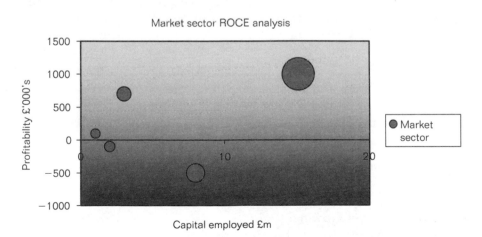

Figure 5.1. Market sector return on capital employed analysis

Benchmark Your Company Performance

The next step is to benchmark your company performance against that of your direct competitors, and companies in other markets. It is amazing what benchmarking can tell you. You know who your main competitors are, and you know your main customers, but how much do you really know about your competition? When was the last time you formally surveyed your customer base and target customers to confirm the size and structure of your market? There are a myriad of sources; market research reports, your existing customers and suppliers, trade associations, and so on. Also, do not accept your own market conditions and assume all other markets perform the same. Go and find out. Learn from other companies how they tick, what makes them produce excellent profits, what makes them successful.

Identify Profitable Markets

Identify profitable markets where there is synergy with your company's existing or potential skills; where customers are developing and growing themselves; where direct competition can be avoided through use of different channels or different processes, and where you define the market broadly enough so you have less than, say, 20 per cent market share. After all, if you consider yourself to have most of the market, where is your hunger for growth? If you want to be profitable, try to avoid mature, commodity markets where you have no competitive advantage and potential for only a small market share. Go for new markets, or niche markets, where you can really add value for your customers, and create entry barriers for your potential competitors to make this a sustainable opportunity.

Find Out the Market Size

Find out the market size, by assessing the turnover of existing and target customers. Put your total potential customer base through filters. Rank those that pass the filter test and make the top ones your target customer base. Filters might include:

▶ Credit rating.
▶ Business complexity (too complex or too simple for your company capability).
▶ Is the customer growing?
▶ Is the customer size too big/too small?
▶ Is your potential customer inside your market's geographic limits?

▶ Can you reach this customer through your preferred channel into the market?

▶ What level of sales support is required?

▶ Is the likely gross margin attractive? (after all we are trying to identify profitable business!).

▶ Are they good payers?

Then indicate your current and target percentages of each customer's business, based on what is possible/desirable.

Capacity

Assess what serving these customers means for your organisation's capacity. This might mean new products, new premises, new computer systems, additional people, and/or new machinery. Do you have or can you afford, the capacity required?

People

Identify the implications for your people. What new skills, training, recruitment possibilities are there? Do you need new languages? What about the organisation structure?

Profit and Loss Account

Now comes one of the most critical stages! You compile a forecast profit and loss account based on all the information you have collated above. Is the proposed business profitable? Does it provide the required ROCE? Is the plan watertight and robust? Test it! Does it achieve what you want to do? Does it add value for your shareholders? Does it make sense? Lots of questions, but all are valid and all need to be answered.

Review the Plan

Finally, review the plan again and confirm whether it does or does not do what you want to achieve. If it does not, have the courage to revisit the whole process again. Figure 5.2 is a schematic summary of the eight steps, which should help you through this process. As an example of strategic flexibility and corporate metamorphosis, the IBM case study that

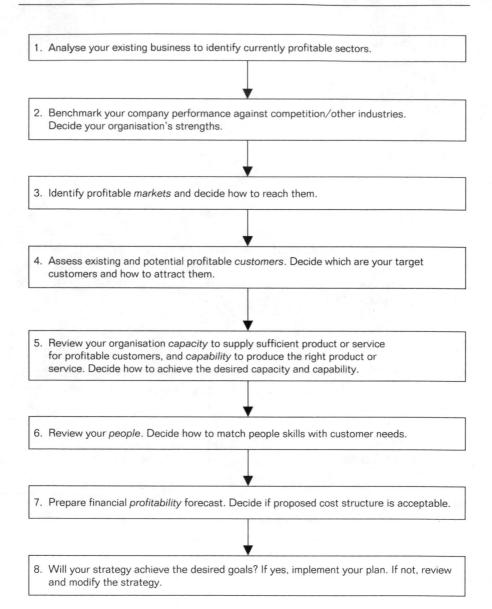

1. Analyse your existing business to identify currently profitable sectors.

2. Benchmark your company performance against competition/other industries. Decide your organisation's strengths.

3. Identify profitable *markets* and decide how to reach them.

4. Assess existing and potential profitable *customers*. Decide which are your target customers and how to attract them.

5. Review your organisation *capacity* to supply sufficient product or service for profitable customers, and *capability* to produce the right product or service. Decide how to achieve the desired capacity and capability.

6. Review your *people*. Decide how to match people skills with customer needs.

7. Prepare financial *profitability* forecast. Decide if proposed cost structure is acceptable.

8. Will your strategy achieve the desired goals? If yes, implement your plan. If not, review and modify the strategy.

Figure 5.2.   Planning your strategy for profitable business

features next is a superb example. It also allows us to look at culture in an e-business; hence the title 'e-culture'.

Chapter 6

IBM Greenock 'E-Culture'

Introduction

In 1951 IBM started to make electric typewriters and punch-card machines at Greenock near Glasgow, employing people with skills developed in the local shipbuilding industry. As IBM Greenock celebrates its fiftieth anniversary, two-thirds of the 5500 employees do not manufacture anything. Instead they provide a service to customers across Europe, the Middle East, and Africa (EMEA). IBM Greenock has become a microcosm of IBM Corporation.

This case study is an amazing story of transformation and innovation. It is also designed to shatter your rose-tinted glasses, to shake you out of any false sense of security with your own business, and to inspire you to rethink your current strategy. The changes described here are so radical that they will force most business models and cultures around the world to be uprooted over the next decade. Be prepared to change or be left behind.

IBM coined the term 'e-business' and describes becoming an 'e-business' as 'the use of Internet technologies to improve and transform key enterprise processes'. Just as the rest of IBM Corporation has transformed itself into an 'e-business', so has Greenock. Others believe similar revolutions will happen elsewhere. For example, Cisco Systems' chief executive officer, John Chambers, stated: 'I believe that a decade from now every major company in the world will be an e-company.'[1]

Before you read the rest of this case study, I do need to issue a brief 'health warning'. As the recent dotcom boom and bust cycle testifies, becoming an 'e-business' is not in itself a reason for success. The transition from 'bricks' to 'clicks' has to be based on a sound strategy where your customers benefit from buying from your website, or where you reduce your unit costs through use of the Internet medium. Blind entrepreneurial enthusiasm, founded on the assumption that $24 \times 7 \times 52$ website availability means orders, invoices and cash generation, is insufficient. The principles that apply to successful traditional business, also apply to 'e-business', and that is why IBM Greenock is a winner.

This case study tells how IBM Greenock developed into an 'e-business' together with its own 'e-culture', where 'e-culture' is 'the way we do things in an "e-business" that affects how our people feel and behave'.

This case study is in three sections:

▶   History.
▶   Culture change.
▶   The future.

We start with an overview of Greenock's history, and then home in on how becoming an e-business has changed the cultures in five key departments at Greenock: communications, the Customer Support Organisation, the Technical HelpCentre, IBM's Global Services (IGS) operation, and e-procurement (i.e. purchasing). Finally we will look into the future!

In this case study there are many general principles to look out for and apply in your own business:

▶   Be prepared for change by ensuring your strategy is adaptable. The case study shows the flexibility of IBM Greenock's strategy, despite the large number of employees on one site. Look out for the examples of wholesale change, and retraining that maintain this agility. Drive, rather than be driven by, market changes if you can.
▶   Take advantage of the Internet to offer new services that add value to your existing products or services. Could/should more of your product be made electronic to aid this Internet access and data transfer?
▶   Rethink your current communication channels with your customers to completely revolutionise the type of work your people are doing. For example, if your customers can place orders themselves more easily and electronically, at their convenience, your people will be able to move from being order entry clerks to higher added value jobs.
▶   Could you improve the after-sales service you offer at drastically reduced cost to you and your customer, by using Internet technology? Could your customers benefit from your website, for example, by being able to order replacement parts to fit by themselves, or by downloading solutions? Ideas abound in the Technical HelpCentre section of this study.

▶ Purchasing systems, information flow, and the service your suppliers can offer you could be revolutionised too. The procurement section contains many examples for you to consider.

▶ Excellent two-way communication is one of the keys to remaining flexible. There are several examples of infrastructure and organisation structure in this case study that facilitate this communication.

▶ General training courses for your people can now be found on the Internet and, if justified, specialist courses can be written and made available on your intranet. Consider, as this case does, the benefit of learning on line rather than through dedicated training courses.

Let us start now by looking at the culture change journey undertaken by IBM Greenock.

History

Greenock started as a manufacturer of mainly electric typewriters and punch-card machines. By the end of the 1950s the plant had moved into electronics, started making printed circuit boards, and sold its first computer. As part of this process, skills began to develop for purchasing and designing/testing electronic products.

In the 1960s, the site focused on mainframe technology with bespoke IBM systems. This increased both hardware and software design skills, but customer support required visits to customers' premises by highly skilled IBM support staff. The next major milestones appeared during the 1970s as optical character readers and display-only terminals.

The 1980s saw the birth of IBM's first PC, with Microsoft operating systems instead of IBM's bespoke ones, and Greenock became the PC manufacturing centre for the whole of EMEA. In 1988 the site made its two millionth PC as well as the associated keyboards and printed circuit boards. By this time it had also invested heavily in front-end logistics capability, with an automated raw-materials distribution centre capable of holding 24,000 one-tonne capacity pallets and a two-mile conveyor system to feed parts directly to the manufacturing lines. This meant the site now also had logistics skills.

In the manufacturing section, the whole production line stopped using robotics in order to be as flexible as possible, because products have to be customised in the right language (e.g. French) as well as hardware configuration. Changes are so frequent that the only continuous improvement to work well in this environment is the one-week assault on a specific issue, which brings a step change in performance each time. The manufacturing section also complemented its capability with test facilities that are so good they now can be offered as services too!

The manufacturing to service revolution really started in earnest in the 1990s, with the arrival in 1993 of Lou Gerstner as chairman and chief executive officer of IBM Corporation. The site management realised theirs was a logistics and information management business, not a manufacturing one. Production of keyboards, printed circuit boards and any commodity products ceased in the search for higher value-added activities. Laptops and Servers replaced PCs, and manufacturing switched from making for stock to build-to-order. Literally hundreds of people at a time retrained to develop new skills – service skills. For example:

▶ In 1995 Greenock opened its Technical HelpCentre, which now holds over 220 technically trained, multilingual staff, providing technical help to over half a million customers throughout EMEA.

▶ A new Customer Support Organisation opened in 1997. Their mission makes sure IBM's customers receive what they order when they want it, across all the countries of EMEA. Today this centralised CSO offers multilingual capability to 70 countries in 20 languages.

▶ In 1998 the ibm.com call centre opened its telephone lines for business. Today ibm.com employs over 750 staff – 600 of these multilingual – offering a variety of customer services including switchboard services, response to general enquiries, fault logging, pre-sales support, data management and telemarketing, again for the whole of EMEA.

Also 1997 saw Lou Gerstner launch the concept of 'e-business', a concept that has proved to be a watershed for IBM.

Between 1997 and 2001 the site accelerated its transformation from manufacturing to service. 1997/98, for example, saw the implementation of SAP software to re-engineer the whole purchasing process throughout IBM, and 1999 started 'e-procurement' in the drive to radically streamline communications with suppliers.

The automated distribution centre mentioned earlier was transformed. It now contains products owned by the suppliers, not IBM Greenock, with transfer of ownership only taking place when raw materials transfer to the just-in-time (JIT) manufacturing areas. It is a 'bonded' warehouse too so there are no import duties until the raw materials are released into production. This has in effect created a virtual warehouse, which opens up yet another new potential service for customers.

Moving now to 2001, IBM Greenock's *products* include NetVista™ Desktops (IBM's range of PCs), Thinkpad Notebooks (IBM's range of laptops), x-Series Servers (IBM's servers), and a range of complementary accessories.

IBM Greenock's *services* now include the whole end-to-end chain from initial enquiry through to warranty and service. This is a very valuable set of competencies, especially in the context of e-businesses.

So far in the history section of this case study, IBM Greenock has:

▶ developed world-class purchasing and raw materials logistics capability
▶ expanded the whole customer service chain to include initial multi-lingual enquiry, specification and ordering, through to post-sales technical help and maintenance
▶ grown the whole arena of product development expertise together with manufacturing and testing.

Culture Change

Now we need to explore the culture changes in each of five departments, to see the impact of all these changes, starting with communications.

Culture Change in Communications

People in IBM used to wonder what was going on in the business elsewhere in the world, wonder about the financial health of the company, and indeed wonder about what the future direction would be. Whether the subject is strategic change, financial performance of their division, or any other significant events, they wonder no longer. Each of the 300,000+ employees knows instantaneously what Lou Gerstner or anyone else has just broadcast, as these broadcasts are televised around each site.

Every employee also has access to the site intranet, and therefore to today's local site news, and also a link to the Greenock site vice president via 'Site Director on-line'. A couple of clicks accesses the Personal Computer Division intranet home page, and a few more clicks displays the IBM worldwide home page where any employee can see what Lou Gerstner said on any given day.

Communication is seen as so important that eight people at Greenock are employed solely to ensure that internal and external communication is accurate, consistent and timely. It will come as no surprise that the site vice president only gets four or five 'Site Director' e-mails each week from his entire 5500 employees. It will also be no surprise that he holds regular site communication meetings with all his people. It is attention to this kind of detail that eradicated historic 'us and them' attitudes, and promoted collaboration. The following two quotes demonstrate this attitude and cooperation throughout IBM admirably:

> *'Cut me down the middle, and you'll find I've got IBM blue blood.*

> *I can phone someone anywhere in the world, explain that I am Robert from Greenock and I need some help; and the response 99.9 per cent of the time is "Sure, how can I help?". This, I find fantastic.'*

Culture Change in the Customer Support Organisation

Prior to January 1997, national teams handled customer orders for a specific country. Greenock received faxed orders and then had to enter these orders onto the Greenock system and liaise with manufacturing to ensure each order was made correctly and on time. Over the next two years, all the national order-taking operations were brought across to Greenock for the whole of EMEA. Around 370 people now support customers, rather than just input their orders, for 70 countries in 20 languages. This upgraded the nature and skill level associated with this role including, of course, the need for languages. Approximately eight years ago there were no significant language skills in this area. Times (and cultures) have changed!

Orders now entered by each customer arrive at Greenock through electronic data interface (EDI) instead of faxes, so the data entry (and potential for mistakes) at Greenock is now history. The system is intelligent, allowing only logical combinations of products to be ordered by each customer.

Automated links through to manufacturing remove the need for paper orders to travel from one department to another. Instead, the single sheet of paper printed out in the manufacturing area and used for the whole manufacturing process, is bar-coded to enable each order to be tracked.

The whole order back-up information is filed automatically and electronically, once approved, which essentially makes this complete order processing system paperless.

A recent innovation, made possible through e-business, is a programme of automatic product replenishment for customers when stock levels reach certain minimum quantities. Currently this requires significant investment and is therefore limited to major customers, but the principle is akin to the paper Kanban system used for raw materials replenishment for many years, but of course without the paper!

Another change as part of becoming an e-business is the development of more informal communication. No longer is it necessary to have meetings to give people information about what is going on in the company, because everybody knows. The difference now is that you can now spend time discussing this information and any implications it may have for the future.

It will already be clear that the kinds of skills required have changed too, which makes it even more important for systems training, customer care training and product training. The key difference with an e-business is that this training no longer requires a whole day or days away from work in a training room with a dedicated trainer; the training is simply downloaded from the Internet and completed in blocks at the individual's convenience.

Culture Change in the Technical HelpCentre

Historically the bespoke mainframe software required very expensive, specialist technical help at the customer's site, but the move to PCs with Microsoft software facilitated remote fixing of problems. In the early 1990s, Greenock decided to develop Technical HelpCentres as a national service in the EMEA countries. The advent of the Internet allowed technical support information to be put on to websites, but otherwise at this point the service was unchanged and still within country. There was another key business driver; that of keeping these national technical help specialists trained, which commonly required six weeks initial training and a further eight weeks product upgrade training each year. This training need, together with the aim of making a centre of excellence, drove the move to centralise to a multilingual Technical HelpCentre at Greenock for the whole of EMEA in 1995.

Many of the employees in the Technical HelpCentre originally worked in the manufacturing areas, the product testing, or product development sections. Their new role, which has changed out of all recognition, is a good example of manufacturing people moving across to a very important service industry role.

The Technical HelpCentre at Greenock receives around 45,000 calls per month. For example, a French Thinkpad customer makes a local call in France. This call is transferred to Greenock where the customer will speak with the next available French-speaking Thinkpad agent. With help, the customers fix around 80 per cent of all these enquiries over the telephone by making settings changes. Of this 80 per cent, around 92 per cent are fixed first time, with the average call duration around ten minutes.

Of the remaining 20 per cent that require other input for ancillary items, or perhaps replacement parts, around one-fifth need parts that the customers can easily replace by themselves. These are called Customer Replacement Units. Being an e-business facilitates this customer part replacement as it makes remote fault diagnosis relatively easy. It works by downloading the whole product configuration to the Technical Help-Centre agents, who find the fault by comparing this with the original product configuration. Greenock simply despatches the required Customer Replacement Unit for the customer to replace.

There is another innovation and improvement in service for the balance of enquiries that require more than remote support. Three years ago a technical help agent visiting the customer would not have known the history of conversations between Greenock and the customer. That history is now documented, and parts to be fitted by an IBM agent are despatched direct to the customer. This speeds up the repair time, and reduces the required skill level of the IBM agent, as on-site diagnosis is normally no longer needed.

With the success of this remote and on-site service, managed by the Technical HelpCentre, these agents at Greenock get much job satisfaction as they own the customer's technical problem until it is fixed. This factor helps explain why the Technical HelpCentre, unlike a typical call centre, has a very low staff turnover.

The HelpCentre is also promoting self-help via the Internet, with multilingual websites. For example, downloading a set of drivers for a printer upgrade from a website is now becoming common practice compared to the slower route of sending a set of drivers on floppy discs through the postal system.

The implication of all this is that the Technical HelpCentre is a centre of excellence. This means it is commercially valuable, rather than being a cost to the organisation. If, for example, another company (e.g. automotive, banking, or airline) wants to establish a help centre, the geographical location is insignificant due to the nature of the communication, so why not let IBM host it? Here is another powerful commercial opportunity that also has major cost and lead-time reduction implications for IBM customers. Thinking of a logical extension to this takes us to IBM Greenock providing a higher level of technical support for, say, the whole of a bank's IT requirements including items such as the telebanking software. The possibilities are endless, and they all originate from being an e-business.

Culture Change in IBM Global Services (IGS)

IGS is IBM's IT organisation, providing software solutions for customers. Greenock's IGS used to provide IT support to Greenock's employees only. These days more of its resources are focusing on external customers, by providing industry specific e-business solutions that range from starter websites through to custom-built applications.

Becoming an e-business means IGS no longer needs to have all its resources on site, so packages of work can be completed by skilled programmers regardless of location. This frees up internal resources that need face-to-face contact with customers, and enables these packages to be managed by project managers rather than be hands-on. This is fortunate because the demand for development people has exploded with the growth of e-business.

Culturally there has been a major change too. The project managers are now empowered to do the whole job, rather than have the commercial aspects handled by business managers. The project managers now know their budget and are accountable for it; indeed it is a key performance indicator (KPI) that affects their remuneration. Project management is now becoming another centre of excellence, with obvious commercial opportunities.

Culture Change in E-Procurement (Purchasing)

The cultural change within procurement is in three phases: organisational change, process re-engineering, and e-procurement.

When Lou Gerstner joined as chief executive officer, he brought with him a new head of procurement. Prior to this there was a national, decentralised structure, leading to multiple interfaces with suppliers and a huge diversity of purchasing systems. The first phase centralised global procurement and decentralised 'fulfilment'. (At Greenock, fulfilment people report to manufacturing and ensure raw materials are available as required for production. Procurement people purchase globally, by commodity, for materials required throughout the Personal Computer Division, not just for Greenock. Procurement people may be based anywhere in the world, and it is common for individuals to relocate for a year or two to China or the USA for a specific project.)

The second phase re-engineered the whole procurement process by implementing SAP and introduced one quality system worldwide too.

Phase three, the move to e-procurement, has changed the supplier relationship. For example, IBM Greenock insists each supplier has its own hub local to Greenock, where it holds inventory prior to delivery to site. This supplier hub concept was new in 1997. It is based on 'replenishment', a little like the regular filling of fresh food display cabinets in food retailers as stocks are sold. Prior to this IBM used to have boats sailing from the Far East for several weeks, with IBM-owned stock on board, to fill the Greenock automated distribution centre. Now materials are shipped to the supplier's hub, and ownership only moves to IBM Greenock when it leaves the bonded automated distribution centre on site. The suppliers are also responsible for configuring every item, in the correct language, for the specific customer order prior to delivery from their hub to Greenock site. This is part of their service to IBM.

These organisational, process and e-business changes, have had the following impacts:

▶ In the old days a buyer from Greenock could meet a buyer from the USA at the same supplier and not know who his colleague was. Certainly there was little scope for economies of scale. Now there is one buyer and plenty of scope for economies of scale. In fact, for the few products that have common items within different divisions of IBM, there is a 'commodity council' to ensure common parts for different divisions are only purchased by one person.

▶ Many layers of bureaucracy have disappeared, particularly jobs for data entry and paper form filling. Skills have been extended and each job now adds far more value than previously.

▶ Two years ago the site had around 200,000 paper invoices annually, which required data entry. Now there are no paper invoices and no data entry people.

▶ The whole procurement process from requisition to payment is now almost fully automated.

▶ 'Requests to quote' are currently sent to suppliers through the Internet Quoting Tool programme. A programme to facilitate open bidding, through quoting on the Internet, is being rolled out now.

▶ Quality engineers used to check the quality of raw materials as they arrived on site. For the past five years there has been no need for receiving inspection, as the supplier quality management systems takes data direct from the suppliers, making the need for incoming inspection redundant. These people have also been transferred to higher value-added, more interesting jobs.

People in e-procurement described the working environment as: 'dynamic', 'everything is changing', 'there's a huge opportunity for changing your job tomorrow if you are willing to change'. 'We are focused on change'.

There is a clear message about innovation and flexibility here.

The Future

Start dreaming!

Imagine your laptop or server is not functioning properly. You contact the IBM Technical HelpCentre via the Internet and hit one key that sends an e-mail, with configuration attached, to the centre. A few moments later your corrected configuration is returned, loaded automatically and you are back in business. Now imagine the whole thing happens automatically without you even realising it. Say your hard drive needs a refurbishment, your Thinkpad software recognises this and arranges the repair automatically with IBM. You carry on your business uninterrupted.

Now take the same concept to a car engine management system. You are driving and the engine management light comes on. Instead of having to visit your nearest garage for maintenance, the fault is sent automatically to the Technical HelpCentre, diagnosed, corrected if possible, and sent back. Your engine management light goes out and you do not need to take any further corrective action. How is that for service?! As the car manufacturer, you focus on your core competence and let IBM handle the software development for this after sales service. What a great way to add value for your customers.

Now consider Greenock. As manufacturing has reduced it has created more space in the automated distribution centre for other companies' raw materials. Add the web to allow e-procurement, and the relevant support software and you suddenly have a very valuable service to offer almost any global company from Coca Cola to BMW. Then consider that you can enable these companies to concentrate on their core competencies by managing their IT environment for them as an added service as well as the 'e-procurement'. This is powerful. This all derives from becoming a world-class supply chain, and from becoming an e-business.

You and your company may be well voiced with the World Wide Web, but now there is something new, something beyond 'the web'. It is being tested now. It is called 'the grid'. In the future, instead of accessing one server and then having to go to a different one for other applications, your data could be stored on a virtual computer consisting of your server and a number of others linked to it. The number of 'others' could be millions; similar to the web but with lower costs, increased access speed and improved access to data. IBM Greenock has already been selected to build the UK's computer grid as a cluster of servers linked together over the Internet. Stand by for another IT and business model revolution!

Summary Action List for Your Business

1. Define and exploit your core competency.
2. Regularly review your strategy and keep it flexible.
3. Move as much as possible of your product or service from a physical one to an electronic one. If you cannot change your current product, bolt on electronic services that add value for your customers. Improve your technical support by offering it remotely.
4. Review your current operation with the aim of offering your skills to other firms as a value-adding service.
5. Improve your communication infrastructure for internal and external communication. Make sure you can communicate information quickly, accurately and consistently to all your employees so they know what is going on, and include suppliers and customers in the communication chain.
6. Foster an innovation culture with systems that support, rather than prevent, change. Make quantum rather than incremental change the norm. This does not mean chaos; it means managed change that keeps ahead of the market progress. Make sure you watch trends in the industry.
7. Use the Internet or company intranet to facilitate e-learning.
8. Ensure you have a broad product portfolio and serve many markets, if you want to survive the next decade and become a successful e-business.

Chapter 7

Quarterly Objectives and Key Performance Indicators

Agreeing objectives stimulates innovation and
continuous improvement

So far, you have benchmarked your culture and decided your mission, vision and values. You have prepared your culture change plan and devised a new strategy for the business. You have kept your teams involved and updated them with the evolving plan. People are prepared for change, but they do not yet know the detail. Nor do they know their future role so they are apprehensive. How are you going to take away this fear? How will you switch *everyone* on to believe in your vision? Implementation starts with a big launch in just a few weeks, but there is one key element still left to introduce. What is this key element all about?

It is about linking the day-to-day actions of each and every person to the strategic and culture change plans (which in practice will be woven into one plan), focusing their attention and time on what matters. It is about creating a sense of purpose and a means for assessing achievements, to motivate higher levels of employee performance and satisfaction. It is about encouraging and repeatedly reinforcing actions and processes to convert this strategic and culture change plan into reality. It is time now to make that link by introducing annual and quarterly objectives, and their associated key performance indicators (KPIs).

Annual objectives, normally established at the start of the new year, are simply what the name suggests; objectives agreed at the start of each year for completion by the end of that year. They should be 'blue sky', blinkers-off types of ideas, normally based on a major step beyond current capability and in the direction the company wants to go.

At departmental manager level, for example, annual objectives should incorporate:

▶ the company's strategic goals
▶ the site manager and departmental manager's aims
▶ continuous improvement objectives as agreed by the Steering Team (to be discussed later in the 'Improving Your Success' section).

Doing this is a good way to align and capture all these different needs in one set of objectives, forcing focus and prioritisation by limiting the number of objectives to five for each department and employee. To ensure success each department's, or person's, objectives should be within their control.

Sometimes, this is a great way of encouraging the radical, new, even breathtaking idea that can revolutionise the way the company thinks and works, as annual objectives apply at both departmental and individual level. For an individual, these would normally be agreed and reviewed with their immediate manager as part of the annual appraisal.

Similarly, quarterly objectives are agreed at the start of each quarter for completion in the same three-month period. The quarterly objectives are also at departmental and individual level, with some quarterly objectives simply breaking up the annual ones into quarterly stages.

KPIs are tangible and measurable criteria (e.g. delivery performance, employee survey results, material utilisation and debtor days) that indicate if the company is on track to meet its strategic objectives. The KPIs, like the quarterly objectives, are also at departmental and individual level.

It is these annual and quarterly objectives, together with the KPIs, that swivel everyone to face the vision and encourage a unified approach to drive the strategy.

Establishing the objectives is a remarkably simple process that is essentially the same whether you are running a local firm of 50 people or a global organisation of 5000. The only key difference is the number of management layers involved. The chief executive officer starts the objectives cascade process each year by taking the strategic plan and agreeing with his immediate subordinates, in this case the board of directors, *measurable* annual and first-quarter objectives for each of them. The objectives must be something they have control over and they must be achievable for the subordinate to buy in to. Each board member in turn cascades objectives to their subordinates and so on. Obviously, the objectives will vary considerably as the process is fragmented further down the organisation, but they should still broadly be in line with the overall corporate plan.

As the process moves on down the organisation, each level has a chance to contribute their ideas; indeed they should be actively encouraged to do so. Who knows, one or a number of these ideas could change the whole future of the company. Five objectives each is the norm simply because this is a reasonable number for an individual or team to focus their attention on. Any more and the focus is watered down; any less and there is too little scope for success, should one of the ideas be blocked.

To indicate how big this could be in terms of a source of ideas, let us take a company with 5000 employees. In each year, each employee has five annual objectives and four sets of five quarterly objectives, making a total of 25 per employee, or 125,000 objectives to improve the whole company each year. In addition, each department agrees to 25 objectives per year, which could easily be a further 5000 objectives for the whole company, making 130,000 objectives in total. These are big numbers!

When agreeing these objectives, make sure your leaders know about the Pareto 80:20 rule and apply the same logic here. Aim for an 80 per cent achievement rate for these objectives, so 80 per cent of your employees can feel like winners. Do not make the objectives unachievable, or so hard to achieve that only 20 per cent make it. Think of the potential to motivate, encourage and reward your staff for performance based on these objectives. Just think of the potential to stimulate innovation too!

Also, presuming you are looking for a pool of ideas to help you grow the company, this has got to be a simple and very effective start point. Since each set of objectives is agreed with the immediate line manager, there is the opportunity for local management to quickly authorise initial investment in those ideas that merit funding, and to feed back further up the organisation any ideas that merit closer scrutiny by the chief executive officer; that little sycamore seed as a germ of an idea that could initiate a flood of activity and major investment to become a real winner.

While we are on the subject of investment in innovation as a subset of quarterly objectives ideas, let us consider the following two scenarios and their respective systems:

▶ Many companies *apportion* funds from a restricted pot that requires each idea to fight for funding on some arbitrary return on capital employed (ROCE), payback period or net present value basis. The system requires approval by several layers of management, and ultimately the chief executive officer, if expenditure exceeds even a few thousand pounds. This inevitably restricts investment to conservative and well-known areas of existing business. It also stifles innovation and de-motivates those employees involved in preparing plans that often get rejected or 'lost' in the approval procedure. Each idea requires much investigation and resource to work the idea into a meaningful plan, resource that is wasted simply because the originators have no real idea whether their plan will be approved or not.

Consider too the impact of your employees believing they are not listened to, that they have to fight through layers of bureaucracy to get to a decision-maker, and that the time frame for approval is measured in terms of years rather than days. Under these conditions how can you possibly expect your company to beat the competition? As Gary Hamel very neatly put it[1] recently (when it comes to investment in new ideas), 'Does your company feel more like Silicon Valley or the Soviet Union?'

▶ Other companies consider ideas should be funded on a *meritocracy* basis, with authorisation well down in the organisation. This is where the values are so important, together with knowledge of the company strategy. With these two simple bits of information, each employee will know whether the idea has potential to help the company when fully developed. It avoids the need for bureaucratic pen-pushing administrators further up the organisation, and allows local approval to encourage innovation. This meritocracy does not mean throwing away large sums of money in an uncontrolled manner, it simply means getting money approved quickly for ideas that have potential, and then allocating resources as appropriate to start making things happen. With informal communication encouraged as part of the culture, any project that is not making quick progress, or has spent its initial funding without building internal support to continue, will soon be killed off by the project team as they will want to work, and be seen to work, only on successful projects. The originator will therefore have to sell the idea to potential project team members to attract the initial resources, and then contribute himself to keep the project going. It is a formula for success.

Now you see why systems that support innovation are so important.

With the quarterly objectives agreed, we now have to ensure they are the focus of every employee's attention. During each quarter, and ideally monthly, each line manager should ask for and receive progress updates on these objectives. This monthly feedback will visibly demonstrate progress and enable corrective action if required.

At the end of each quarter, it is especially satisfying to be able to look back and see just how much progress has been made against these objectives. Each employee assesses their achievements, quantifies them where appropriate, and then agrees the status with their line manager as part of the next quarter's objective setting meeting. Publishing these 'Quarterly Achievements' is a great way to demonstrate progress has been made, both at a local level and also to the most senior personnel. My recommendation, based on personal experience, is to have a front summary sheet to ensure busy senior executives at least know the main achievements, even if they have not time to read the more detailed ones.

So, motivate your employees by agreeing rather than imposing objectives. Leave the 'how' to the employees. Empower your teams to achieve, to innovate and to become masters of their own destiny within the strategic direction of your business!

Simon Jersey shows us how by 'Delivering the Best' in the next case study.

Chapter 8

Simon Jersey
'Delivering the Best'

Introduction

Simon Jersey is a leading designer and supplier of clothing to business and industry worldwide, recognised as the pioneer of fashionable work wear, and famous through its excellent catalogue and corporate/bespoke service for its 'clothes for people to work in' (see their website www.simonjersey.com for further details). The firm has grown from two employees and two major UK customers who allowed Simon Jersey to offer new, vibrant and imaginative colours not seen before in their market, to a £30 million business with 280 staff and over 60,000 customers worldwide.

Simon Jersey is no ordinary company. This is made clear even as you approach reception down a cascade of curved steps towards the circular glass and steel structure that accommodates all the employees. On the wall in reception are the Excellence Northwest Award 2000; two North West 1999 special awards for leadership and people satisfaction; plus Investor in People 2000 and a myriad of other signs of success, which confirm that Simon Jersey is different.

As you will find out shortly, everything at Simon Jersey is focused on the culture for 'Delivering the Best', particularly in terms of customer service. Simon jersey developed this special culture over its 30-year history; one that reflects its heritage and its desire to trust, value, and care for its employees. Even the building is purpose-built to be open-plan and barrier-free to support this customer service ethic. As an example of customer feedback, here is a quote from Hertz:

'It is a pleasure to work with a responsive and innovative company. The customer service and commitment is outstanding and runs

through the whole organisation from the managing director all the way down.'

In this case study we will concentrate on three things:

▶ Simon Jersey's 'Delivering the Best' strategy
▶ the role played by the Leadership Development programme
▶ Simon Jersey's internal customer (i.e. employee opinion) survey.

As you would expect from this special company, there are many general principles in this case study that potentially apply to literally any organisation regardless of industry sector or geographic location:

▶ Be prepared to ask for outside help when formulating your strategy. Non-executive directors are a potential source of expertise for you.
▶ Communicate your strategy to every employee and make it easy to understand. Simon Jersey have developed a very simple, and effective, single page format.
▶ Link your strategy to the daily activities of each employee to ensure everyone is focused on what you want them to concentrate on. Look at how Simon Jersey has achieved this.
▶ The Simon Jersey case study highlights the importance of having a dedicated culture champion (called customer focus manager in this example); to encourage people to focus on customers' needs, to implement the EFQM Excellence Model, and to drive continuous improvement throughout the company.
▶ If you want to make work fun, here are a myriad of initiatives.
▶ Also be prepared to ask for outside help to develop leaders throughout your company. Here is a programme that worked well for Simon Jersey. You could apply a similar programme in your own company.
▶ Employee opinion surveys are invaluable when you ask the right questions. The sample questionnaire in this case study will give you some ideas of questions, format and process.

Let us look now at Simon Jersey's culture change experience.

Simon Jersey's 'Delivering the Best' Strategy

Around 1995, the senior management team asked themselves 'What do we want to achieve?' They decided to:

▶ develop a strategy with five or six key objectives each year
▶ communicate this strategy to every single person at Simon Jersey

▶ ask managers to put together their objectives in line with the over-all plan

▶ have a very open, honest, down-to-earth culture which involved and cared for their people

▶ focus on profitable business

▶ learn how to lead the company more professionally.

They added complementary skills of a non-executive director on the board, to help define what they wanted to have as their strategy. They reviewed the possible UK markets, customers and margins available. They also looked at their export business. For their strategy they decided:

▶ in addition to the UK business, to focus their export drive on four countries

▶ to specialise in design, marketing and distribution rather than establish manufacturing capabilities (although they do have some employees to make clothes on site, to cope with just-in-time supply)

▶ to concentrate on two channels into their market; the catalogue (which accounts for the majority of sales turnover) and the bespoke service for blue-chip clients.

Simon Jersey complemented the above strategy by achieving ISO 9001 in 1995. The next, highly significant step, involved creating the role of customer focus manager; to be a catalyst for encouraging people to focus on customers, for driving continuous improvement, and also for implementing the EFQM Excellence Model. In 1997 Simon Jersey started the EFQM Excellence Model journey by entering the North West Quality Awards process to get feedback; hence the awards in the Simon Jersey reception today. Although 'Delivering the Best' is based around the EFQM Excellence Model, few people within Simon Jersey would link the two as it has been simplified and branded internally as 'Delivering the Best'.

The current strategy for Simon Jersey is to increase market share in the UK, to promote further catalogue sales overseas, to establish more pan-European customers, and to add further e-commerce. Currently, only existing customers can order from the Simon Jersey website. The aim, during 2001, is to facilitate new customers to also be able to use this channel. Clearly, exciting times are ahead for Simon Jersey.

Back in 1998 the technical director, whose role includes business excellence and customer focus strategy, wanted to summarise on one sheet of paper what the organisation was trying to achieve. He intended to make it easy to communicate the strategy to all employees. The top team brainstormed and decided what was important to the company:

▶ customers
▶ people
▶ processes
▶ business performance.

These four titles form the horizontal headings for 'Delivering the Best'. He proposed that for each of the above headings there should be:

▶ a mission
▶ desired outcomes
▶ key objectives
▶ key performance indicators (KPIs)
▶ key measurement tools.

These five subjects form the vertical headings for 'Delivering the Best'.

During this strategic review meeting they re-defined the company motto as:

> *We will offer the finest service in the design and supply of clothes for people to work in.*

The net result is a one-page matrix that neatly summarises the company objectives and strategy (see Figure 8.1).

With the aim of making 'Delivering the Best' crystal clear to all employees, and to end up with a double-sided laminate for each employee, the reverse side of the laminate defines each heading. For example:

▶ customers are 'people who buy from us'
▶ people are 'you and I'
▶ processes are 'the way we do things'
▶ business performance is 'achieving better results'.

Similarly the Simon Jersey definitions are:

▶ motto (what we do)
▶ mission (how we will do it)
▶ desired outcomes (what we need to have)
▶ key objectives (what we need to achieve this year)
▶ KPIs (what things we need to check)
▶ key measurement tools (what we use to check things).

Delivering the Best 2001[1]

Our motto: 'We will offer the finest service in the design and supply of clothes for people to work in'

	Customers	People	Processes	Business performance
Mission	We will meet the demands and expectations of our customers to the highest standard of quality and service within our industry	We care about our people and will maintain our position as a fair employer	We will continually identify better ways of working through innovation and involvement	We are committed to improving the financial performance of our business by focusing on profitable clothing products in appropriate European markets, to maximise shareholder value
Desired outcomes	Delighted customers Innovative design of products	An enthusiastic, inspired trained, involved and stable workforce	Creative marketing and selling of our products Production of quality products at value for money prices Flexibility and ability to handle large volumes of small transactions Timely distribution of products	Maintaining a strong and profitable business Timely collection of payment from our customers
Key objectives	Increase customer satisfaction to 97 per cent	Increase people satisfaction to 88 per cent	Implement two main improvements and one improvement from each manager	Increase sales to £32 million Maintain stocks at 20 weeks Increase PBIT to £3.7 million
Key performance indicators (KPIs)	Customer perceptions Customer retention Stock availability Order despatch performance Market penetration	Employee perceptions	ISO 9000 Supplier performance Material utilisation	Sales Stockholding Budgets Bank balance Debtor days Gross margin Profit
Key measurement tools	Customer surveys Marketing retention report Out of stock report Despatch performance report Market penetration report	Employee surveys Investors in People accreditation	ISO 9000 accreditation Supplier performance analysis Material utilisation report	Sales report Stock report Budget report Debtors report Gross margin report Management accounts

Note 1: Credit is given here to Simon Jersey who in 1998 defined and created 'Delivering the Best' in this one-page format.

Figure 8.1. 'Delivering the Best 2001'

Not content with just establishing the 'Delivering the Best' strategy, the board made a director responsible for each KPI (e.g. stock availability) and established the following *monthly* communication process. After each board meeting, *all* the directors review the KPIs in a single management meeting to consider the operational issues within the business. A meeting follows this with all the managers and within an hour of this managers' meeting, there is a further briefing by each manager to their team to make sure everyone knows the same message. The feedback loop on this process is closed by the internal customer survey asking people to respond either yes or no to the statement 'I am aware of our key performance indicators'.

Now that we have briefly covered the scope of Simon Jersey's 'Delivering the Best' strategy, we will now take three examples from the matrix and explore in more detail how the company implemented these. Let us start with customer satisfaction.

The target for 2001 is to increase overall customer satisfaction to 97 per cent. To know whether or not this has been achieved requires customer satisfaction surveys. For Simon Jersey this is based on feedback twice a year from catalogue customers and bespoke customers, including the people who buy the clothing and the people who wear it. With a database of over 60,000 customers and over two million garments sold each year, this objective requires careful management but can produce invaluable information to guide future product and service developments.

The second example, this time from the people mission, says, 'We care about our people and will maintain our position as a fair employer.' Here are a few examples. Simon Jersey installed showers for use by staff that come to work by bike. 'It is good for the environment and it is good for our staff. We try to keep our people happy as they are the core of our business.' Simon Jersey employees are also shareholders after three year's service. They also receive profit-related pay (PRP), which helps the employee and helps the company too, especially when you hear comments such as 'Turn the lights out, think of the PRP.'

Thirdly, the key people objective is to 'increase people satisfaction to 88 per cent in 2001', as measured by the employee surveys. Simon Jersey keeps coming up with new initiatives to make work fun. Examples include:

▶ 'Bright Spark', where employee improvement ideas are fed through to the customer focus manager and published on e-mail to each department. Staff receive recognition for all implemented ideas.

▶ 'Employee of the quarter' for the employee that has most demon-
strated behaviour beyond the call of duty. The people vote for this
award.

▶ 'Department of the year' for the best service to other departments.
This is a silver trophy and certificate for the winning team. The
people vote for this award.

▶ Each employee receives a personalised birthday card, box of
chocolates and a Christmas gift.

▶ 'Employee evenings' where employees are invited to social events held
in the workplace.

▶ Fund raising activities, from sponsored walks to cycle rides, to
support local charities selected by the employees.

Simon Jersey's managing director gets involved with the award presentations and makes each event lots of fun. You can see many examples
of the caring attitude, the visible demonstration that employees are
valued, and the implicit trust that is so engrained it does not even need
mentioning.

Leadership Development Programme

Simon Jersey directors worked on the premise that to improve the
company required improved leadership. They wanted three things:

▶ to grow the company
▶ to focus their people on what was important
▶ to be better leaders.

Simon Jersey's managing director and technical director decided that
external help was what they wanted for the company. Following a
couple of meetings with a consultant, they defined what was 'missing'
from the company and hence established the 'results to be achieved' as
the first step of an 11-stage programme. The key need was for improved
leadership.

They then started to get the rest of the team on board through an
'awareness seminar'. The top people (board level plus one level down)
attended the awareness seminar at Simon Jersey, where they were asked
questions such as: 'What are some of the changes you have seen? Where
is the company going? Where is it now? How do you feel you need to
grow and develop?' The aim was to help make the team realise that they
needed new skills and changed attitudes to really stimulate faster growth

for the company. This top team, called the Communications Group, had to make a decision as to whether or not this was the right move for the company.

There was only one criteria set by the two directors for the Leadership Development programme to proceed; the need for each person attending the awareness seminar to come up with and implement an improvement that would save the company in excess of £5000, or a total of £130,000 between them. The final savings figure actually signed off by the directors was £400,000.

Following the awareness seminar the directors decided that Simon Jersey would continue with the Leadership Development programme, and agreed that it would be the board plus one level down who would be involved.

A series of one-to-one interviews followed between the consultant and the 26 members of the Communications Group. There were two main reasons:

▶ For the consultant to better understand what the directors and managers wanted to get out of the programme. (The directors wanted coaching, increased manager 'buy-in', and support. The managers asked for improved leadership style, personal confidence, team building and the ability to prioritise.)

▶ To complete manager and individual assessment forms for the 26 attendees. This identified gaps between the required and current skill levels. For example, a gap might be the need 'to be more proactive and innovative'. This step also focused on 'This is why I am doing this', to initiate some buy-in and accountability of both manager and individual. For the individuals this meant putting things into practice, with the consultant as the coach. This implementation element turned the whole programme into one of business development rather than simply training.

Feedback from the 26 interviews confirmed the programme design would meet the needs identified earlier. Simon Jersey had good people but needed more leadership. The senior people had to think more strategically; for example, how to double the business in five years. The programme aim was to get people to think differently – to be a coach, guide, leader, to set challenging targets, and to think, 'What value do I add to the organisation?' The next stage was to tell them *how*, which required behavioural change – to *start* coaching, encouraging, inspiring.

This stimulated a kick-off meeting with the directors and top 20 managers, to let them know what they were going to do, to agree some goals and objectives for each person, and to encourage everyone to share what they wanted to achieve from the programme.

The heart of the programme contained 10 sessions for all 26 people to be developed *together*, in-house, at the rate of one half-day session every two weeks. Each topic was practical; tools learned on Wednesday could be implemented on Thursday. Subjects included time management, being positive (e.g. try saying 'I feel fantastic today' when you arrive at work and see what sort of reaction you get!), leadership, planning, and many others.

One of the best sessions for Simon Jersey was 'the organisation required to make monitoring and measuring easy', which produced a list of 'key result areas' (KRAs) for each person. The KRAs must be measurable and fully support the Simon Jersey 'Delivering the Best' strategy and company KPIs. This process ensures that people and their activities are fully focused on what is important to the organisation. These KRAs are now included as part of the annual appraisal process, thus ensuring a direct link between the company, departmental, and individual objectives.

Major benefits from this training package were a common language for the whole top team, the same knowledge base for all, and the realisation that a strategy was vital for the future success of the business. It also was a great way to build relationships and, of course, trust. The programme included a 360-degree appraisal.

During the series of programme sessions, the consultant regularly reviewed the progress of each individual, crosschecking with his manager, and at the end of the programme held a full review with the directors to confirm what had been achieved. In particular they assessed the achievements against the KRAs, with the end goal being to get the directors to coach their managers monthly and quarterly to help achieve the KRAs, rather than tell them what to do. Finally the team held a 'What is next?' meeting which agreed a number of follow-up sessions each year.

Simon Jersey's technical director thanked the consultancy firm by writing, 'It was a real pleasure to receive my diploma at our closing session yesterday and the thing that struck me most was how proud I felt seeing the strength, confidence and inspirational ability of each member of our team, which is quite a shift from just six months ago.' He also summed up the three main things Simon Jersey got out of the programme as:

► highly improved leaders
► a stronger, more integrated and more focused senior management team

▶ £400,000 forecasted bottom line savings in one year by the introduction of continuous improvement money saving projects.

Now that we have briefly reviewed the Leadership Development programme in Simon Jersey, we still have to find out what the Simon Jersey employees think of the company. What better way to find out than by asking them through an employee opinion survey, in this case called 'internal customer survey'.

Internal Customer (i.e. Employee Opinion) Survey

Twice each year, Simon Jersey constructs a one-page questionnaire (see Figure 8.2 overleaf) to gauge employees' opinions and feelings about the company. The only identification is by department. The answers are all collated and analysed by the marketing department. Some questions look at the interdepartmental customer service and thereby help managers to identify and correct internal issues. Other core questions, repeated in each survey, help establish trends. For example, over a three-year timeframe the statement, 'I enjoy my work' increased from 80 to 90 per cent satisfaction (defined by those who tick 'agree' or 'strongly agree'); 'I feel motivated' increased from 65 to 75 per cent, and 'We co-operate with each other' increased from 70 to 83 per cent. The whole questionnaire is included as Figure 8.2 to help you with ideas for your own internal customer (employee opinion) survey.

Summary

To summarise, Simon Jersey is a thriving company with a strategy that has changed the way people perceive industrial work-wear. The managing director and her management team encourage a professional, enthusiastic and highly motivated team culture dedicated to product quality and customer service. They are indeed 'Delivering the Best'.

INTERNAL CUSTOMER SURVEY Department name _____

To answer a question COMPLETELY FILL IN the box of your choice as ● Yes ○ No

		Up to 1 yr	Up to 2 yrs	Up to 3 yrs	Up to 5 yrs	More than 5 yrs
1.	I have worked at Simon Jersey for:	○	○	○	○	○

2. The person who conducts my appraisal is: ○ Teamleader ○ Manager

○ Supervisor ○ Director

○ Assistant Manager

We want to continue to improve internal customer service, in order to further improve our organisation and achieve our key business objectives.

3. Please state which department you work with the most

_____ department

	Strongly Agree	Agree	Disagree	Strongly Disagree
We co-operate with each other	○	○	○	○
I get what I need from this department	○	○	○	○

Can you suggest changes which could be made in order to improve the service you need from this department. Please use the space overleaf for any additional comments you may have.

_____

_____

4. Is there any other department that could improve the service it gives you?

_____ department

	Strongly Agree	Agree	Disagree	Strongly Disagree
We co-operate with each other	○	○	○	○
I get what I need from this department	○	○	○	○

Can you suggest changes which could be made in order to improve the service you need from this department. Please use the space overleaf for any additional comments you may have.

_____

_____

We need you to understand the objectives of the company and contribute to achieving them by continuously improving the tasks you perform.

		Y	N
5a.	I am aware of our key performance indicators	○	○
5b.	I understand how I contribute to them	○	○
5c.	I feel I receive enough information on our progress against our key performance indicators	○	○

We want you to get satisfaction from your work and feel motivated to do your tasks well.

		Strongly Agree	Agree	Disagree	Strongly Disagree
6.	I get satisfaction from my work	O	O	O	O
7.	I feel motivated at work	O	O	O	O
8.	I enjoy my work	O	O	O	O
9.	I feel good performance is recognised by my manager	O	O	O	O
10.	My manager encourages high morale	O	O	O	O
11.	I have two-way effective communication with my manager	O	O	O	O
12.	I receive regular information from monthly communication meetings	O	O	O	O
13.	My comments from the last internal survey have been actioned	O	O	O	O
14.	These actions have brought positive changes	O	O	O	O
15.	I would recommend Simon Jersey to a friend as being a good company to work for	O	O	O	O
16.	I feel adequately trained for the job that I do	O	O	O	O
17.	I am encouraged to improve my knowledge and skills	O	O	O	O
18.	I feel that annual appraisals are beneficial to me	O	O	O	O

Figure 8.2. Internal customer survey

Summary Action List for Your Business

1. Decide your company strategy, give it a name, and make it easy for your employees to understand. A one-page format similar to Figure 8.1 is a clear way to do this.
2. At each employee appraisal, agree individual objectives (KRAs) that align and focus each person on the same areas of importance as the company objectives.
3. Initiate a programme of leadership development, rather than just leadership training, to improve both your people and business performance.
4. Complete and action an employee opinion survey annually.
5. Make work fun, be positive, and trust your employees.

Chapter 9

Create the Environment for Communication

Excellent communication starts and ends with listening.

Introduction

When people talk about what makes a successful retail business, they normally use three words: 'location, location, location'. Culture change has the equivalent: 'communication, communication, communication'. There cannot be too much communication where culture change is concerned, but it does not happen automatically; you have to create the right environment. Remember there is informal as well as formal communication; talking to, talking with, and listening to; plus the unspoken body language and physical environment that send just as many communication signals to customers and employees as the spoken word. We will look at implementing your culture change from three key viewpoints: communicating your culture change plan, channels for listening, and creating the physical environment for communication.

Communicating Your Culture Change Plan

Successful companies take communication very seriously. For example:

▶ British Airways recently brought 30,000 employees from all over the world to talk to them face to face about 'Putting People First Again' (PPFA); a programme covering the company strategy, brands, and each employee's role in this global customer service business.

▶ Mortgage Express launched a veritable volley of new initiatives such as 'The Way Ahead', 'MARS' (Mortgage Applications Review System) and 'Exceeding Expectations'; all with much razzmatazz to reinforce their 'customer-service, one big family', culture. Their people know they are valued.

▶ IBM has a complete company-wide intranet, making it easy for every employee to know within seconds what Lou Gerstner, chairman and chief executive officer, has broadcast. IBM people know what is going on in their company without having to ask.

Go on, shout about it! You are the leader and you have got a great plan. This is your chance to really inspire your people, to really start leading them to success! You may be talking with one person or one thousand; the numbers do not matter. If you want to inspire, then communicate from the heart, positively, with passion, belief, and enthusiasm. Paint a picture of the future; explain what this means for everyone, and why it is bigger, better and more valuable than what they have today. Name and broadcast your plan. Timetable your plan. And then deliver what you promise.

Do something similar to British Airways and Mortgage Express. Make your presentations high impact. Get your messages across so people remember them; ideally incorporating feedback from your employees. Phrases like 'You told us ... so we have done ... ' will go down very well! Use this as an opportunity to get out of your pinstriped straightjackets. Let your people see your real character; make the whole event great fun. It is okay to have fun! People outside work have fun, so let us shake things up in here and make work fun too. We are changing the culture, and this is what we are going to do!

Ensure your message is consistent and includes 'what happens next'. Communicate your vision and answer questions directly. Explain what your culture change team is planning to do, and when the audience can expect to hear more. Your culture change journey is just starting and the road may be paved, but still misty. You will not have all the answers, but do not worry. As long as the vision makes sense and you can see a way to achieve it, leave the details of the strategy to your small culture change team.

Maintain consistent, regular, and timely communications during your culture change. This is vital. For example, in addition to your critical face-to-face communication, you might support this by explaining your culture change vision in a professional video, especially if there is bad news involved. It gets the same message across to each individual and his/her family. It makes the message simple to understand. It can empathise and sympathise with anyone that could lose his job. It is effective communication. The video will have backup from other written and verbal communication too. Do not hide behind the video though; just use it as a tool to help deliver a consistent message. The regular face-to-face presentations to each team are the vital element. Assuming, however, your message is good news, use these as great opportunities to feedback the latest successes and, of course, to celebrate the future outlook too!

Communicate your important culture change messages to employees through your line management channels, not via human resources. Line managers have the responsibility for implementing these initiatives, so they must be seen to own them by communicating them too. Human resources provide technical expertise, but the delivery must come from the first line managers.

The main point to make is that during a culture change there cannot be too much communication, especially as open communication helps build trust. Go for overkill, make sure it is consistent, frequent, and keep everyone well informed. To confirm this you also need to keep your antennae alert for feedback.

Listening for Feedback

You can tell a good listener a mile away! Listening is an art, and also a prerequisite for showing respect for your employees. In researching for this book, I came across employees (in companies outside the case study sample) who indicated that they do not feel valued because

- ▶ 'they (managers) do not listen'
- ▶ 'you can have a one-to-one conversation and they say what you want to hear, but later actions do not back these statements up and nothing changes'.

Not listening results in feedback akin to, or stronger than: 'happiness is not a word that would feature in a straw poll around the office'. Just contrast this for a minute with feedback from the case study companies. Statements like:

- ▶ 'the company is a big family'
- ▶ 'I am passionate about what we are doing in the business'
- ▶ 'I think they are a fantastic company'.

Do you get feedback like this? Would you love to get feedback like this? Next time you get feedback, listen carefully to what your team are really saying. Take action to rectify any weaknesses you detect. Ask for outside help if appropriate. Make yourself approachable. Relocate yourself and occupy an existing desk in amongst your team, in the middle of the open plan office. Get back in touch. Remember, inspiring your team takes two-way communication; listening in addition to speaking.

We are going to explore 'the daily walk round' in more detail later. For now, suffice it to say that with you and your managers walking around your organisation regularly (I do *not* mean as chief executive officer plus entourage on a formal well-announced visit) will encourage informal feed-back, ensure managers are proactive rather than reactive, and make you all available to talk to, as the open door policy then becomes a no door one!

Other communication channels also need to be wide open, easily access-ible and bi-directional – for both formal and informal communication. For example, give everyone his or her own personal e-mail address and access to the company intranet. Make sure any employee can e-mail the chief executive officer, and get a personal answer.

Provide regular access to directors – through question and answer sessions broadcast on the intranet if your company is too large for regular face-to-face feedback, or via line communication meetings with directors present. Provide access and interaction outside normal work-ing hours too, to get to know your people as individuals rather than just 'Fred, who works in the test lab'. Fred might be chairman of the local sports club, or have gained an honours degree in his spare time that you did not know about! Find out about your people. It is amazing how much talent is there to be released if only you know which interest buttons to press. Imagine what your company could do to your com-petitors, and for your customers, if only you could get everyone to be as fired up and motivated at work as they are in their leisure interests. Simply making work fun is a good start, as we will discuss in more detail later.

Two-way team communication is another great channel for listening. One good example is the 'Morning market' meeting, where a team briefly discusses yesterday's events and the plan for today, with the team leader listening and asking team members to suggest how to improve on what was done yesterday. This applies just as much to a team of estate agents telling each other about new business they have just won, as to the uphol-stery department in a furniture manufacturer.

Another good two-way communication example is the whole contin-uous improvement process detailed in Improving Your Success later in the book; everything from continuous improvement meetings, to open style suggestion schemes. Nothing is hidden and anyone can 'listen' to this feedback $24 \times 7 \times 52$. To listen, all you have to do is visit the work area.

Take all your training matrices (spreadsheets that show the current status of each employee's training), health and safety meeting minutes, and accident performance figures out of the filing cabinets, and display them in your restaurant where most people can see them. Keep them all current and highlight any training completed each month. Use the same medium to publicise social events/competitions.

Finally, employee opinion surveys (see Simon Jersey for an example) are critical in terms of listening to your employees. I have two pointers for you to help the questionnaire design. First, test each question to know what the range of possible answers tells you, and decide what action you are going to take when you get these answers. Second, make sure you involve a cross-section of people throughout the company when preparing the questions. The questions must be relevant, target the controversial areas, and be repeatable so you can confirm next quarter or next year whether your perceived improvements are real. It is so obvious, but oh so critical, to act on the answers!

Create the Physical Environment for Communication

Do you remember the loyal employee, Mabel, who used to bring round the coffee and chocolate digestive biscuits on a tea trolley many years ago? Unfortunately a cost-cutting exercise removed her job, but perhaps Mabel's job needs reconsideration; not for the coffee and biscuits, but as a means of encouraging informal communication throughout the business. I will bet you Mabel probably knew more about what was really going on in the company than most senior executives. I wonder why!

If you do not want to re-employ Mabel, then at least make sure your employees get a proper break by banning them from eating and drinking at their desks. Provide easily accessible, centralised cafeteria (or vending machine) areas that are light and airy and pleasant to be in. Simply furnish these cafeteria areas with upholstered chairs and small tables to encourage informal meetings and use these facilities yourself, to signal that it is okay to meet and mingle informally in the cafeteria areas.

If you have a separate restaurant, furnish this with tables for at least eight people (rather than for four or two), and encourage everyone to use the restaurant. If you have planned the layout correctly, you should find people come into contact with those they do not directly work with, which will promote knowledge transfer throughout your organisation. If you have a combined cafeteria/restaurant/vending machine area, use the long table, restaurant layout as a preference.

Remember too those long 'corridors of power', where you could walk from one end of the corridor to the other without seeing anyone; with door after door made of solid panelling, firmly closed, with some cryptic department name or number attached? What a brilliant barrier to communication! Here is the next part of this culture change. Rip those offices out and make everyone visible, including those personal secretaries in office anterooms. You will soon find out who is 'dead wood' when you do this. Make the office areas open plan, with no individual offices; just glass meeting rooms to be used on the rare occasion that needs a private meeting. Well-designed open plan offices encourage more informal communication, which helps everyone know what everyone else is doing. Directors, too, should be in amongst their teams, rather than hidden away in offices or on separate floors of the building. Any 'us and them' needs to be buried.

I will finish this chapter now by reiterating the following to you because communication is so important for culture change: 'Provide the physical environment for communication. Talk *to* your people. Talk *with* your people … and … probably most importantly, listen to them, too.'

The third case study company has definitely created the environment for communication. Find out how, by reading about – British Airways.

Chapter 10

British Airways and the 'Putting People First Again' Programme

Introduction

In an organisation of almost 60,000 people, consistent and accurate communication of *any* subject is a major challenge, but when you wish to explain the company values, mission statement and strategy, something special is called for; and that is exactly what the British Airways team has done by creating the 'Putting People First Again' (PPFA) programme. This is the fifth in a series of major communication programmes held over a 20-year period. By the time the two-year long show closed in March 2001, around 30,000 British Airways employees from all over the world had come together to hear, see and experience for themselves what British Airways is all about and, most importantly, their role in the company's success.

Although most companies are smaller than British Airways, and therefore will not need the scope and scale of the PPFA programme, the following general principles are still likely to apply to your firm:

▶ Ensure your employees know the company mission, vision, values and strategy, and keep people up to date by communicating this regularly. Look out for the various communication methods employed here.

▶ Encourage informal communication and reduce any 'us and them' by using open-plan offices, with directors in amongst their teams rather than in separate offices. If you can, it really is worth visiting Waterside, the British Airways head office near Heathrow, to really appreciate how the building affects the culture. You will read about Waterside in the case study.

By the end of this case study, you should have some great ideas that can be moulded to the size and nature of your own organisation in terms of what, how, where, when and to whom you communicate, regardless of whether you are speaking to 30, or 300 or even 30,000 people. Linking investment in product brands to the company strategy, plus the role played by employees to consistently achieve the brand promise, is also included. Finally, simply allowing access for your employees to talk to senior management is put into practice. Applying the techniques and training contained here will ensure your employees understand where the company is going, what it stands for, and increase their confidence and pride in working for a truly excellent company.

How is a programme like this planned, created and enacted? What should it contain? Where is it best held? Why is this programme necessary at all, and what is the history behind it? This study aims to answer these questions, starting with the background to set the scene. Fasten your seatbelts!

Culture Change

In 1981, when John King (now Lord King) was chief executive officer of British Airways, the company was a giant government-owned and heavily subsidised business. At that time, there were around 61,000 employees of which 8500 were classed as having customer contact. Contrast this with today; circa 58,000 people employed with over 26,000 classed as customer facing. His aim was to prepare a survival plan and to start to prepare the business for privatisation. A clean sweep of loss-making routes, old inefficient aircraft, and many people, resulted.

In 1982, Colin Marshall (now Lord Marshall) became the new chief executive officer and started the process of cultural change together with establishing the British Airways brand. He asked the customers what they wanted. He listened to the employees and came up for the first time with missions, values and goals. He brought in the culture of customer service, and he prepared the business for intense competition resulting from the impending deregulation. No longer would British Airways be the only carrier flying certain routes.

The first 'Putting People First' programme took place in 1983/84 to get the company message across to the employees; 50,000 attendees, 100 per day for two years! This led to changes in livery, uniforms and the advertising slogan 'The World's Favourite Airline' emerged. Cross-functional 'Customer First Teams' were launched as part of a continuous improvement initiative to make changes proactively rather than reactively. For example, users as well as designers would be involved in deciding how various items were laid out in developing a new galley. Five new values for the business were defined as vision, urgency, take responsibility, trust and motivation.

There were follow-up programmes to Putting People First: in 1985 'A Day In The Life', in 1987 (the year of privatisation) 'To Be The Best' and in 1992 'Winners'. These programmes gave people a chance to show others what they did, benchmarking against the competition, and customer retention respectively.

In 1996, Bob Ayling became chief executive officer of British Airways. He focused on making British Airways the best managed company and launched the 'Putting People First Again' (PPFA) programme to put across the message 'it is the people, not the planes, that makes the airline'.

In 1997, the global tailfin-painting programme called Utopia was introduced. The introduction of the new corporate image proved to be a challenging time for the company as public reaction to the new designs was mixed and the launch coincided with industrial unrest that culminated in a three-day strike by some cabin crew. The strike acted as a major catalyst for change. Planning started for the PPFA programme, to be run by internal people, as just one of those changes needed to lift the staff and give the whole company a sense of purpose and direction.

Also undertaken in 1997 was an employee opinion survey, which had a 50 per cent response rate. Although 90 per cent of people returning the form said they were proud to work for British Airways, most employees felt the management team would not do anything with the survey results and most employees said their managers did not listen to them. So the Listener programme was launched, to break down the departmental barriers and get people to understand better their role in the overall company performance. People were allocated time to visit other departments, to find out rather than speculate what their colleagues actually did. Regular employee opinion surveys are now completed.

Despite all these initiatives to boost the feelings of the British Airways staff, morale remained pretty low until, in 2000, Rod Eddington joined as chief executive officer. So far he is credited with the consolidation of the British Airways family and for driving the '3Cs' strategy that focuses on capacity, customers and costs.

He has also had to restructure the company's finances and significantly reduce operating costs and headcount in the wake of the terrorist attacks in the USA. The incursions inevitably resulted in fewer passengers, particularly on the profitable trans-Atlantic routes. Despite these enforced changes, British Airways has continued to put people first; not just its own people, but also its passengers. Here are a few initiatives put in place shortly after the terrorist attacks, that demonstrate how Rod Eddington and his team have so far approached this challenge:

► Adopt a voluntary approach to headcount reduction and preserve cash in the business to protect the airline's future:
 – offering options, such as voluntary unpaid leave and temporary or permanent part-time work
 – retraining existing employees to fill vacancies internally rather than recruiting externally
 – directors taking a 15 per cent pay cut
 – asking senior managers and managers to take a pay cut (10 per cent and 5 per cent, respectively)
 – agreeing with the trade unions to defer a staff bonus payment, until the company's financial position allows.
► Invest in passenger and crew safety and security:
 – reinforcing cockpit doors to prevent unauthorised access to the cockpit
 – extra security checks at boarding gates.
► Introduce regular briefings to discuss and brief people about business issues and actions:
 – weekly briefing for managers, hosted by Rod Eddington
 – regular contact with the trade unions including a special weekly briefing.

Rod Eddington's mission is to have motivated people and a successful airline that offers world-class customer service. You will see later the three-pronged strategic approach to achieving this objective.

So you can see that the British Airways staff has gone through some major highs and lows in the past 20 years. Now we understand the need for the PPFA programme, let us mentally attend it as a delegate and see what messages come out from the day. Let us join the British Airways PPFA programme at Waterside, the British Airways head office near Heathrow airport.

Waterside

When you enter Waterside, you quickly realise why this building is described as an inspirational place to work and why it is such a great venue for the PPFA programme. It is definitely worth taking a little time out before the course to briefly explore Waterside. Created at a cost of £200 million, and opened in 1998, Waterside covers around 40 acres out of 280 acres of parkland. It houses some 4000 people in open-plan offices designed so each person is never more than three seats from a window. Built around an open rectangular centre, there are six C-shaped extensions, each named after a continent, which facilitate this access to light. Running through the middle of the rectangular heart is what is quaintly termed 'the street', complete with cane tables and chairs, pot plants, coffee bar, Waitrose, banking facilities and the undercarriage of a Boeing 747. The latter might sound out of place, but it actually is entirely appropriate in this environment. Underneath the street are additional facilities for the staff that include a gym, mock-up fuselage for cabin crew training, hairdressing salon and limited car parking. Way up above the street is the central glass roof. Together with the predominance of glass panels round the sides of the building, this leads to an open, warm and relaxed setting in which to work.

Waterside is described as a catalyst for change, for flexible working and an efficient, comfortable environment. It is also saving British Airways around £15 million, per year in operating costs. Since Waterside opened, the culture has gradually changed to make it perfectly acceptable to use the cane chairs and coffee bar area in the street to hold meetings; indeed this is actively encouraged and led by the directors to facilitate the desired open communication style. You are as likely to see a director in 'the street' as at a desk in the middle of the open-plan office area. Separate offices for directors are now history.

Putting People First Again Programme

Coming back to the Waterside entrance again you meet 'hosts' wearing distinctive blue T-shirts and holding up the PPFA logo to guide you to the training area. The facilitators and hosts are volunteers from every area of the business who play a key role in the training throughout the day. They also act as a psychological catalyst for employee acceptance of the PPFA messages, rather than having an independent or management led approach to the training. This multi-disciplined, multi-departmental and international cross-section of facilitators approach is one of the reasons this programme is so successful. Guided by the hosts, delegates find that half way along the street is the entrance to the PPFA programme.

Each PPFA day, up to 250 employees from all round the world meet and are allocated into teams of 16–20, each with its own facilitator. At 09.30 the 'doors are opened'. This happens together with powerful music, dry-ice smoke and blue lighting into which people disappear as they enter the auditorium. You are greeted with a wide cinema-screen display with the PPFA logo. Someone enters centre-stage and says:

> *'Imagine a play with no actors. Imagine a school with no children. Imagine British Airways without us!'*

On screen, the clock rolls back in time and a whole range of special events where British Airways staff have excelled are flashed up; the crew of flight BA09 who rescued the aeroplane when all four engines failed at the same time on the 24 June 1982; Richard Harrison, an engineer, in April 1988, who stopped a flight from taking off. ... Because he saw fuel leaking from an engine and saved a potential disaster; and the £12 million collected for UNICEF in loose change from passengers and staff.

Two people enter the stage this time with 'Hi. I'm Ian, cabin crew at Gatwick. I'm proud to be working for British Airways.' and 'Hello. I'm Maggie from Finance. I'm passionate about what we are doing in the business. Today is about our past, our present and our future.'

Ian and Maggie then give some one-line descriptions of high and low points in the past 20 years, including the fluctuating profit and loss figures, plus more recent announcements culminating in two statements:

> *'Research shows that how our employees feel has a direct impact on how customers feel'*

(which is a reference to the work undertaken by the Judge Institute of Cambridge University and supports the need for the PPFA programme) and

> *'Our challenge now is to increase profitability and regain the confidence of our shareholders.'*

Ian ends the introduction session by summarising the British Airways strategy as 'The 3Cs':

- ▶ *capacity* in line with profitable demand
- ▶ attract and retain profitable *customers*
- ▶ tackle inefficiencies and reduce *costs*.

With the general introduction complete, we now follow one team through the main programme, highlighting any generic points that could be useful to your business.

Note that facilitators run the first three sessions below, which somewhat overturns the usual hierarchical organisation structure. Regardless of their normal job within British Airways, each facilitator is well trained to lead discussions about specific parts of the PPFA day and delivers this knowledge with confidence. The aim is for the delegates to learn from each other and their groups rather than for the facilitators to 'train'. However, facilitators who are baggage handlers lead discussions with captains, customer service agent facilitators coach cabin crew at all levels, and accounts people discuss their subject matter with engineering managers. Well, why not?

The structure of the main day is:

▶ *matching the promise*: a look at the brand values of McDonalds, Mercedes and British Airways
▶ *meeting the challenge*: a review of the British Airways product brands and their 'promises'
▶ *four activities*: 'people not planes', 'the game plan', 'e-revolution' and 'the bottom line'
▶ *question time*: your opportunity to ask a director directly.

Matching the Promise

Holding a bottle of Perrier with the label hidden, a facilitator asks, 'What is this?' He gets an immediate response from the audience that is correct because they recognise the green bottle with its unique shape, even before the label is shown. Then he asks 'What does this mean to you?'. He gets the response 'Expensive fizzy water. Healthy living.' The questions are repeated for McDonalds' yellow arches and the Mercedes triangular star. Again very specific answers highlight the strength of these brands. These strong brands all conjure up an image for the consumer, an expectation and a promise. A promise that is consistent.

Asking the audience 'What does the British Airways brand mean to you?' got responses from employees such as 'safe, on-time, good customer service' and on the video-takes from customers 'It's like setting foot on the first piece of British soil when you enter the cabin.' and 'In the past year I've received both the best service and the worst service from the same carrier, British Airways.' This latter quote highlights the need for consistency, as does 'There's always good teamwork, however there is clockwork teamwork where everything is sterile and then there are the times when the crew have really gelled and they become a team with the passengers. And [then] on a long flight time goes faster.'

Feedback from customers identifies the five key values now associated with the British Airways *parent* brand as:

▶ quality (of service and product) throughout British Airways
▶ innovation (e.g. the lounge procedures, new product services provided)
▶ customer focus (vital in a customer service industry)
▶ safety and security (in terms of confidence and sense of responsibility)
▶ British heritage (the positive elements of being a British *company* in a global market).

With regard to the customer focus value, Martin George as director of marketing, says 'We are all in a customer service industry and if we are not serving a customer or supporting those who serve customers then we really should be asking ourselves how we are contributing.'

The last of these parent-brand values links in with the current tailfin-painting programme. Here the global designs from the Utopia programme are being replaced by the 'Chatham Design', depicting the Union Flag with its traditional British red white and blue colours in a wavy, softer, design. This started in 1999, in response to customer feedback about the new British Airways identity, when it was decided that the Chatham Design tailfin would be extended to half the main fleet. The second stage of this evolution is extending the Chatham Design to the whole fleet, with aircraft being painted only when they are due for repainting and at no extra cost. The Chatham Design was introduced as one of the Utopia designs and has proved to be one of the most popular amongst the British Airways passengers and staff. The Utopia identity was designed around the intention to position the airline as 'global and caring', in support of a business strategy that focused on volume growth in the international leisure market. British Airways has since readdressed its business goals; focusing on premium products and delivering the highest standards in customer service. The Chatham Design reintroduces Britishness to the identity in a more modern, less formal way, reflecting the direction the company is now heading.

Also as part of the product launches aimed at the premium traveller market, the latest advertising slogan now is: 'Defining air travel in the 21st century', which establishes a powerful promise for British Airways to deliver for its customers.

Finally, 'being passionate about providing excellent service to customers, that recognises them as individuals, is the essence of the British Airways brand'.

Another key question asked by the facilitator is 'What is your role in portraying these brand values?'. The varied responses all revolved around everyone having customers either within the company and/or externally, so it is clearly everyone's responsibility to give the best *service* possible.

Another message that comes across clearly is that unlike McDonalds or Mercedes who can physically offer a product, each customer of British Airways has received an 'experience'. The key is to ensure that British Airways customers come away with a good 'feeling' or 'emotion' because of the way they were treated.

> *Research shows that 80 per cent of the reason people are loyal to a brand is because of the service they receive.*

Many manufacturing companies would do well to note and act on this research, especially in their drive to differentiate themselves from the competition.

Meeting the Challenge

Having indicated in 'matching the promise' how important the parent brand is to British Airways and that all staff have their own key role to play in portraying these values to each and every individual customer, this section 'meeting the challenge' focuses on the *product* brands and what each 'promises'. The teams have great fun defining what each product brand means to them, clarifying one or two minor misunderstandings en route. Knowledge here is vital to be able to sell the benefits to customers. Note too that later in the afternoon, the link is made between the corporate strategy and the investment in specific product brands.

Having discussed the 'hard' aspects of each brand, for example, the six-foot flat beds introduced into Club World, the facilitator moves on to the 'soft' aspects of the service offered, namely the role played by each employee in providing every customer with a positive feeling about their experience with British Airways. Also covered is what enables each one to give this high standard of service that they have talked about, on a daily basis – it is about their choice of attitude and the service style behaviours they adopt. This is particularly important, as chief executive officer Rod Eddington said to the team on video, 'We are all in the customer service business. We have to work together as a team.'

British Airways is a service business.

Four Activities

People Not Planes

Team working is emphasised in a very simple but effective game called 'people not planes' where four teams (each called a different colour) represent different departments within the same company. Each team has to answer questions to get parts of a jigsaw. Initially, correct answers get parts that match the team's colour, but then the game gets interesting as parts for other teams are given as reward for correct answers and that is when the bartering starts, company working disappears and departmental teams dominate. Only when the whole jigsaw is complete, which then reads 'only by working together will we succeed', is it clear what the game is all about. The message gets through loud and clear.

The Game Plan

This is the very clever strategic review of the British Airways portfolio. This 'game plan' helps the employees understand why British Airways is investing in certain aircraft and products (to increase value and hence justify a price premium), and the general move out of the low price market.

E-Revolution

An insight into the potential for Internet transactions for British Airways, with annual transaction growth rates as multiples rather than percentages, show the employees that investment in this technology is critical for future revenues. In 2000, the online revenue was £60 million; in 2003, it is forecast to be £700 million. That is how fast it is growing.

The Bottom Line

Since 71 per cent of British Airways staff own shares in the company, the share price and company profits are important to them. This session gave a chance to learn some basic statistics about the company; from the annual cost of fuel, number of people employed, and of course the share price!

Question Time

The final part of the PPFA day is a chance to question a British Airways director about any current or future concerns. This particular team was lucky to have Peter Read, Director of London Heathrow Customer Services, available to answer questions. Maggie (who introduced herself at the start of the PPFA day) led the session and Peter Read was very open, answering all the questions that he could. Any he could not, he referred the questioner to another person within the organisation.

Current issues then for British Airways were twofold; to ensure the service is consistent, and to provide an adequate return on investment. Following the events of 11 September 2001, there is now a third issue; demonstrating the core value of safety and security.

British Airways' success in the future also depends on the service provided by their people, which is why programmes like 'PPFA' are so important.

Summary Action List for Your Business

1. Break down barriers between departments by giving employees time to visit and understand what their colleagues do in other areas of the business.
2. At home you live in a community. Try to create the same sort of environment at work by providing areas for work, rest and play.
3. Eradicate physical barriers to communication, such as separate offices for directors and staff.
4. When communicating your business strategy, mission, vision and values, or indeed undertaking any training programme, ask for and train volunteers from throughout the organisation to be part of this team, so that the overall message is not entirely management led.
5. Ensure your employees know what the company brand values are, and the employees' role in supporting these values.
6. Promote excellent customer service; in particular, the way customers are treated and the experience they have each time they come into contact with your company, as this is critical to achieve customer loyalty.
7. Give your employees a chance to question you and your directors about any current or future concerns face-to-face on a regular, frequent, basis.

Part 3

Investing In Success

This part will be hard work for you and your company, but really exciting! It is where you move the teams from reluctantly accepting change to enlightened optimism for the future; where each person can become a leader in his/her own right, and where the teams make their own decisions rather than referring to 'managers'. It's where employees start achieving the best possible skill levels, begin stretching each other and commence moving (where appropriate) from hourly paid to monthly paid.

This seven-chapter section (which links closely with the Wates Group, Colman's of Norwich, and Alcan Foil case studies) breaks the investment down into the role of your culture champion, raising standards, training and the Investors in People Standard; plus changing attitudes, your 'walk rounds' and making work fun! This is where you really start to give your company a major competitive advantage. First, we need to look briefly at *why* we need to undertake these changes.

Here I need to mention Maslow's Hierarchy of Needs, and Hertzberg's Hygiene Factors and Motivators. This territory is well trampled by other authors, so I will keep it concise.

Maslow defined a hierarchy of five 'needs' (physiological, security, affiliation, esteem and self-actualisation), representing the order most people seek to satisfy these needs. Once the lowest need is fulfilled, the next becomes important, and so on. Bearing in mind that a 'need' is only a motivator until that need is fulfilled, our target is for everyone to be seeking to satisfy the highest need of self-actualisation by achieving the highest possible personal goals. The team is then fully charged with motivation fuel!

Similarly, Hertzberg identified elements to motivation; hygiene factors and motivators. Hygiene factors are the conditions surrounding a job (e.g. working conditions and salary). In the same way that good hygiene will prevent you from becoming ill but it will not normally make you better, satisfying these hygiene factors only prevents dissatisfaction. Motivators (e.g. achievement and positive feedback about performance) are all about the job itself; get these factors right and you improve both motivation and performance.

So, the aim of this section of the culture change is to satisfy the hygiene factors and lower level needs, and to promote the motivators and esteem/self-actualisation needs. This can be done by:

▶   raising standards of basic site cleanliness, tidiness, and safety
▶   training in new skills, including multi-skilling and leadership
▶   changing attitudes
▶   visiting your people where they work
▶   making work fun!
▶   implementing many other initiatives already covered in Planning Future Success, together with those about to follow in the Improving Your Success section.

We will start now by exploring the role of your culture champion in satisfying these needs.

Chapter 11

Your Culture Champion

*Value Your Culture Champion; for His Values, together with Your
Values, form the Heart of Your Culture.*

So far you have been the driving force for change, and we have simply
talked about having a small team to prepare the culture change plan with
you. Now it is time for your right-hand man in the culture change organisation, your 'Culture Champion', to move into overdrive for the implementation phase. Let us look at:

▶ the kind of person you should choose
▶ their role during the culture change process.

The kind of person you will need is someone who can act as a catalyst
for the cultural change; ideally a person near the top of your organisation
with the ability to influence strategically. Bear in mind he will need to be
able to take a customer-focused approach to the training skills, especially if
you decide to follow Simon Jersey or Mortgage Express along the European
Foundation Quality Management (EFQM) Excellence Model route.

The role of your culture champion will have an impact at all levels in
your organisation, especially from the training and development
perspective. Bear in mind that the training will include most of your
employees and, if multi-skilling is required, this could take between six
and 12 months to plan and implement. (The Shell Chemicals case study
will help you find out more about training and the facilities required.)
This is not a small role.

Also, if your organisation is unionised, there will be the local and possibly national union representatives, plus site convenors and shop stewards, for your culture champion to involve and get help from as early as
possible (refer to the approach taken by Alcan Foil Europe – Glasgow).

Similarly your culture champion will obtain independent help; for coaching, advisory and arbitration purposes.

Your culture champion will also probably establish new recruitment, appraisal and other personnel systems as part of the culture change planning process, as well as help in the 'change him or change him' process, which we will cover later in this section.

There are many other aspects to this role, too numerous to mention here; suffice it to say that your culture champion has a critical role in both planning and implementing the culture change process. The final content and detail of this role obviously depends on the nature of your current organisation and your vision of the future, but you can be certain that an excellent plan followed up by professional and timely implementation, is the recipe for success.

We see an external culture champion in action, next in the case study about Wates Group.

Chapter 12

Wates Group Culture Facilitates 'Best Value' in the Construction Industry

Introduction

Wates Group Ltd is the ultimate parent company of Wates Construction Ltd, one of the largest, privately owned construction companies in the UK. The 1999 annual report for Wates Construction Ltd begins:

> Four years ago we began, through Wates Action, a commitment and a programme involving cultural change for the sustained renewal of our company. The fruit of this work is now being seen in the projects that we deliver and, in this year's report, we reveal our fifth successive annual increase in revenue and profit.

In 1995, the business had survived recession but as a result had halved the number of employees and still had serious concerns about the future. Sir Christopher Wates, then group chief executive officer and now chairman of the holdings board, initiated a major programme of cultural change with external help.

In this case study, the senior management review section reveals the issues and heartache around prior to the culture change programme. It then takes you through the workshops that started to transform the culture and fundamentally change the nature of the Wates business. The case study covers the two approaches used to communicate the 'Wates Action' plan, and follows this with employee and customer feedback about the culture change. Finally the study brings us up to date with two examples of how the culture change gives Wates a competitive advantage in the construction industry; 'Wates Action improving construction', and 'delivering best value'.

Although this case study is about a company in the construction industry, it includes many general principles that are equally true of any company wishing to change its culture:

▶ Having a chief executive officer with the strength of character to accept the need for change, and then make it happen, is something many companies can learn from.

▶ A consultant from outside the organisation can often be perceived as politically neutral and therefore be allowed to explore the thoughts and feelings of senior employees more readily than an existing employee. This case study is a good example of this neutrality at work, uncovering the real issues in the business.

▶ Respect and open communication is vital for a top team to work together effectively. The three off-site workshops in this case study show the team dynamics in action and the deeper respect and broader relationships that result from opening up and sharing thoughts about each other.

▶ The case study shows the difficulty of communicating the thoughts of a small team, fired up with enthusiasm about the impending change, to the rest of the employees. The examples of both unsuccessful and successful attempts at communicating should save you from going up the same learning curve as Wates.

▶ Autocratic control, in the style of an owner manager, stifles company development once the business gets too large for one person to efficiently lead it. Delegating responsibility to your management team, and inviting them to accept authority for this responsibility, makes a huge difference to motivation and leadership further down your organisation. This principle is shown at work in the second workshop.

Wates is a great example of a cultural change that has turned the company round. Let us join Sir Christopher back in 1995 at the very beginning of this cultural revolution.

Senior Management Review

Christopher Wates meets a consultant whom he decides could help his company, but he is unsure where they should start and what the consultant should do.

The consultant starts at the top. He surveys the directors, shareholders and senior management, in a no-holds barred, confidential approach. What do people really think of Christopher Wates? Where is the company going? What improvement opportunities are there? What is the top management crying out for? What is the management style at Wates? Amongst the many statements received were the following:

▶ 'we do not have a strategy, the marketplace is dictating what we do'
▶ 'no space for innovation, creativity and fun'
▶ 'managers will not do things differently'
▶ 'the sites have no idea what is happening in the ivory tower'
▶ 'the Wates way is unchangeable' (due to command control from the top)
▶ 'management does not listen'
▶ 'decisions go really fast – unless you want to do something different'.

Six themes emerged from this survey:

▶ we must change to survive
▶ what is our strategy?
▶ we want better management and leadership
▶ relationships need to be stronger both internally and externally
▶ we want one big team and better communication
▶ we have a company culture, but is it the right one?

Underlying these themes were specific requests such as:

▶ marketing vigour – PR and corporate identity
▶ expand Wates' share of the leisure business market
▶ improve the office environment
▶ negotiated and partnered business rather than tendering. (Tendering typically means putting in your best price for a contract in a sealed envelope, and presenting this at the same time as several of your competitors, with the lowest price winning the tender. Negotiating literally means agreeing a price directly with the client based on the value added rather than just the cost.)

Workshops

There was clearly a need for change, but how? The consultant suggested the top team start with a series of three three-day workshops for

40 people, all to be held in neutral territory. Two more would follow these, each for 200 people.

The first workshop, called *personal transformation*, took place in November 1995. Led by the consultant, this in essence helped the team to open up and share their thoughts about each other, with the understanding that anything said in this three-day session would have no consequences for any individual. On this basis the conversations were full and very frank, with lots of soul searching; but they cleared the air, changed perceptions, and developed new broader and deeper relationships previously missing. For the first time in a long time the top team became able to talk openly to each other. They also established 'Catalytic Management Teams' tasked with implementing actions agreed at this first workshop.

The initial interviews with senior management had identified specific requests for strategic as well as cultural change. The 40 leaders that had attended were really charged up with enthusiasm and started to spread the message 'change is coming' by meeting fortnightly in their 'Catalytic Management Teams' with a further 30 people. The aim was to work out how the move from tender to negotiate could happen, how the office environment could improve, and how changes to staff rewards, empowerment, and information technology could be implemented.

Four months later, the consultant ran the second workshop, aimed at igniting *strategic transformation*. Another three-day session, this time all about 'How are we going to create a new business strategy?' This helped the team to realise they are: *collectively responsible* for the company future; *accountable* for their part in a specific project; *with authority* over all areas for which they are accountable; and perhaps most importantly, able to replace the former 'Wates way' with fresh ideas that will be listened to and implemented rather than simply allowed to die as happened historically. These ideas paved the way for a new strategy for the business to be drawn up by the management team over the next six months. Then came the third workshop.

Entitled *organisational sustainability*, the third workshop asked: 'What is missing to take the company forward and increase both performance and profit?' It also covered how to translate what was missing into an action plan and, of course, how to share this plan to enrol the rest of the organisation.

The key success that came out of the initial set of three workshops was called Wates Action. Wates Action is made up of the 'commitment' and the five 'guiding principles' that together still form the bedrock of the Wates culture today. The Wates Action message is in two parts:

▶ Wates' commitment, which is: 'We commit to the sustained renewal of our company.'
▶ Wates' guiding principles, which are:
  – giving extraordinary value to our customers and shareholders
  – being the best place to work in our industry
  – having communication based on trust and openness
  – having freedom to take initiatives in a no-blame culture
  – giving accountability and authority deep within the company.

There were two stages to sharing Wates Action, each of which involved a different communication method.

Communicating the 'Wates Action' Plan

The first method of communicating Wates Action was simply to repeat the first and second workshops, but this time with 200 people from throughout the company, plus the original 40 who attended as hosts. After each workshop the idea was for each of the 240 attendees to share what they had experienced with another four colleagues. This process did not work well as there was no clear edict about 'what happens next' and the non-attendees were reticent to accept any message as they saw themselves as 'excluded'. Wates needed to find another way of sharing the results of these workshops.

The second communication method was 'Wates Action learning', which proved successful. The senior management team held communication forums for 40 people each time. This sustained and spread the values of Wates Action throughout the organisation, with the same message being transmitted each time. It also gave employees the chance to ask questions to clear up any misunderstandings. The end result was consistent knowledge of where the company was going and why, including 'what happens next'. This took place during most of 1997, making completion of this 'Wates Action' initiation and enrolment process a full two-year time frame.

Employee and Customer Surveys

Instinctively the company could say its workforce genuinely owned Wates Action, but to confirm this it decided to complete a confidential staff attitude survey managed externally. It also asked its customers and supply chain what they thought.

The staff attitude survey covered:

▶ the company and the future
▶ you and your job
▶ management style and team working
▶ communications effectiveness
▶ developing your potential.

This fed back positive news about knowledge of the strategic plan, improved communication and morale, plus benchmarked employee satisfaction for the first time. It also confirmed that people find Wates a friendly place to work and the majority believe that team working is an important feature of the way they work.

The latest employee opinion survey published in 2001 shows that communication has improved with people now feeling better informed about Wates performance generally. Also, people now have a clearer view of the company's vision and strategy.

The customer survey, directed at key customers and other professionals within the industry, showed that the company had definitely changed its approach to business. However, the other message received said this changed approach was not always getting through to employees on the construction sites, so when times became tough it was 'reversion to type'.

The Culture Change Results

The culture change from Wates Action has enabled Wates to develop a business strategy and implement two major new initiatives.

Wates Action Improving Construction

One recent undertaking is 'Wates Action improving construction' (WAIC), implemented in January 2000. This initiative won Wates the 'achievement through innovation' section of the 'Quality in Construction Awards 2001', *in recognition of a company's commitment to the future through innovative management and construction techniques.*

WAIC has four core objectives: to improve on-site delivery of construction projects; to improve performance along the supply chain; to improve service to customers; and to measure, learn and profit from these improvements. The five components to achieve these objectives are: right first time, supply chain management, measurement and benchmarking, coaching and technical training.

The Wates innovation team fully business-planned this programme, with ten full-time project managers driving the implementation throughout 2000. This commitment cost over £1 million, however the returns by 2004 are expected to be £20 million.

Delivering Best Value

The final, but key result of this culture change, is that Wates is winning business through 'delivering best value'. Delivering best value is about developing long-term business relationships and also about being the selected construction company on the basis of best value, not price. This requires negotiation directly with the client rather than just tendering.

Wates has grasped this delivering best value initiative and trained coaches to introduce the best practice tools into the client/consultant/ contractor/specialist sub-contractor meetings. Instead of the historic, adversarial communication chain from client down to specialist sub-contractors, with claims against the client for additional work done by the contractor during the course of the project, this best value initiative aims for a right first time approach. In order to help the partnering and best value process, all parties get together to better understand the client's project requirements. Trained coaches facilitate the meetings. This process is at the cutting edge for the construction industry and is definitely a significant factor that has facilitated Wates to move the majority of its business from tendered to negotiated.

To give you an example of this in practice, consider that Construction Industry contracts are normally awarded on a project-by-project basis, with long-term projects tendered annually. In 2001, Wates won a £50 million project planned to take five years to complete, where Wates are the contractor for the whole five-year period. This is extremely unusual, but it has been made possible because of the best value approach, the open culture achieved through Wates Action and the opportunity that this introduces for continuous improvement through the life of the project. This is proof that changing your company culture can win you extra profitable business.

Summary Action List for Your Business

1. If you need external help to transform your business, be strong enough to ask.
2. If your top team is not working as a team, be honest, be open, and share your thoughts and concerns together, ideally with a facilitator. Get beyond the personalities to the fundamental business needs.
3. Take 'time out' to gel as a team and together decide the way forward.
4. Transmit your message to manageable numbers of people. (Wates found 40 people at each session to be about right for them.)

Chapter 13

Raising Standards

Raising standards starts with improving the basics.

Speaking fine words about the corporate mission, vision, values and strategy, alters nothing at grass roots level; apart from preparing your teams to expect change and giving them an idea of where the company is heading. Your employees may, if you are lucky, have started to buy in to this, but the service provided and/or products made are still the same. Customer complaints, quality concerns and all the other day-to-day fire-fighting issues continue unabated. Now comes the implementation phase, the really challenging section of your culture change.

We need to start training to achieve desired skill levels, but in parallel we must also start changing attitudes by raising basic standards.

Any well run company, whether service or manufacturing based, is a clean, tidy and safe place to work. There are, however, degrees of cleanliness, tidiness and safety. To be 'the best' you will need to achieve standards of excellence in these three basics. Let us look at the reasons why raising these standards is important, from both the customer and employee perspective.

From the customer viewpoint, imagine you have the choice of purchasing from two companies (company A and company B) and you want to visit both of them to gain confidence in their ability to supply a consistent quality product, on time, every time. Their approach to you as a potential customer is markedly different. Here are a few examples of these differences to illustrate the point.

Company A e-mails clear travel instructions to you prior to your visit, and has the company name on a large sign on the front of the building that makes finding the firm very easy. Car parking space is reserved for visitors. Initial impressions are of a clean and well-maintained building and frontage. The reception entrance is obvious and the receptionist welcomes you with a warm friendly smile. We are off to a good start.

Company B faxes an almost illegible photocopy of their directions and has its name attached to the building on a tatty wooden sign in need of painting. To get to a car parking space you have to drive round to the back of the building, negotiating your way around broken wooden pallets and pieces of polythene flapping in the wind. After parking in an unmarked space that you have to assume is available for your vehicle, you then try to find the reception entrance. A piece of paper stuck to a possible entrance door indicates with an arrow that reception is one way and deliveries are in the opposite direction. It fails to indicate whether you should enter this doorway or not. In the absence of any obvious alternative entry points, you enter this door and are met with a hostile reaction from the people inside telling you that reception is 'around the front'. The front door is locked and you have to wait there until the person you arranged to meet opens it, as there is no receptionist. Draw your own conclusions, but both are live examples.

Company A sales person offers you a walk round the site, which due to the technical nature of the product made, involves a visit to the production area and maintenance workshop as well as the administration offices. Although the focus of the conversation is on what the company could do for you, during this walk round you also notice that the whole site has been recently swept and there is no evidence of any litter. There are, however, many wheelie-bins each with their own lid (I will explain the significance of this shortly). There are also painted lines on the floor that designate where certain equipment should be. Each area has a label identifying what it should contain. It is clear that there is a place for everything and everything is in its place unless it is actually in use. Walking through the engineering workshop you are greeted with welcoming acknowledgements from the employees and once again everything is clean and tidy. There are no superfluous items visible. Even the tools are hanging on 'shadow boards' where the tool shape is marked on the board as a shadow that matches the shape of the real item. It is easy to see if tools are missing with this system.

Company B sales person offers you a walk round the site, including a visit to the production area and maintenance workshop. This time you see rubbish that has fallen out of full open-top waste bins. It appears that people have simply thrown the waste at the bins rather than into the bins. This is one good reason for having the wheelie-bins with lids; it induces a discipline of having to make a conscious effort to throw the waste away rather than simply being too lazy to tidy it up properly. Machinery being utilised is dirty, has safety guards missing or not in use, and 'walkways' are cluttered with items that have simply been dumped. There are certainly no lines to indicate what should be where, and plenty of evidence that what is there probably should not be! You also see some girlie calendars hanging up displaying favourite pictures, and plenty of evidence of people smoking at their workplace rather than in a designated area. You also overhear some cynical banter between colleagues. Although some people acknowledge your presence, most carry on with their work and ignore you completely.

Clearly the culture of company B is less conducive to inspiring confidence in prospective customers. It also visibly indicates a lack of discipline, organisation, and potential ability to supply the quality product you are looking for.

Most of the above tour description gives visual and verbal clues about the way the company is managed. Company A has set and achieved higher standards than its competitor. This is likely to give you as a potential customer, higher confidence levels in terms of the supplier's 'ability to perform'.

Now let us look at the same two companies from the employee viewpoint. The nature of your business, as well as the particular job under consideration, will affect the physical working conditions of your staff. Regardless of whether your employees are principally office-based, in a production area or perhaps outside, however, the obligation still exists to make sure the working environment is clean, tidy and safe. I asked myself, when touring company B:

▶ When had they last completed and acted on an employee opinion questionnaire?
▶ What was their current overtime bill as a percentage of basic wages?
▶ How high were their absence and staff turnover percentages?
▶ What was their hospital accident rate?

With all other things being equal, employees in company A should have a lower accident rate because there are fewer situations where the employee is exposed to danger. The company A employees are also likely to be more efficient than their counterparts because they will not waste time looking for things. They appear to take pride in their workplace, which is a good indicator that they are also happier. Finally, their management demonstrates that they put the clean and safe working environment high on the priority list, which shows a caring attitude towards their staff. So how do we create this improved physical environment if we are not happy with the current level of cleanliness? Not surprisingly, although paint helps, it takes more than one coat to arrive at the desired cleanliness!

A major part of changing from company B mentality to the clean and tidy culture of company A, is a radical change of employee and management attitude. This goes much deeper than a blitz of spring-cleaning or providing the tools and resources to facilitate the gradual improvements expected in cleanliness. Yes, you need to set and maintain high standards at the top of the organisation, but you also need to align company and employee goals and instil the values of 'trust' and 'respect for the individual'. Completing and acting on an employee opinion survey would be a good start; in fact this could provide the ammunition for a full culture change programme if it makes 'someone see the need'. You will probably also require annualised hours (see Colman's of Norwich) and its associated staff status, plus leaders within each team and ideally aim for 'self-managed teams' (see Alcan Foil Europe – Glasgow).

Although the standard raising is much more than a surface effect, encouraging a refurbishment programme will send visible signals of change. When, for example, did you or your site manager last walk round the site with paper and pen in hand making notes on where improvements to paintwork, buildings, windows, etc. are needed? A programme of building and site maintenance, particularly repairs to leaking roofs together with painting and general upgrading of the communal areas such as toilets, will quickly show the employees that you are serious about raising standards. Encouraging and implementing further suggestions for improvement through the Health and Safety Continuous Improvement Teams (see Improving Your Success section), and employee involvement meetings, will also help foster this process of change.

Another important area of action that leads to a tidier environment is the process of identifying and 'tagging' any equipment that is redundant or has not been used for perhaps three months. After checking that this tagged equipment is no longer required, it is either sold or simply scrapped. It is amazing how much 'stuff' (and here I include old papers filed in desk drawers and filing cabinets as 'stuff' too), literally tonnes of it in many cases, is kept 'just-in-case'. If it is not needed, remove it. Let the scrap metal merchants and paper recyclers earn a living! This is a very effective way of clearing space that can be better utilised, and it also helps make the site safer.

You need to back up this site clearance and refurbishment programme with other actions that point towards raising standards. Simple things like removing any girlie calendars, and eliminating graffiti from toilet walls, are also quick ways of sending a message to your workforce that times are changing and standards are on the way up.

Creating a light, airy and well-maintained working environment that enables all of you to work together efficiently and safely, will satisfy the hygiene needs. It will enable your culture change implementation team to refocus its energy on the motivation and, ultimately, the inspiration of your employees. Raising standards is just the start of this process.

Chapter 14

Training

He who is trained can transform his performance.

I am conscious that the mere mention of change, let alone a culture change, is enough to trigger cold sweats and panic for some employees; especially if this means learning new skills on training courses held away from the normal working environment. There is little point in being blasé about training; it needs to be planned well and accomplished with both emotional understanding and yet also sword-like precision to be effective.

In considering the training required for your culture change, we need to look at the needs of new recruits as they join, as well as existing employees; after all, there is little point in diluting investment in the majority if we ignore the inevitable staff turnover and its associated injection of new recruits. So, after touching on the importance of training, we will briefly follow the logical process of recruitment, induction and appraisals from the culture change perspective. Then, we will focus on training as a major part of the culture change implementation. Within training there are six sections: planning, teamwork, skills training, visits to other firms, a range of practical steps including training matrices, and finally, measuring success.

The key points to be revealed in this chapter are why a strong culture based on values rather than rules helps deselect unsuitable applicants, why administration of the whole recruitment process is simplified, and an indication of the sheer scale of training required.

The Importance of Training

Let me paint a picture for you about skiing, to illustrate why training is so important for your culture change. I am working on the presumably safe assumption that you want to accomplish a significantly improved performance, as well as have a highly motivated team.

In my experience there are three kinds of skier:

▶ The 'poser': complete with all the latest gear including one-piece ski suit, brand new skis, the reflective sunglasses and the essential sun-protection cream. Only to be found on sunny days in low-lying resorts, the sum total of skiing done by the poser is the one-minute dash to the mountain restaurant to sunbathe. This is the complete non-performer.

▶ The 'enthusiastic amateur': skis one week a year and has to make the most of every available minute's ski lift time. Plans routes carefully to maximise skiing time, but queues with the rest of the bucket shop enthusiasts for second-rate ski hire equipment. Thinks he is good but the ungainly style on the way down the mogul field indicates other-wise. Amateur by name and amateur in his performance.

▶ The 'seasoned professional': lives for skiing and hopes to take part in the Olympics in three-year time. He is on a mission, physically fit and with all the best (not latest) equipment. And his black run ski-ing is so effortless you hardly notice him. Expertly trained, with all the right tools for the job. Professional by name and sparkling in his performance.

We are aiming for the 'seasoned professional' performance; hence the need for training. Your people need the training, then the best equipment, and ultimately the motivation, in that order, to really perform. So we need to sort out more of the basics again. This time it is the training.

The great thing about training is that, despite any trepidation before starting the training programme, the resulting confidence boost from achiev-ing new skills can produce a real buzz of excitement. It is just like learn-ing to drive. Do you remember desperately trying to master the mechanics of hill starts and parking? Do you recall the adrenalin rush at passing your test? And now, can you remember your drive to work today? Such is the natural move from unconscious incompetence through to unconscious competence (via conscious incompetence and conscious competence).

Recruitment

Introducing new employees into the company is a little like selecting con-taminated oil instead of fresh oil to put into the oil filler of a car engine. Unless the contaminated oil can be filtered and upgraded before adding it to the rest of the oil, or at least pass it through a gradual cleansing process after it has been added, it will soon damage any moving parts.

This is where the strength of your culture, combined with evidence of the values in action, really helps the filtration process. Applicants exposed to a really strong company culture and distinct values during the recruitment procedure, should feedback reactions that are polarised into either a dislike for the company culture or a desire to join. These differing opinions, teased out during interviews, should help you decide whom to employ.

Since you are looking for excellent performance and competitive advantage from your people, put yourself in the position of being able to select the best candidates by paying relatively high salaries as part of your strategy. Employing an average 'Joe Soap' is no longer enough. Being an average company is not acceptable either. Raise standards! Remember, 'success breeds success!'

Induction

Then there is the induction programme. Familiarisation and initial training certainly form major components, but exposure to the proposed as well as the current culture and values are paramount. Establish your new recruit during this honeymoon period. Let him get his feet under the nearest proverbial desk, and ensure he has a mentor to provide support and knowledge through the first few weeks of getting to know people and systems. The mentor role is an important part of establishing employee expectations and the ground rules; achieved simply by reinforcing the company culture.

During the induction, the mentor will presumably explain various administrative details, including the presence of the 'employee manual'. I would not be surprised if your current manual measures several centimetres thick, especially if it gives example letters and detailed rules about how to handle various situations. Here is another part of the culture change. Look forward to replacing it with a booklet based on values rather than rules; one that you can fit in your shirt pocket, as Alcan Foil Europe – Glasgow has done.

Appraisal

Let us move on to the appraisal. It may sound obvious, but motivation often boils down to three main factors; the job itself, feedback on performance, and career development. Since the culture change situation is not the norm, any appraisal done at this time will also be unusual. You may be selecting people for redundancy, for new jobs, or for training to do current roles in different ways as part of the culture change. Professional handling of appraisals as well as other interviews becomes even more important than normal. Part of your culture change preparation should therefore include training line managers in how to hold these reviews.

In general terms, the appraisal gives the employee a chance to communicate with his supervisor, not about the daily needs of the job, but how he feels about himself, and the people he interacts with both up and down in the organisation. It is also an opportune time to review performance against annual and quarterly key performance indicators (KPIs), so that the appraisal feedback is based on genuine achievements rather than just opinions. Use the appraisal to find out what each person can do now that they could not do before, how they have developed, and get some feedback for your company to confirm whether or not the training provided has been fruitful. Have we moved from enthusiastic amateurs to seasoned professionals yet?

The appraisal is not just an historic review, however, it also looks forward at career development; agreeing new goals and establishing training needs, including those that will improve performance not just in today's job, but also in the job they are going to do tomorrow.

Training

So, on now to a core component of your culture change – training. There are six elements to consider.

Planning for Training

Developing your new culture definitely requires training focused on the skills required in the 'new organisation'. The training also involves revisiting the culture change plan, by opening up about what it means for the individual being trained and what his/her role is in this 'new organisation'. Without this more detailed examination you run the risk of alienating your employees. With proper training, however, plus feedback that confirms comprehension and enlightenment, you will gradually begin to see attitude changes. The initial shock from the culture change announcements will turn to reconciliation, to understanding, to optimism and eventually heightened enthusiasm, as people realise they have a future; a better future than the working life they had historically.

Planning this major training initiative may in itself be a significant culture shock for the leaders as well as followers, but it really is a vital element of the culture change. You can communicate and wave your arms about painting as many pictures as you like, but if you and your people do not have the requisite skills embedded within you, your vision is not going to happen. To complete your successful culture change, you will definitely have to spend considerable time, resources and money, on training and coaching both you and your team. My recommendation for the culture change is to treat training as you would any other capital investment in machinery or buildings; decide where it needs to go and plump for best value, not lowest cost. Give the training the respect it deserves by asking your most proficient people to arrange it.

You will have already noted that all the case study companies completed major training programmes for their culture change – 30,000 people brought from all round the world by British Airways for their Putting People First Again (PPFA) programme, and IBM Greenock's wholesale training during its transformation from manufacturing to service. This training is a deliberate, strategic act to enable the culture to change.

Teamwork Training

Where to start training in your own company depends on your current culture. If, for example, there is a history of adversarial interaction between management and employees, creating an entrenched 'us and them', you will need to break down these barriers first. This requires teamwork training. 'Teams' should consist of employees with their team leader and any union representatives, together with middle and senior line managers, to help this bonding process.

Prior to each team being trained, you will probably need to arrange a separate coaching session with the team leaders. The purpose is to air and iron out any concerns the team leaders may have (e.g. belligerent characters in the audience!), to explain the purpose of the teamwork training, and to ensure the team leader genuinely leads the teamwork training session; with the support of a professional coach in attendance. It helps if this coach has managed a culture change before, to be able to foresee and therefore avoid potential pitfalls.

This teamwork training is not about job titles or current roles in the organisation, it is about having a congruent focus on the culture change and what this means to individuals. It is about airing concerns about the culture change, and about getting to know each other as individuals rather than as managers/subordinates. Bearing in mind my opening comments about the possible range of employee reactions to training, some of these sessions may be awkward at first but they will pay real dividends by developing a team spirit and breaking down barriers to communication. These sessions will also help develop respect for, and trust between, the individuals involved.

Beware the credibility trap! Actions agreed at the team training discussions must be followed up with solutions that eradicate any concerns. The task force for this could be the Steering Team. (See Improving Your Success section later.)

Skills Training

There is also the need to arrange training for all the other skills required in the new culture. This is where the amount of training can vary enormously from one company to another; from the leadership development of 26 people at Simon Jersey, through to the multi-skilling of literally hundreds of technicians in former workshops at Shell Chemicals. If you have ever experienced this scale of effort, you will appreciate just how amazing this sight is.

Since we are discussing and arranging peoples' futures now, we have to get the training right. The training programme therefore also covers and explains the mechanics of how the new culture will work; multi-skilling technicians (Shell Chemicals), why annualised hours are calculated this way (Colman's of Norwich), new mortgage application and review systems (Mortgage Express), and so on. It also includes training on any new capital equipment purchased as part of the company strategy.

It is worth noting here that a culture change normally involves working smarter rather than harder; simply because the changes are thought through from start to finish, rather than the relatively simple, but far more destructive, 'numbers reduction' game.

Another revelation for many firms is the concept of promoting informal communication, especially from the lower echelons upwards rather than in the opposite direction. Here is your chance to reverse the tide. To at least give this a nudge in the right direction, the culture change training should help improve two-way communication throughout your organisation. For example, include PC skills training, allocate e-mail addresses for everyone, provide access to the company intranet, and invest in widespread employee knowledge of integrated company systems (e.g. SAP).

Training Through Visits to Other Firms

'Training', in this culture change context, also includes employee benchmark visits to other firms; to see for themselves the principles of your vision already in place. It is a tangible demonstration of your vision that neatly removes any incredulity and replaces this with credibility. Since you will probably have already benchmarked during the initial phase of your own vision creating process, these visits should be relatively easy to arrange and well worth the effort.

Assuming you are changing to staff status in your culture change, look for examples in these benchmark visits where firms have switched to annualised hours. Look for firms where the teams, as well as management, are continuously improving the processes. Ask these team members to tell your teams what happens when the job is complete; to confirm they go home to their families rather than working to the end of the shift. This, for hourly paid employees, can be a real culture shock; although really it is simply a result of aligning company and employee goals.

Training also includes visits to customers and suppliers:

▶ For forklift truck drivers, to see beyond the trailer that they have just placed palletised product onto; or customer service personnel to meet the customers they talk with daily, to name just two examples.
▶ To interact with suppliers, so they understand your needs; for example, delivery timing, product quality, or the information supplied.

If your vision is to be the best, then your people have to understand *why* they are doing something in order to move from doing a job to having a mission. Remember the two 'rock breaking convicts' earlier? Just imagine the difference it would make to your own company performance if all your employees were genuinely on a mission!

There is a significant motivator associated with training and that is the tangible demonstration that you are investing in your employees. Assuming the training is relevant, this sends a signal to the individual being trained, and their colleagues, that says, 'You are valued'. As I mentioned in the introduction, if you want to move from the 'number two' position to market leader, investing in your employees so they can contribute more in return is a vital element for success.

Practical Steps for Training

So, what practical steps do we need to take to facilitate training as part of the culture change programme?

For each department, there will need to be at least one 'trainer'. It does not matter whether you are talking about an accounts department, airline cabin crew or travel agency; this departmental trainer role is another vital cog in the training wheel. The trainer will be asked to implement the agreed programme according to a training plan developed with the culture champion.

First, each departmental manager has to discuss and decide with his employees the skills required to operate efficiently in the 'new organisation'. Keep the training needs as simple as possible, particularly if you have several departments doing similar things, by standardising the training programme. This will help minimise the cost of achieving uniform standards around the company.

Training matrices are the next key tool. Bold and colourful, yet simple and clear! They double too, as a publicity medium! The idea is for the departmental trainer to put the training status of each employee on a departmental training matrix (see Figure 14.1). Employee names stretch across the top and required skills form the left-hand border. The legends are coloured (normally in the rainbow colour order, Red, Orange, Yellow, Green and Blue for 'Training required' through to 'Trainer') to indicate each employees' status in the training programme, and the date in each cell confirms when each section was completed.

From the publicity viewpoint, training matrices publish well on the site intranet, or alternatively a hard copy adds colour, as well as information, to the departmental training board. These matrices really should be A3 size as a minimum to make the information easy to read. The colour scheme also makes it obvious, even to a passing casual observer, whether most of the team is fully trained and which people or skill types need further attention.

With many departments on one site, why not bring the departmental training matrices together onto the training board in the restaurant? The aim is to show other employees that training is taking place. You could, for example, show on the restaurant copy each week, that a particular employee has progressed from one training status to another. You might wish to stick stars of the appropriate colour, or highlight cells to signify training completed that week, and then follow this up with a new updated matrix printout monthly. One small word of caution is if you do use the stars system; do not leave stars freely available by the matrices unless you want to see considerably more training progress indicated than has actually taken place! The aim is to keep the matrices 'live' and current, which in turn adds credibility to the training

..............................DEPARTMENT SKILLS MATRIX

Reviewed by: Review Date:

Training Subject	John Briggs	Ruth Brown	Charles Davidson	Duncan Fairway	Liz Roberts
Company Induction	15/09/97	10/09/01	07/05/01	22/03/01	06/06/94
Company Culture	01/11/01	01/11/01	01/11/01	01/11/01	01/11/01
Mission, Vision & Values	01/11/01	01/11/01	01/11/01	01/11/01	01/11/01
Investors in People					
Continuous Improvement philosophy	05/02/02	05/02/02	05/02/02	05/02/02	05/02/02
Suggestion scheme	05/02/02	05/02/02	05/02/02	05/02/02	05/02/02
Quarterly Objectives & KPIs	08/01/02	08/01/02	08/01/02	08/01/02	08/01/02
Self-managed teams system	08/11/00	10/10/01	07/06/01	24/04/01	08/11/00
Health & Safety Induction	15/09/97	10/09/01	07/05/01	22/10/01	06/06/94
ZAP 'Observations' system					
First Aider	18/01/02	18/01/02	N/A	N/A	N/A
Safety Representative	N/A	N/A	22/10/01	22/10/01	N/A
Intranet/e-mail	24/04/01	10/10/01	07/06/01	24/04/01	24/04/01
Word	15/07/99				15/07/99
Excel	16/07/99		23/08/01		16/07/99
Presentation skills	03/04/98				03/04/98
Leadership skills	08/11/00				08/11/00
Customer visits	1	2	0	1	2
Supplier visits	0	0	0	1	1

DEPARTMENTAL JOB SKILLS
(As appropriate to each individual, so no individual colours or subjects shown)
LEGEND

| Training Required | Learning | Proficient | Fully Trained | Trainer |

Figure 14.1. Departmental training matrix

programme. Providing each departmental trainer updates his matrix regularly, these hard copies should be a simple, living, pictorial representation of the site training status.

You will also need a plan that forecasts completion dates for each major section. Similar to the training matrices, this will also be in a matrix format, with months across the top and skill types down the left-hand side. The culture champion should publish this training plan after discussion with the departmental managers and their respective trainers.

Measuring the Success of Your Training Programmes

So, now that we have taken steps to facilitate a training programme, how do we confirm it has been a success? Although this is a simple question, the answer is not obvious but it is a question we should know how to answer before we spend serious sums of money on internal and external training.

We should start with a few baseline measures against which we can measure tangible progress. How many of your team can, for example, work in more than one department? What percentage of your workforce has completed all training and therefore only has green boxes on the training matrix? What percentage of boxes that were red at the start of the training period are now green? These are just a few quantifiable questions that can help demonstrate 'success'.

Then we have the less tangible factors such as improved employee morale or happiness. By definition, these aspects of 'success' are extremely difficult to measure. This, however, does not prevent a follow-up of each training course in three parts:

▶   before the course to show why the training is needed
▶   immediately afterwards to get feedback on the expected usefulness
▶   three months later to find out whether the training is actually being used and if so, what difference it has made.

This feedback can be incorporated in the overall training evaluation. Again the departmental manager, trainer and culture champion will all have a role to play in assessing how successful this training has been. The key is to invest in your employees' training, so they too can become 'seasoned professionals'.

This chapter has indicated the scale and importance of training in your culture change. Before you start wondering how your team is going to manage this ... its time to introduce Investors in People.

Chapter 15

Investors in People

Achieve Business Improvement through People Development.

Introduction

You may be looking for a structured and focused approach to managing your people development, and/or a major initiative to help drive and support your culture change. If so, you will be pleased to know that help is available. It comes in the form of a standard that in October 2001 celebrated its tenth anniversary; the 'Investors in People' Standard.

This chapter covers the purpose, content and benefits of the Standard so you can assess the potential of its role in your culture change. As well as my own personal experience with the Standard, this chapter incorporates feedback from thousands of employers and employees. It will give you a balanced view that may well change your perception of the Standard, especially if your experience is prior to its revision in 2000.

The Investors in People Standard is included here for four main reasons:

▶ It remains unique in that it is the only standard in the world that successfully integrates business strategy with people strategy.
▶ Taking the actions required to satisfy the Standard's 12 indicators will actively support your culture change implementation.
▶ It provides both a benchmark and a structure for improving your company, through investing in and developing your employees.
▶ It is rapidly becoming a global standard (with long-term partnerships and projects in 17 countries so far), so will be available to most readers of this book.

Since the inauguration of the Investors in People Standard in 1991, over 25,000 companies (mainly in the UK but also throughout Europe, in Australasia, and also South America) have achieved recognition as an 'Investor in People'. This means over 5.8 million people now benefit from being employed by Investors in People organisations.

Almost a further 3.5 million people are employed in companies that have committed to achieve the standard; making over 9 million people in total who are either enjoying the benefits, or are working towards recognition.

These large employee numbers are the sort of figures that change not just a company's working culture, but also potentially a country's working culture.

So, in case you are wondering if this standard applies to your company, the answer is yes providing you employ two or more people! Over 11,000 companies with less than 50 employees, over 8000 with 50 to 199, and over 5000 with 200+ employees have already been recognised as Investors in People.

The Investors in People Standard

Let us start by looking at the *purpose* of the Standard:

> *The purpose of Investors in People is business improvement through people development.*

In essence, the Investors in People Standard is all about improving the performance of your organisation through a planned approach to setting and communicating business objectives, and developing people to meet these objectives. The standard is, however, not simply a recommendation for more training. It is the link it contains between 'training that develops your people', and 'business performance improvement', that is critical. It is this unique aspect of the Standard that really justifies its inclusion in your culture change plans.

The Standard is based on the four *principles* of commitment, planning, action and evaluation, which together make up a continuous improvement cycle. Twelve *indicators* of good practice underpin these principles.

The Standard was revised in 2000 to focus on the 'outcomes' rather than the 'processes'; that is, what you can do now that you could not do before being trained, rather than whether a specific training record form is completed.

Now, for example, you do not have to provide any extra paperwork to achieve the Standard. This sensible change, which also removed the need to provide a portfolio of evidence to back up your application, was as a result of feedback from companies indicating the administration aspect of the Standard had become onerous without significant benefit.

In its revised format the Standard is a practical, value-adding tool that requires you to have the 12 indicators well established and clearly working to achieve recognition as an Investor in People. It is working with the Standard, not just achieving it, that is important; or as the Standard itself says, 'It is important that you treat Investors in People as part of your culture rather than as a separate project.'

Investors in People UK is responsible for the Standard's national marketing, development and quality assurance, but (apart from companies with 3000+ employees) not the individual company reviews.

In the UK the Standard is delivered through a network of advisers (who give advice about how to achieve the Standard), and assessors (who make the recognition assessments and recommendations).

Internationally, Investors in People UK has strategic partners based in the relevant country. Initially each strategic partner completes a pilot study, during which the UK team trains and mentors the national advisors and assessors. Thereafter the delivery process is similar to that in the UK.

Historically it has been difficult to sustain a consistent minimum Standard for recognition, but much corrective action has been implemented, particularly since introducing the revised Standard in 2000. This corrective action includes training, mentoring and auditing of the whole delivery channel, including advisers and assessors. It is now harder to just 'get the badge', and of course there is a reassessment every three years as well as the initial review.

Although there is input from the management team as well, the review consists mainly of interviewing a representative cross-section of employees from the company or site being assessed. It is the employee feedback that determines whether or not the company achieves the Standard. To give you some examples, the main four (out of 12) indicators the assessor is looking for are

▶ the organisation is committed to supporting the development of its people
▶ the organisation has a plan with clear aims and objectives, which are understood by everyone

▶ managers are effective in supporting the development of people
▶ the development of people improves the performance of the organisation, teams and individuals.

Achieving recognition as an Investor in People is therefore external acknowledgement that helps demonstrate to your customers and employees that you are investing in and developing your people.

To help you gain recognition, Investors in People UK has published a toolkit 'how to become an Investor in People', which uses case studies, checklists, questionnaires and other tools to assist your firm towards achieving the Standard.

Let us now start to find out more about how your organisation can benefit from becoming an Investor in People.

Investors in People Benefits

There is no doubt that working towards the Investors in People Standard will move your culture closer to the success culture you rated your firm against in the Benchmarking chapter. Many of the issues in the poor performance culture; like 'no teamwork', 'no time for continuous improvement' and so on, are all countered through implementing the Standard but there is still the question about the impact that achieving the Standard has on productivity.

Although there is no research study yet that demonstrates a *quantifiable* improvement in productivity by achieving Investors in People, there is plenty of *qualitative* evidence. We will look briefly at two UK research studies commissioned by Investors in People UK and carried out by CREATE,[1] and Planet Research.[2]

Create

The first piece of research, '*Building Capability for the 21st Century*', was published by CREATE in 1999. This looks at over 2000 firms, all of whom are recognised as Investors in People. It reports the following powerful statistics:

- 70 per cent of organisations with the Standard have improved their competitive edge and productivity
- 80 per cent have increased customer satisfaction
- 90 per cent have improved communication, clarified culture and values, and achieved a motivated workforce.

Planet Research

Planet Research published the second survey 'satisfaction at work' in 1999. It covers 600 UK companies, half of which are working with Investors in People. As you will soon see in Table 15.1, the results from the employee perspective are markedly different in the two sets of companies.

As these two research reports all clearly indicate, there are major benefits from having the culture of an Investor in People.

Table 15.1.   Employee 'satisfaction at work' survey results (percentage of employees agreeing with statements)

Statement	Employees in companies working with Investors in People	Employees in other companies
I like my job	94	37
I feel secure in my job	82	42
I get on well with my colleagues	92	37
I feel real involvement with the business	57	3
I have experienced promotion in my present company	55	32
I agree with the company's ambition/focus	39	1
I rate my rewards and pay well	67	45
I have been offered training	97	51
I feel valued	91	74
I feel 'invested in'	95	69

Investors in People – The Future

From the culture change perspective, whether your company is already recognised as an Investor in People, or has yet to make that commitment, Investors in People UK has three key intentions that are likely to help the Standard act as a catalyst for your culture change.

The first is the vision for the Standard, which is to be:

> *An internationally recognised standard that enables organisations to maximise their success by developing the potential of their people.*

As the Standard becomes more international there should be better access both to the Standard and to advisers and assessors who can support your implementation, regardless of your company size and irrespective of which country or countries your firm is based in. This is why there are long-term partnerships and projects in 17 countries already, together with a concerted effort to increase this number.

The second intention is for 50 per cent of the UK workforce to be working in Investors in People organisations by 2005. The main target market for this growth is firms with five to 49 people.

The third is to add to the scope of the Standard. In addition to the core Investors in People Standard, there are two additional elements that 'stretch' the Standard. The first is the Recruitment and Selection Model, launched in July 2001. The second, due to be launched in mid 2002, is Management and Leadership. These two modules are aimed at adding further value for companies already with the core Standard.

Finally, I hope this chapter has given you an overview of the Investors in People Standard and what it can do to support your culture change. Let us move on now to the next element of leading your people to success; changing attitudes.

Chapter 16

Changing Attitudes

Rather than your words, it is your attitude that conveys the real message.

To change your company culture you have two distinct challenges to overcome. The first challenge consists of your company systems. These are relatively quick and easy to dismantle, as most are paper or electronic information. New formats, some reprogramming, or perhaps commissioning a new system, will normally take just *months* to accomplish. Add in the relevant training so people are competent, and you are virtually there. Modifying systems to support your desired culture is merely a project; it can be planned, resourced, monitored, and completed.

The second barrier, however, is a much bigger challenge. It is a critical, rate-determining factor en route to your new culture, and certainly one that requires a much heavier arsenal of skills and communication to achieve. This second barrier is called 'changing attitudes', and it applies to you and all your employees from the top to the very base of your organisation. It is likely to take considerable effort, for a few *years*, to accomplish these attitude changes; but it is a swamp that needs draining and clearing to make it safe to cross to the other side. Changing attitudes is simply a requirement to progress from a 'poor performance culture' to a 'success culture'.

In this chapter we will revisit the characteristics of these two extreme cultures; those same aspects that you ranked your company against in the benchmarking chapter. This time we will look at the underlying attitudes associated with many of these 'poor performance culture' and 'success culture' characteristics. We will explore the likely reasons why these attitudes prevail, make suggestions as how to change these attitudes into those present in the success culture, and finally look at some of the outcomes (e.g. reduced absence and employee turnover, and improved accident record). Particular areas to be revealed include:

▶ senior management changes
▶ employee changes, including 'change him or change him' and structural changes, such as introducing 'annualised hours' and 'self-managed teams'.

Senior Management Changes

Your own personal attitude and behaviour have a huge bearing on the way people around you, and lower down your organisation, feel and behave. In other words you personally affect your organisation's culture, perhaps even more than you realise.

The mere fact that you are reading this book indicates you are interested in culture change. You are likely, therefore, to have already spent some time leading your own culture change, or certainly have that desire to improve your peoples' working lives and company performance. For simplicity, however, and to be able to illustrate typical changes required, the assumption for now is that your culture is currently firmly in the 'poor performance' bracket. On this basis, we are about to divulge how changing your own attitude and behaviour in six important areas will do two things. Firstly start to move your culture towards that of success, and secondly send the equivalent of Apache smoke signals to the rest of your people as signs of change. As it is your own behaviour and attitude in this situation, the changes should be relatively quick to make. All you have to do is be open to change, realise the benefits for your organisation, and have the desire to initiate them.

Us and Them vs Equality

Some people have an egocentric and arrogant attitude that requires feeding by physically or verbally differentiating themselves from the rest of their colleagues. Differentiate it may do, but in the process it also creates barriers; an 'us and them' situation. (Physical status symbols include: a larger desk or office, different colour of office carpet, or a requirement to be on a higher floor of the office building; type of company car, or perhaps an allocated car parking space as close as possible to the reception entrance. Verbal indicators usually involve conversations that become right/wrong rather than constructive, where you win or lose arguments, or when you either dominate or are dominated in discussions.)

Actions to signify change could be to relocate yourself to an open plan office area with your team, simply as another member of that team, and to eliminate all allocated car parking spaces apart from those for visitors. Next time someone asks for something to satisfy his ego rather than improve the company performance (e.g. upgraded office furniture), you might just ask yourself 'Am I prepared for *all* my employees to receive this same benefit?' You will have moved to equality when the directors are physically, verbally and contractually treated the same as the rest of your employees.

Blame/Fear Culture vs Coaching/Supportive Culture

When you visit a site (e.g. retail outlet, call centre, research centre, hotel, or hospital department) is it announced well in advance, is it formal, and are your people afraid of your visit? Do you get angry with your employees if something is not as you expected? Is the person to blame regularly sought after if a mistake is made? If the answer is yes to any of these questions, there is a high probability that your organisation has a blame culture, or worse still, a fear culture. This argument about blame/fear cultures vs coaching/supportive cultures is not about standards, it is about employee performance and encouraging innovation and leaders. Working in a blame/fear culture is a great way to achieve conformance to rules, but an even better way to completely snuff out any risk taking or innovation.

Perhaps there is another way of achieving the excellent performance you crave; one based on coaching and supporting your employees. Rather than seeing an artificial performance specially orchestrated for your arrival, you could try regularly visiting completely unannounced. The first time you will find out what really happens while you are away, but after that standards will genuinely improve. Noting these improvements and encouraging further changes, giving people the benefit of your experience rather than saying 'My way is the right way', and freeing up your people to act on their own initiative with decision making at local level, will make a tremendous difference to the culture. It might even surprise you how much the site performance improves too.

Eradication of the blame/fear culture will be evident when people thoroughly investigate each mistake; not to pinpoint who to blame, but to identify what went wrong and to prevent a repeat of the same error. When this is combined with more training or other preventative measures, you will have completed the move to a coaching/supportive culture.

Parent/Child Relationship vs Adult-to-Adult Trust

Peters and Waterman[1] include a poem, written by the 'auto workers' underground', that paraphrases into how each individual outside work may be a father, husband, voter, lover and adult; and yet for eight hours each day, once he takes his place on the car production line, transforms from a man into a child.

It is a poignant poem that hints at the parent/child relationship employed by the management. It conjures up a picture of 'telling people what to do rather than asking for their opinion', assuming each person is a 'body without a responsible brain', and 'watching their every move, just as you would a young child that is learning to walk, because you cannot trust them to be unsupervised'.

My personal experience and that of my colleagues over the years (of asking for opinions, sharing knowledge, explaining the bigger picture, answering questions honestly and trying to treat everyone fairly) is that it demonstrates respect for the individual. It makes every person feel valued, shows them that they have an important role to play, and it makes them feel good. Most importantly it helps change their attitude towards the company; from having a job in order to live, towards the desired 'I live to work' mentality. If you genuinely do trust your employees, give them as much responsibility as they are capable of accepting, and let them make themselves accountable for this responsibility. Then you have accomplished the move to a relationship built on trust.

Autocratic Control at the Top vs Responsibility and Accountability Accepted and Thriving at the Lowest Levels in the Organisation

One of the characteristics of an owner-managed company is that its growth becomes constrained by the owner's desire to make all the decisions. Only when the owner is prepared to let go, to trust subordinates to make decisions without continually checking and double-checking, can the organisation move into its next phase of growth.

Another characteristic of an organisation with autocratic control is the endemic bureaucracy and rules established purely to force all key decisions to be filtered upwards. It means the senior management become puppets, administrating the business rather than leading it. It makes the people at the base of the company feel powerless to make even simple decisions in case they get told they should not have done it this way. It wastes energy, slows down decision making, drains profits from the business because of the bureaucracy, and it is a great demotivator for all except the chief executive officer!

If you want your people to be able to perform, you have the key inside you to unlock this; but you must let go of this autocratic control. You must be prepared to demonstrate your trust in your senior colleagues and indeed in all your employees by letting them make important decisions too. Strip out layers of bureaucracy, and let decisions be made locally. Focus your attention on the strategy and values rather than the minutiae of the day-to-day administration. Start leading rather than managing, and empower your people at the lowest levels to make significant decisions (within generous pre-defined limits) without the need to continuously refer upwards.

You will know you have empowered your people to make decisions and act on them, when you hear about new initiatives and innovative ideas that are already implemented, or being developed, rather than waiting for a decision from you.

Personal Standards and Values

Living the values and raising standards is all about changing attitudes further down in your organisation. Promoting the values of honesty, fairness, openness, fun, pride, happiness and safety will all be on your daily agenda if you expect them to filter out to people at the extremities of your organisation. You will eventually hear stories on your walk rounds that confirm these values are becoming embedded throughout the company culture.

Do You Consider Your Employees as an Asset Rather than as a Cost?

Finally in the senior management changes section, your view of your employees as an asset for your business, rather than as a necessary evil, will be reflected in your approach and interest in them. Being in the 'asset' camp implies hiring and firing should be a relatively rare activity, replaced instead with more training and development in times of quiet trading. The aim should be to build still more service skills to enhance an already excellent customer service, and thereby win additional business in new markets as part of the company growth strategy.

Employee Changes

In this employee attitude changes section we shall explore four areas:

No Teamwork vs Cohesive Teams

When customer demand suddenly escalates so your resources are stretched, your well co-ordinated team can suddenly transform into a series of separate departments that end up fighting against each other rather than working together. (Do you remember the game 'people not planes', in the British Airways case study, that vividly demonstrates the importance of working together as a team?) Communication breaks down, tempers fray, and people move into reaction mode. Fire fighting becomes the norm, and customer service suffers as a result. Cohesive teamwork is replaced with little or no teamwork and your management time is spent resolving issues that should have been sorted out much earlier by people lower down the organisation. In short, responsibility is abdicated to higher management where the accountability really lies, stress levels increase and the quality of working life plummets.

In a poor performance culture, the 'our department's okay' attitude dominates. In bad cases, information is perceived as power and can actively be withheld by one department to the detriment of another. You have probably heard this next argument before too. Transport department to production department: 'Why did not you tell me it was ready?' Production department replies: 'You did not ask.' The outside world does not care about the internal wrangling of your organisation. All they want is to have the best product or service, at the right time, at the agreed price. So, what can we do about this?

The answer may sound obvious when it is mentioned in a minute, but first let us look briefly at the group dynamics in this situation. What incentive is there for *hourly paid* employees to finish their job efficiently and early? There is not one; in fact there is an active disincentive because taking longer to produce the required goods or service can lead to employees being paid more, for overtime. What is more we even load the scales further in the wrong direction by paying a premium rate for the overtime. This means 'mistakes' and 'inefficiencies' are rewarded with higher incomes at higher cost to the company. Could there be a better way? There certainly is.

It involves trust. It involves removing your clock card machines for hourly paid employees. It involves making all your employees monthly paid, with the same salary each month regardless of the hours worked.

'What about fluctuations in demand?' I hear you ask. 'What about seasonality?'

Let us ask a few key questions in return, and offer a potential solution. What about peer pressure, rather than management effort, to control your teams? What about giving your employees an incentive to work efficiently so that they can go home when the job is done rather than at the end of the normal working day? How can you get your teams to reduce absence themselves? How can you get them to think of, and implement, continuous improvements to processes throughout your organisation? How can you get your teams to be 'self-managed'? The potential answer lies in the journey from hourly paid to 'annualised hours'.

Annualised hours is a concept that applies to any industry that exhibits seasonality or variations in demand that can be reasonably well planned in to the working pattern. This might include demands that regularly peak on a Thursday each week with troughs on, say, Mondays and Tuesdays. Another scenario might be summer and winter seasonality, or pre-Christmas surges in demand. Instead of manning your process or service to run smoothly at normal demand levels, and then asking (and paying) for extra hours to be worked at peak periods through overtime or employing temporary labour, you might wish to consider the option of annualised hours.

Annualised hours is simply a system that takes the total annual hours required to provide the desired service or production, and pays the same for these hours each month, regardless of the hours actually worked. It is just like paying a monthly direct debit for your domestic gas and/or electricity consumption. The monthly payments are constant even though in the summer months your demand is low and conversely high in the winter. The monthly payments normally cover the annual consumption costs, without need for change, unless the demand trend alters significantly. In company terms a trend change could be the result of gaining additional new business that increases the total annual hours required; or investing in new more efficient systems or equipment that require less time each year to accomplish the same output. Under these circumstances the annualised hours would change. If the hours increase, you might need additional people. If the hours reduce, you may release time for further training or continuous improvement activities. However, since the investment in more efficient systems or equipment would probably have been justified by a planned increase in output, it should not be long before the time released for training is reabsorbed.

For more details and an example of implementing annualised hours, refer to the Colman's of Norwich case study. Annualised hours is also the backdrop to creating teams that are 'self-managed', as discussed in the Alcan Foil Europe – Glasgow case study. The Alcan Foil Europe – Glasgow case study shows how the site reached 'Agreement 2000', which is founded on values rather than rules, and how they built their teams that incorporate several leaders, each responsible for a specific aspect of the team's needs. The Alcan Foil Europe – Glasgow case study is a great example of developing leaders throughout an organisation.

You will know that your teams are really cohesive when your management time is freed up to concentrate on genuinely leading and improving the organisation rather than bogged down in the day-to-day administration.

Working to Live vs Living to Work

Give a person control over his/her working environment and you will increase that person's motivation significantly. Explain why a particular job is vital in the overall company strategy and you will help give it purpose and meaning, which again increases motivation. Encourage and implement new ideas originated by your employees, and you will raise motivation yet another notch. Combine this influence with increased responsibility, open peoples' eyes to the need for change so they begin to see it for themselves even without your help, and you begin to have the recipe for developing leaders in the team. You will soon have leaders who start to live to work; leaders who demonstrate this by occasionally coming in on rest days to ensure their particular project is progressing to their satisfaction. You will have leaders that begin to innovate, without being encouraged, to the point where innovation cannot be suppressed; and leaders throughout your organisation that want to make things better, that believe in the company, and are proud to work for your firm. You will recognise this transformation every time it happens, as the signs are so obvious. All it takes is a change of attitude.

'I Am Not Sure We Can Do That' Attitude vs 'Can-Do' Attitude

Lack of confidence in an employee shows itself in many guises; but even a strong character in a subordinate position will eventually submit or get out of an organisation if continually given negative feedback, if threatened rather than supported, or if reprimanded every time he makes a suggestion. Similarly organisations that promote individuals based on length of service rather than on merit, stand a very strong chance of ending up with people at the top of the organisation that have achieved this position by not making mistakes, rather than through making good decisions. They are likely themselves to build barriers to change, rather than actively remove these barriers.

The move towards a 'can-do' attitude may require a close look at your senior people, their history, and how they achieved their current position. It will definitely require a meritocracy, and it will take positive leaders throughout your organisation that support, coach and mentor their people. To have a 'can-do' attitude demands confidence, but like living to work, it will be transparently obvious when this 'can-do' attitude prevails.

Change Him or Change Him

The old adage, 'You can take a horse to water but you can't make him drink', is just as true today. Even in the 'employee changes' section, management initiate most of the modifications to enable employees to respond with a change of attitude. Just like the horses, not all employees will respond without further effort; hence the need for 'change him or change him', to prevent one bad apple from turning others rotten too.

The expression 'change him or change him' succinctly describes what happens to an employee with a 'bad attitude'; either the attitude changes or the employee leaves the organisation. Someone with a 'bad attitude' might exhibit this through a poor attendance, sickness, or accident record; or less tangible aspects such as laziness, disrespect for others, selfishness or other similar characteristics that fall outside the desired company culture or values.

The first element of change him is to show a genuine concern for the employee's welfare by finding out if there are underlying reasons for the poor attitude. If not, take steps to improve an employee's attitude by ensuring the employee knows what is expected. Once set, these standards and expectations form a benchmark for performance measurement. Most employees mend their ways so the end result is a positive one. In a minority of cases, however, it becomes obvious fairly quickly that the desired outcome is never going to happen, especially when the disciplinary procedures progress without success. Hence the second part of change him, which neatly describes the employee's exit from the company.

Change him or change him is a long, steady process that reinforces the company values. It calls for support from the recruitment process as we discussed earlier. It needs line managers to invest time with each person to keep them in tune with the company values. It requires a commitment to take tough decisions for the long-term good of the business; and it demands support from the top of the organisation to make this cultural change.

This policy brings benefits that can be very significant, particularly in terms of reduced sickness and absence figures, lower accident rates, higher morale and greater productivity. Trusting and respecting your people is one thing, but if someone abuses that trust and respect, they have to know that they are liable to suffer the consequences.

The aim, at the end of the day, is to steadily increase the calibre, flexibility and motivation of your team through training and career development. Trying to do this with high absence and employee turnover rates is virtually impossible, so picking out the bad apples is one way of creating the culture for accomplishing this objective. Sometimes you just have to go through this 'change him or change him' pain barrier to arrive significantly stronger and more competitive at the other side.

In the next case study we will integrate many aspects of this chapter by travelling a culture change journey founded on the implementation of annualised hours. Let us join Colman's of Norwich now to see how they achieve their vision.

Chapter 17

Colman's of Norwich Annualised Hours Helps Make Colman's a Great Place to Work

Introduction

Figure 17.1 shows you the vision of what Colman's of Norwich wishes to be in the future, together with their values down either side. This case study is a story of culture change that has been carefully and strategically implemented to realise this vision.

People development		Inspired people
Spreading brilliance	**A great place to work**	Learning organisation
Trust		Ownership
Responsibility	To be Unilever's most successful factory	Happy people
Passionate people		Understanding

Figure 17.1. Colman's of Norwich factory vision

Included in this case study, as with the preceding ones, are many general principles that will appeal to a wide audience spanning both service and manufacturing sectors:

► 'Seeing the need' and then leading the culture change. Colman's of Norwich is a good example of leading in practice.

► The whole principle of aligning employee and company goals by introducing the right systems, in this case annualised hours. Look out for the resulting continuous improvement driven by the teams.

► Demonstrating that you trust your employees – there are many examples to look out for where trust has removed the need for bureaucratic systems and the associated employees.

► Replace an 'overtime' culture where hourly paid people 'live' at their workplace, to one that is virtually free of overtime, by moving to monthly paid as part of the transition to annualised hours. See how the journey to introduce annualised hours is travelled in practice; and consider what it could do to reduce your own overtime costs. Bear in mind that this principle applies across all industry sectors where there are reasonably predictable demand patterns.

The case study walks you quickly through Colman's history. Initially we reach the point where employee and company goals need re-aligning. Shortly afterwards the managing director calls for a 'leap of faith', and then negotiations, to initiate the introduction of 'annualised hours'. Then we explore annualised hours in more detail; in particular the scheme structure, and how to calculate the hours required. Discussing the many benefits of annualised hours brings us up to date, and the study concludes with where Colman's of Norwich are now. You will note how different the company culture is today compared to when the journey first started eight years earlier. You will note too, the important role annualised hours has played in this process.

Just before we start the history, here is a brief definition of annualised hours. 'Annualised hours' is essentially a plan that takes the total hours worked in a standard year, and matches the hours in each period to the anticipated demand in that period. For example, it might take a standard 40-hour week for the whole year, add on the overtime worked, and then reschedule these hours to match the anticipated demand. To appreciate what annualised hours is really all about and how this helps make Colman's a 'great place to work', we need first to review a little history.

History

Colman's of Norwich started in 1814, when Jeremiah Colman took over a mustard manufacturing business just south of Norwich. His great nephew, Jeremiah James Colman, became head of the Colman's mustard manufacturing firm in 1851. Jeremiah James Colman was a visionary with ideas on employment well ahead of his time, including the realisation that a healthy and happy workforce would be more productive. In 1864, nearly 20 years before education became compulsory, he built and subsidised a school for his employees. In 1868, he established a kitchen to provide hot meals at reasonable prices. Ten years later he employed one of the first industrial nurses, to assist the company doctor and to visit sick employees in their homes.

The Colman mustard manufacturing business was so successful that the company was able to buy its main rivals, especially Keen Robinson & Company (which is where the phrase 'as keen as mustard' originates). In 1938, Colman's of Norwich merged with Reckitt & Sons to form Reckitt & Colman. Then in 1995 Unilever bought the Colman's food business and incorporated it into Van den Bergh Foods Ltd, its largest UK food company. Colman's of Norwich now produces products for three market areas: dry foods, culinary and, of course, mustards. Throughout this long history, Colman's has continued its caring and supportive approach to its employees. This is reflected in 'our factory vision' above. It is also a key reason for introducing annualised hours.

Goal Alignment

I would like to start this case study about annualised hours by asking you a fundamental question about alignment of employee aims and business goals. How do we ensure these two are really heading in the same direction, rather than opposing each other?

Let me give you an example. Assume your company, perhaps a traditional manufacturing firm, has some 'monthly paid' employees who are paid the same salary each month regardless of how long they work for. You also have other employees called 'hourly paid', who clock in and out each day, get paid weekly, and earn more money the more hours they work. They also earn at a higher rate for any overtime worked. Now, lets assume that the hourly paid production people have a 'bad week', with many niggling breakdowns and stoppages that prevent the weekly orders from being fulfilled in the standard working week. In order to ensure the customers receive their orders, some overtime is needed on a Saturday at the rate of time and a half, or perhaps even on a Sunday when the pay moves to double-time. Does the employee benefit financially? Yes. Does it cost the company more? Yes. Does the employee have to work longer hours and therefore have less time for family and other interests? Yes. Are the employee objectives and business goals aligned? No.

At Colman's there were times when the team members used to 'know' on a Tuesday that they would be needed for overtime on a Saturday. How did they know? I will leave that question unanswered for you to work out yourself!

There was also the vital element, called trust, which was missing at Colman's. Having hourly paid employees clocking in and out is like lighting a neon sign that says, 'We don't trust you'. It also creates a them and us environment between the hourly paid and salaried staff. Colman's decided in 1991 to extinguish the neon sign, remove this differentiation, and align the employee and business goals. Annualised hours proved to be the main mechanism to achieve these objectives and the resultant cultural change. Note too that 'trust' is one element of the factory vision.

Leap of Faith

In 1991 there were five key issues.

Wage Agreements

Colman's hourly paid were on five grades for operators, four grades for engineers, and there were various rates for different jobs. The GMB (General, Municipal and Boilermakers Union) and AEEU (Amalgamated Engineering and Electrical Union) represented the employees. Colman's used to work 40 hours per week, get paid for 38 hours and have every fourth Monday off. There were agreements in place where you were paid the average of your previous 4–6 weeks pay if you were off sick, or absent. This implied that after a period of sustained overtime, an employee who was absent or off sick would be paid more than his colleague who was actually in work. Also, after the peak demand periods, the average hours worked could be kept high by working overtime to cover for absent colleagues.

Absence

Absence ran at around six per cent.

'Floaters'

There were then, and still are, significant peaks and troughs in demand during the year. Departments with peak demands had to bring in 'floaters' (people working elsewhere on site, contractors, or temporary workers) to supplement the full-time resources. These people were often resented and given the more menial tasks to do, and there was an increased requirement for training and retraining. This meant expensive labour was adding little value to the business.

Payroll Administration

In peak demand periods, around half of an administration assistant's time would be spent arranging weekend overtime. Also a significant number of hours each week would be needed to correct mistakes made with the clock cards. Plus a payroll clerk spent effort to keep the hourly paid system going. Most of this work added no value.

Engineers' Pay

In 1991, every shift engineer earned more than £30,000 per year. They worked long hours to earn that amount and there was a question mark over the value of some of this work. From a management perspective there was scope and a need to change.

Colman's of Norwich employed a new managing director in 1991. He wanted to change the culture. He wanted a better relationship with the unions. He also wanted people to be excited about product development, and to encourage people to use their own initiative.

He started at the top by asking senior managers to buy in to the proposed culture. He was a strong leader with great vision and desire to change. He realised the need to take senior management with him on this journey of change and was prepared to stand by his beliefs. He held management conferences and meetings and got 'buy in' to the Norwich site strategic plan.

One of the elements of this process was a belief, a leap of faith, that annualised hours would be beneficial for the site. Members of the Human Resources department and union delegates worked together to gain full understanding of annualised hours and how it might be implemented. This leap of faith conversion to start using annualised hours turned out to be the key factor in the whole cultural change process for Colman's, one that required a major injection of trust by all concerned.

Negotiations for Annualised Hours

Colman's started in one production unit as a one-year trial. They consolidated all the different operator pay rates, whilst engineers had some differentials based on qualifications (i.e. apprentices/single skilled/dual skilled/technician). The company committed to multi-skilling all operators and engineers. One production manager spent much time prior to the formal negotiations, educating the shift teams about different shift patterns, what reserve hours were all about, and preparing the way for the GMB and AEEU negotiations.

In Colman's case the overall wage cost for annualised hours increased by ten per cent , including a new five per cent performance bonus. The new operator salary was set at the level previously earned by 60 per cent of the operator team, with an agreement reached in just two formal meetings. The proposed engineers' salaries, however, were lower because of the overtime previously available. Although the new basic salary rate was extremely attractive, the engineers really tested management's commitment to annualised hours. It took a meeting between the site managing director and the engineers, where he stated his full commitment to the implementation of annualised hours and gave them the choice of accepting annualised hours or redundancy, to gain the engineers' agreement.

The annualised hours agreement had very specific written rules about when and how reserved hours could be asked for. This proved essential at the start but now is hardly ever referred to as the mutual understanding and trust makes this redundant.

Rostered and Reserve Hours

The annualised hours process started its journey in 1993 with the following initial plan based on a 38-hour working week. Let us look at the basic calculations, starting with the two components of annualised hours; rostered hours and reserve hours.

Rostered hours are those that make up the normal shift pattern averaging 38 hours per week over a year to reflect the previous hourly paid 38-hour week.

Reserve hours are there to give some flexibility in the amount of production required if there are unplanned fluctuations in customer demand. They allow extra production time if breakdowns prevent the target production from being made during the rostered hours of any particular week. Alternatively they can be used to extend the original rostered hours should the plan required for a given week exceed the original roster. If demand increases, for example, then eight-hour shifts extend to ten or 12 hours to increase the production hours available to the planner. This would normally be advised to the teams some weeks in advance, although not always. *Note*: Reserve hours are not 'overtime'. They are paid as part of the annual salary whether they are used up or not.

Having defined rostered and reserve hours, we will now look at the basic calculations behind annualised hours and how this links in with the shift structures used. Based on a 38-hour week, the annualised hours derive from:

Rostered Hours

Allowing for leap years there are an average of 52.18 weeks per year	52.18
Eight bank holidays/year is equivalent to 1.6 weeks. Deduct this	(1.60)
Assuming five weeks for holidays, deduct this too	(5.00)
Total number of working weeks available each year	45.58
At 38 hours per week	× 38
Total number of working hours available each year for each person	1732

Reserve Hours

Add 168 'reserve hours' to cover poor line performance, demand changes and breakdowns	168
Total hours available to be worked in annual contract	1900

Colman's chose this figure of 168 reserve hours for two simple reasons. Firstly it equated to just under ten per cent of the basic hours, which provided sufficient flexibility to cope with unplanned swings in production demand, and secondly 1900 seemed a nice round number! If, for example, the week's production is below target, the reserve hours allows additional production on a Saturday morning, or through increased mid-week shift hours at no extra cost.

Calculating the Hours Required

If the total number of hours required for all processes is estimated at, say 5050, then three teams are needed ($3 \times 1732 = 5196$, which is more than 5050). The other consideration is whether you invest sufficient capacity to allow a 5 × 24 rather than a 7 × 24 working week. Colman's had historically worked a five-day week in all but severe seasonal increases in demand and had machine capacity within their plants to continue on five days. There was no push towards seven days, although if future demand dictated then this might occur, which would require more than three teams. For example, working seven days per week for half the year, and five days for the other half, normally requires four teams. Similarly, if working a constant seven days throughout the year then five teams will be required.

I mentioned earlier that the customer demand for Colman's fluctuates during the year. This demand is fairly accurately forecasted and allows different shift patterns to be planned in at the start of the year to cope with this demand change. For example Colman's has three shift teams working a three-shift rota, with numerous working pattern possibilities for 80 and 120 hours per week:

For 80 hours per week:

1.   Two teams on eight-hour shifts × five days, one team off.
2.   Two teams on 12-hour shifts (three days × 12 and one day × 8, three nights × 12 = 80), one team off.
3.   Three teams on eight-hour shifts working continuously from Monday 06:00 to Thursday 14:00, no teams off.

For 120 hours per week:

1.   Two teams on 12 hour shifts × five days, one team off.
2.   Three teams on eight-hour shifts × five days, no teams off.

At Colman's it is now the team members themselves who generate the annual shift pattern to suit both the factory demand and their preference for working hours. Interestingly, when Colman's started there were many 12-hour shifts (working two weeks on and one week off, with 17 weeks rostered off per year). Now most factories have replaced some of the 12-hour shifts with eight-hour shifts (three teams working, no teams off) with a reduction to approximately 12 weeks rostered off per year.

Benefits of Annualised Hours

So, the total of 1900 hours per year is equivalent to an average of 41.68 hours per week if all the reserve hours are worked. In practice the number of reserve hours actually worked each year tends to be cyclical over a two to three year time frame. Let us follow the logic. A small initial increase in demand will require use of reserved hours. As demand increases, so does the need for reserved hours until further investment is justified (unless performance/capacity increases through continuous improvement keep pace with this demand). When extra capacity is in place, the number of reserve hours required drops back towards zero. Further demand increases simply encourage additional reserve hour cycles. If demand remains static, the number of reserve hours should fall over a period of time as continuous improvement adds capacity and efficiency improvements. Both of these scenarios are win–win situations for the company and its employees, because over a period of time the company gains extra output capacity, and the employees earn themselves extra time off as shown below.

To make the annualised hours work well needs trust between the manager and his team. At Colman's this trust took time to build up, and required the managers to realise and respect that once the team had met its target for the week, the team could go home. It also needed the operators to realise that they were not going to be asked to work extra hours once their target had been met, a concept that seemed very foreign at first. For example, a manager could not suddenly add extra weekend working simply because he wanted to increase the agreed weekly production plan. Had he done so, then the incentive for working efficiently would be lost, as well as the element of trust that is inevitably required between the team members and managers in these situations.

Taking this job-and-finish incentive a step further means that when a team makes a process improvement, they win extra time off for a while. The company gains in the medium term, however, by gradually but fairly increasing the production targets. The key is not to abuse the trust built up through this process. An example demonstrates the principle well. The dry foods team decided they wanted to reduce the time taken to change from one product to another going through a sachet filler. Team members designed different improvements for the engineers to make and install. Previously the engineers waited to be called before helping the operators. This time they helped the operators do the design work too. These improvements resulted in changeover times dropping from 45 to 12 minutes. With usually about 12 changeovers per line each week, this improvement saved about six hours production time (approximately five per cent), increased the unit's flexibility and capacity, and reduced the workload of employees. This was a win–win for both the factory and its employees that probably would not have been achieved in the old hourly paid era, as the operators would then have denied themselves potential overtime. Now they reward themselves with the opportunity to finish early or avoid the need to work reserve hours. A small group of employees from different areas of the business implemented this change as part of a three-day workshop that concentrated on the one problem of changeovers.

It is also worth noting that with annualised hours in place, you have to get the planned quantity made, but also ensure the time required for continuous improvement is available, regardless of production pressures. Although this could be perceived as a conflict in times of high production demand, you have to ensure the continuous improvement carries on otherwise you can go down the slippery slope of focusing purely on production. Colman's have suspended continuous improvement for short periods in the past but soon learned that this is counter-productive. It also sends the wrong message to all employees.

Holiday entitlement is restricted to the rostered weeks off, but it is possible for shift team members on different shifts to swop weeks with each other. This creates flexibility for holidays, is normally arranged within the team, and does not take up any management time. This means the teams are again getting the best from the scheme without harming the factory's production.

Where are Colman's Now?

▶ Clock cards are history, with everyone on a monthly salary.
▶ Absence has dropped from around six to three per cent.
▶ There are no people employed to cover for absence. If someone is off sick, the other two teams must cover for the sick person. This change has created significant peer pressure, which in turn has reduced absence. If the illness is long-term, then temporary labour covers.
▶ Shift changeovers now happen in the workplace, rather than in the changing rooms, to make the whole handover process more efficient.
▶ Overall output has increased by around 30 per cent for the same number of employees.
▶ There is no payroll department any more.
▶ Overlapping two shifts at shift changeover provides time for continuous improvement. The teams implement major improvement projects when capacity is planned to be available.

▶ If interested, team members are encouraged to look at potential new machinery investments once or twice per year, in their rostered time off.

▶ Some team members come in voluntarily on their days off to help their team, or to work on specific projects. This is not removed from their reserve hours.

▶ Dry food overall efficiency increased from 55 to 85 per cent over three years.

▶ There is now a 'can-do' attitude on site.

▶ The teams are actually using around 50–60 hours reserve time when averaged over several years.

▶ Twice each year the whole site stops work for a vision and strategy day, which gives all 200 employees an update on the company progress and the latest thinking about the company strategy.

Colman's of Norwich took the decision to move to annualised hours back in 1993. The driving force then was the desire to change the culture. Now working for Colman's is described with expressions such as: 'It's great fun', 'You get plenty of support', 'I really enjoy working for Colman's and I think they're a fantastic company', 'People have a lot of pride in working for Colman's', and 'Colman's is a great place to work.' Although not all of this can be attributed to annualised hours, the operators and production managers certainly describe annualised hours as 'the hub' of the Colman's cultural change journey.

Summary Action List for Your Business

1. Assess if your customer demand fluctuates in a reasonably predictable way, whether seasonally or weekly, to make annualised hours a viable proposition.
2. Assess if making everyone salaried, by introducing annualised hours, would help align your business and employee goals.
3. Ensure you and your team fully understand that annualised hours is a culture change journey involving trust and win–win situations, rather than a simple system you can introduce tomorrow.
4. Decide an appropriate level of reserve hours as well as rostered hours, and design the shift structure accordingly.
5. Bear in mind the need to build in time for continuous improvement as part of the annualised hours culture.

Chapter 18

The 'Walk Round'

*If you want to find out what is really going on,
go for an informal Walk Round.*

Now we come to the personal touch that makes such a difference to your employees.

Put yourself in your employee's shoes for a minute. Imagine you are a chef, one of a brigade of ten, in a large hotel where functions are often for several hundred guests at a sitting. The kitchen is well equipped and everyone from head chef to washer-up knows his or her daily routine. The hotel is lucky to have a really good team. You and the other chefs have to work quickly and efficiently to ensure you serve the highest quality food that is piping hot at *exactly* the right time. Heads are down to concentrate on the preparation required amidst the general hubbub of activity, so there is very little talking apart from brief instructions shouted between you and the other chefs. As you have been with the company for a long time, however, much of your work is done automatically with a rhythm gained from the years of experience. Despite the pace required to complete your own preparation, you still have time to keep an eye on what is going on around you.

The kitchen is near a walkway used by waitresses, reception staff and housekeepers from all over the hotel. They pass by on a fairly regular basis during the day to visit another area or to go for their breaks. Occasionally your hotel manager also walks straight past without even looking into the kitchen. Sometimes you wonder if the hotel manager knows you at all, or cares what you do so long as customers are satisfied and the hotel makes money. It is a general moan among your fellow chefs and waitresses that he spends most days in his office and never comes to say hello or ask how you all are, so you do not feel valued and sometimes that leaves a feeling of insecurity...

As hotel manager do you really know what is going on in your hotel? I do not mean have you looked at yesterday's sales figures, seen today's room occupation rates, or noticed your wages bill for last week. All this can be gleaned from your computer without talking to anyone.

I mean have you visited your employees today? Have you walked into those physical extremities where they work (whether top floor bedrooms, hotel maintenance workshop or restaurant), and talked with them not just about the latest figures, but also asked about and listened to what is happening in their lives? Did you discover a new recipe being developed by a sous chef that you were not previously aware of? What did today's lunch look like as it was being served? Was the hotel lobby clean and tidy today? Are we ready to check-in the two coach loads of customers when they arrive this afternoon? What other issues have we got today? You would be hard-pressed to find answers to these questions on your PC.

Some leaders are more effective than others at finding time for motivating and staying in touch with their team. The 'walk round' is one of the most important means of maintaining your finger on the pulse, it confirms that what you want to happen is actually taking place, and it can do great things for motivating your people too. Provided the walk round is carried out with sincerity and a genuine desire to find out not just about work-related issues but also more about the interests and home lives of your employees, it shows you are interested, care about them, and value what they do.

It does not matter whether you are chief executive officer or managing director of an ambulance service, retail chain or an oil major; making the effort to visit your people when they are at work (e.g. the night shift) rather than when you are, joining them at their workplace rather than at your head office, and taking an interest in them as individuals instead of treating them simply as those forgotten faces who turn up on time at work every day, makes such a difference. It is tangible, memorable and meaningful for those employees. It is a snapshot for you of what they are trying to do and the conditions they work in. It is a chance for informal communication, a golden opportunity to receive direct feedback from your people at the sharp end, and a key moment to hear opinions, concerns and even funny stories!

The most effective managers and leaders are those who make a habit of daily informal walk rounds. The emphasis is on informal so that it avoids the 'standby your beds, this is a kit-inspection' syndrome, which would promote an 'us and them' environment rather than the empathetic one intended.

A 'walk round' provides your people with an opportunity to show you their successes.

A 'walk round' also gives you a chance to encourage your people rather than tell them what they cannot do; to coach rather than scold, to make them enjoy rather than fear your visits, and to make yourself approachable instead of being boxed up in an ivory tower. It is a chance for you to actively reinforce the company values such as safety, and to seek out training matrices and training plans to confirm employee development is taking place.

The walk round is such a simple and effective way of staying in touch, and yet so many chief executive officers and managing directors forget, or prefer to talk only to the senior management, or only focus on the machinery. And yet it is your people that make your company tick, not the machines. It is your people that look for your support and interest. It is your people who can be motivated, or totally switched off, by you. If you have just flown thousands of miles overnight to visit the site today, surely it would pay dividends to walk those extra few yards to visit some of the research, administration, sales, or other people you do not normally meet. Surely you owe it to your employees to make time in your schedule to do a 'walk round'. Allow time in your programme so you can talk with and listen to your most important asset; your people.

Although not directly linked to the 'walk round', the next and penultimate case study is positioned here as it neatly brings together many aspects of the book so far. Let us see how 'Agreement 2000', at Alcan Foil Europe – Glasgow, establishes leaders throughout the organisation as well as self-managed teams.

Chapter 19

Alcan Foil Europe – Glasgow 'Agreement 2000' Produces Self-managed Teams

Introduction

Through 'Agreement 2000', Alcan Foil Europe – Glasgow (simply referred to as Alcan Glasgow from now on in this case study) is now a much leaner and sharper business, with a ten per cent reduction in labour costs. There is a self-managed teams culture that encourages *all* employees to develop, contribute and become leaders in their own area of expertise. Responsibility has been successfully pushed down through the organisation, freeing up time for managers to focus on improvements rather than the day-to-day administration of their department.

General principles for you to consider in this case study include:

▶ If you want to know how to lead a culture change, then this case study has got to be on your reading list. It gives you a step-by-step guide that will apply in principle to most culture changes.
▶ Establish systems that encourage peer pressure to manage teams instead of management effort. See how Alcan Glasgow has created this peer pressure and how this results in self-managed teams. Also note the decision-making grid and its role in defining when consultation is required.
▶ Each person in each self-managed team agrees to lead the team in a discipline. This means the whole organisation is seeded with leaders trained in both the leadership role and leader behaviour. This is a great

way to empower your people in addition to aligning their activities with the company goals. The ideas are there for you to apply in your own business.

So, this case study takes you through the Agreement 2000 journey and how a 'self-managed' team works at Alcan, starting with a short resume about Alcan Glasgow.

Alcan Glasgow

Alcan Glasgow is a leading manufacturer of plain and converted aluminium foil products for flexible packaging and industrial markets, including dairy, food, confectionery, tobacco, and container, along with a range of products for industrial applications. The Glasgow business unit is part of the Alcan Foil Rolling and Technology Group (AFR&TG) comprising businesses in the UK, France, Italy, Germany and Switzerland. AFR&TG is part of Alcan Global Packaging, which in turn is a wholly owned subsidiary of Alcan Inc., Montreal, Canada.

The company employs around 200 people on a continuous shift rota basis, selling approximately 20,000 tonnes of foil annually. Union representation on site is Transport and General Workers Union (T&GWU), Amalgamated Engineering and Electrical Union (AEEU), and Association of Clerical and Technical Staffs (ACTS).

Agreement 2000

In the early part of 1999 the new general manager delivered the hard message 'change now or die later' to the people of Alcan Glasgow. His explanation, told to everyone on site in small groups, included falling selling prices, poor manufacturing performance, the strength of Sterling, and costs not reduced fast enough to compensate for reduced gross margins. During the previous decade the company had improved its profits but still not recovered the cost of its capital, so the threat of closure was very real. Internal factors holding back the company performance included:

▶ Overtime had become a way of life; with the new 48 hours per week limit contained in the Working Time Regulations, new systems were needed.

▶ To make the retained profit exceed the cost of capital required a ten per cent reduction in labour costs.

▶ Business drivers were out of line. For example, if repairing a machine took longer a craftsman would earn more money but the company would make less. Also, if people were absent their colleagues made more money on overtime, which increased the company's costs.
▶ Employees were not responding fast enough to customer and process issues.

The medium for change, Agreement 2000, aimed to achieve a retained profit at least equal to the cost of capital invested in the business, together with a ten per cent reduction in labour cost. How was the agreement achieved?

Prepare for Change
Step 1, in February 1999:

▶ Established and communicated the above target.
▶ Created a joint Union/Management Team to negotiate the Agreement 2000.
▶ Employed the Advisory Conciliation and Arbitration Service (ACAS) as facilitators.
▶ Trained *all* managers in a series of workshops about how to manage change.
▶ Benchmarked Alcan Glasgow against other companies (which included visits to companies registered on the Inside UK Enterprise scheme (IUKE)).
▶ Brought in the trade union district officers to ask for their help.

Establish New Values
Step 2, also in February 1999, established new business values and behaviours as fundamental to the way ahead. These values and behaviours, incorporated in the Agreement 2000 are shown in Table 19.1.

Framework Document Prepared
In March 1999 the general manager tasked the joint management/union/ACAS team to produce a framework document for the agreement. The ACAS facilitator worked wonders in these offsite meetings to ensure the whole process maintained momentum, without getting bogged down in detail or personality issues. This team was sworn to secrecy to prevent possible mandates from outside being introduced through leaking the

Table 19.1. Alcan Glasgow's Agreement 2000 values and behaviours

Safety	*Performance*
Works safely	Works hard
Looks out for others	Improves work methods
Keeps workplace safe	Sets tough targets
Keeps place clean	Meets targets
Takes long route if safer	Challenges poor performance
Challenges unsafe behaviour	Has high personal standards
	Adapts to business situation
	Is open to change
	Takes initiative
Customer driven	Is flexible
Knows customers	
Exceeds customer needs	*People focus*
Responds fast	Respects self and others
Forms customer partnerships	Develops self
	Develops others
	Treats people fairly
	Expresses views openly
	Respects others viewpoint
Teamwork	
	Integrity
Helps others	Is always honest
Co-operates well	Does what they say
Leads when needed	Delivers on commitments
Puts team needs first	Respects confidentiality
Listens well	Is dependable and trustworthy
Communicates well	

meeting contents. The aim was to change working practices, plus introduce improved systems and procedures to facilitate the reduction in people, instead of simply chopping ten per cent of the workforce. Money was not on the agenda at any stage in this process. The team had to get the ground rules right, and then talk money.

Update the Employees
In step 4, in May 1999, the general manager updated everyone at Alcan Glasgow on the business position and the main elements of the framework document. Again this was to a series of small groups to make sure everyone received his message and had a chance to ask questions.

Finalising Agreement 2000

Step 5, also in May 1999, saw the ACAS facilitator disappear from the meetings as she was no longer needed, and the joint management/union team started to negotiate/decide the final contents of the Agreement 2000.

Agreement 2000 is Published

In step 6, in June 1999, the team signs off each chapter of Agreement 2000 as complete, allowing publication of Agreement 2000 in small pocket book format and the contents to be communicated by the general manager to all employees at Alcan Glasgow. Agreement 2000 is now considered to be the Alcan Glasgow 'bible'.

Moves Towards Acceptance

In July 1999, a series of question and answer sessions clarifies the content of Agreement 2000 and helps move the site towards acceptance at a ballot.

Agreement 2000 Approved

Step 8, in August/September 1999, held site ballots with full recommendation for acceptance by the Union Officials and Representatives. Two unions and the non-union employees voted yes in the first ballot. The remaining union members voted yes in the second ballot. Agreement 2000 is in place, it just needs to be implemented!

Implementation Begins

Step 9, September 1999, sees the Agreement 2000 design team change role to become the implementation team and the implementation begins in earnest. The team gets training programmes under way and prepares system changes ready for January 2000.

Go-live

Step 10, January 2000. Agreement 2000 goes live after natural Christmas break!

Let us look now at the key features of Agreement 2000, and then focus in on the self-managed teams element of this agreement.

Agreement 2000 has the following key attributes:

▶   The whole agreement is based on the values and behaviours (see Table 19.1) rather than on a series of rules and regulations, 'to create and sustain an atmosphere of goodwill, co-operation, mutual trust and respect'.

▶ *Everyone* is paid a monthly salary and there is no clocking in or out any more.

▶ Annualised hours apply to all shift, day, and support staff, including the financial accountant, etc. 'The annualised hours scheme is introduced to create a salaried environment where people work flexibly to meet customer requirements, to help team working and continuous improvement, and to treat people fairly in relation to each other and the company.' The annualised hours are made up of 'rostered' hours and 'reserve' hours. The rostered hours ensure continuous operation of the capital equipment and provide Alcan Glasgow's people with 'time off to fulfil their lives'. The reserve hours are used 'to cover absence, training and work demand'. The annualised hours contract is averaged over five years rather than the more normal two years.

▶ All parties agree to 'continuously review and improve operations, systems, methods and procedures, implementing changes where necessary, including continuous training and re-training of its people'.

▶ The agreement aims to 'achieve the most effective utilisation of manufacturing facilities'.

▶ It maintains 'open and direct communication with all our people on matters of mutual interest and concern'. For example, *every* employee has access to e-mail, with his or her own unique e-mail address.

▶ 'Team working is seen as an essential part of the Alcan Glasgow culture.' 'The team culture is based on mutual trust, recognising that people are responsible, disciplined, and capable of working together.' The agreement also promotes self-managed team working.

Self-managed Teams

When we talk about self-managed teams in this case we are really focusing on the continuous shift people (i.e. as each shift finishes, the next one starts without a break). Each of these teams consists of former operators and former maintenance fitters, now amalgamated into one job role called process technician. The role of process technician is to 'operate production or ancillary equipment and maintain that equipment to established standards, maximising production up time, and be fully flexible.' The Agreement 2000 defines the process technician team member role as:

- ▶ 'a team member should pull their own weight' by doing their fair share of the team's workload
- ▶ 'improves work output and work quality' by identifying and implementing better ways of doing things
- ▶ 'co-operates and communicates' to help others and to share knowledge and information freely
- ▶ 'takes responsibility and acts with integrity' by admitting mistakes, taking ownership of problems and by doing what he says he will do;
- ▶ 'learns, changes and is adaptable'
- ▶ 'plans and organises own work'
- ▶ 'takes the initiative, troubleshoots, makes decisions and solves problems'
- ▶ 'jointly selects and trains team members'
- ▶ 'gives input on staff changes which impact them directly'. For example if a team's developer retires, the departmental manager who has all five self-managed teams reporting to him, seeks and gets input from the team on his/her replacement
- ▶ 'evaluates team and individual performance, giving and receiving both positive and negative feedback'
- ▶ 'works safely and looks out for the safety of others'.

Now that we have defined the process technician team member role, we need next to go into some detail about the shift structure in order to appreciate how the reserve hours part of the annualised hours helps each team to be self-managed.

The continuous shift system is made up of five teams each working 2×12-hour days, 2×12-hour nights and then four days off as a repeat cycle. Built in to the shift pattern is the five weeks holiday. Bank holidays are worked and the only complete shut down is over the Christmas period. After deducting holiday entitlement from the nominal 38-hour week, means an average of 32.68 hours per week actually rostered at work. Careful rostering allows two 18-day breaks for each team each year, as well as their regular four days off work.

On top of the rostered hours are the 192 reserve hours (= 16×12-hour shifts) to cover absence, training and work demand. The target is to use less than half of these reserve hours on average, and also to write off any unused reserve hours at the end of each quarter to prevent them from accumulating until the end of each year. Let us look first at how these reserve hours are used in the event of short-term absence.

Alcan Glasgow established a call-in system for short-term absence cover, where each person is required to standby for potential call-in on ten shifts per year (equivalent to one person on call for every 15 people working per shift, or two people on standby each shift). The people on call must be contactable for one hour after the relevant shift start times. If the call-in is exercised (30 minutes after the shift start time) the person comes to work and 12 hours are written off from that person's reserve hours. If the call-in is not exercised, six hours are written off.

The handover from one shift to the next takes place by the relevant production machine, and each individual must remain in the appropriate machine area for up to one hour after the normal shift finish, until the handover is completed. So if someone arrives late, his colleague will have to wait for him without being paid any more for this extra time. This is a simple way to apply peer pressure for timely arrivals! Also, if the person arrives more than 30 minutes late and has failed to notify the shift team, he will find himself *and* a callout person on the same shift. This also acts as a major incentive to communicate! Being late is an easy way to make yourself unpopular with the rest of your team, although there is the option of making this time up to your colleague on the next shift. This is the first example of self-managed teams in operation.

The next example shows the leadership element for each individual in the team (rather than simply for the team supervisor in the old system). Each self-managed team would normally have between five and 15 people, and each person is asked which three leadership roles would he prefer in order to have some choice in the final selection of individuals for each leadership role. 'People in self-managed teams take on lead responsibilities as required to facilitate the achievement of team meetings, planning, safety and other key activities for the team. Role leadership responsibilities can rotate among team members to help understanding and currency of roles. Team members assume responsibility for monitoring performance, solving performance problems, and planning. Team members will participate in the selection of new team members and ensure team self-discipline.' So, lets now give you an example of how this works.

There are six leader roles (people/communication, maintenance, productivity, quality, housekeeping, safety/environment), each of which has a mentor from the senior management team with support from the departmental managers as required. On each shift, each department has a maximum of two people acting as leaders for each leader role. Their *leadership* role is to:

▶ 'set direction' in terms of what the team is going to do
▶ 'organise action' in terms of who does what, when
▶ 'track performance' of how the team is performing, what the problems are, and how we tackle them
▶ 'resolve conflicts' within the team and between the teams
▶ 'handle inbound/outbound communication' to and from management.

Similarly their leader *behaviour* role is to:

▶ lead by example
▶ be passionate about performance
▶ communicate well
▶ live the values. Note again how the values underpin all the self-managed teams' activities.

The final, structural element of the self-managed teams is the decision-making grid (see Table 19.2) that sets out what the team can decide itself, what it needs to consult on, what needs a joint decision, and what the team has no say in. This grid makes it very clear to all concerned what they can and cannot decide as a team.

Each team has a team board as a visible management tool. On each board is:

▶ the team charter (a form of mission statement)
▶ leadership roles and leadership matrix clearly displayed
▶ absence recorded by people/communication leaders with a red dot
▶ timekeeping recorded by people/communication with a green dot
▶ skills matrix, plus future training requirements identified
▶ contact numbers, as everyone needs to be contactable
▶ reserve hour balances, maintained by the teams
▶ failed call-ins and no answer via the phone identified with a red dot
▶ monthly team targets displayed.

Other symbols of the change to Agreement 2000 are:

▶ there is new work wear (blue trousers and polo shirt) for *everyone* to be dressed the same when on site
▶ the Agreement 2000 booklet is copied to every employee
▶ clocking in/out is withdrawn and the old clocking stations are represented as a simple in/out card system, so that in the event of a fire the information is available about who is on the premises
▶ catering facilities have been extended to reflect the new shift rotas

Table 19.2. Decision-making grid for self-managed team

Given[1]	*Consult*[2]
Values and behaviours	Changes to values and behaviours
Engineering standards	Changes to engineering standards
Annual budget	Next year's budget
Quality standards	Changes to safety procedures
Safety procedures	Staff changes which impact them directly
Business plan	De-selection or termination of team member
Conditions of employment	Changes to employment conditions
Legislation	Preparing objectives
Annual company objectives	Changes to salary
Salary	Changes to team headcount
Environmental standards	
Joint decision[3]	*Individual/Team*[4]
Further education and development	Work allocation
Pre-selection: screening of external candidates	Selection of internal and external team members
People planning (time off)	Training delivery and release
Maintenance and local budgets	Equipment rotation
Team development	Improvement
Process control	Performance reviews (team and individual)
Next year's plant objectives and local objectives	Daily work planning
Implement improvement	People planning (day-to-day)
Set objectives	Team self-discipline
Performance vs objectives review	Individual performance feedback
Training needs identification	

[1] Team has no say in these decisions.
[2] Team is consulted or can make suggestions on these issues. Final decision is outside the team.
[3] Consensus decision between team, teams developer, and support.
[4] Team has final say in decision but may consult other groups to make this decision.

▶ learning centres are now established
▶ there were special team briefings on each shift first day back signifying formal handover to self-managed teams.

The general manager puts the success down to several critical factors, including:

▶ good communication
▶ ACAS external facilitation of the framework document

▶ union full time officers involved from day one of the Agreement 2000 creation

▶ the joint union/management team meetings

▶ joint benchmarking, including IUKE visits to other best-practice companies.

He also identified several learning points. If they were to repeat this process again they would

▶ increase the amount/frequency of communication

▶ make the Agreement 2000 pocket book and shift rotas information available earlier, to allow it to be tested more thoroughly

▶ have revised terms and conditions/contract ready for the date the switch to Agreement 2000 takes place

▶ work on the flexibility skills training sooner (some contract workers were employed from June to December to facilitate the multi-skilling programme)

▶ forward plan any simple systems requirements

▶ state a target for full attendance (in other words zero absence)

▶ involve more the salaried staff people

▶ think again about 'total' integration of engineering maintenance as some dedicated maintenance people are still needed

▶ include a skill-based salary development track for works salaried people

▶ reconsider the chosen shift pattern, as the lifestyle for the employees is excellent, but it is not so good for the business needs as the managers' contact time with each person is very limited, and the time spent at work is so little that it almost becomes an interference in the rest of their life rather than the dominating factor! An alternative shift system that would redress the balance is a four-crew system with additional people on each crew for holiday and absence cover, and also a variable roster (i.e. crew members are rostered off on different days but must cover their own team's absence)

▶ there have been some difficulties with reserve hours cover, as it is difficult to contact some people and a few frequently make themselves unavailable.

In an environment of survival, Alcan Glasgow people have changed their structure, systems and culture to support their strategy, not just reduced the number of people employed to make the rest work harder. As a direct consequence of Agreement 2000 and the self-managed teams, work previously done by highly paid experts is now done by each team, whole layers of middle management have been removed, and each team member is able to lead in his designated area of expertise. Record output performances have already been achieved and the site is on target to meet its key aim, a retained profit that exceeds the cost of capital in 2001/2002.

Summary Action List for Your Business

1. Start leading your culture change.
2. Benchmark your business against other firms operating 'best practice', and implement relevant improvements in your own organisation.
3. Create a joint management/union/employee agreement based on values rather than rules.
4. Provide a framework for creating self-managed teams, with the key elements of mutual trust, responsible people, self-discipline and annualised hours.
5. Recognise that in a self-managed team everyone has a chance to shine, so empower everyone to lead in their designated area of expertise.
6. Provide a clear decision-making grid for the self-managed team to identify the scope of their empowerment.

Chapter 20

Developing a Fun Team Spirit

The happiness that is genuinely satisfying is accompanied by the fullest exercise of our faculties, and the fullest realization of the world in which we live.
Bertrand Russell, The Conquest of Happiness

'Leading Your People To Success' is a journey founded on the mission to achieve two fundamental goals; to improve people's working lives and to increase companies' economic prosperity.

As we have already discovered, to satisfy the first goal takes many changes to the company culture; with each incremental change in its own small way satisfying a human need. Our aspiration is for each employee to be stretching his or her capabilities towards achieving the best possible results, and therefore to be realising self-actualisation. To do this demands both the affiliation and esteem needs from Maslow's hierarchy to be satisfied. It also requires future challenges to be achievable, and above all for employees to be happy and to have fun.

In this chapter, we will look at three fundamental arguments for promoting fun as part of your company's culture, together with ideas from two firms that consider fun so important they have made it a core value. Then we will consider the following four ways of having fun:

▶ Holding external events that deliberately reach out to include all employees and their families.
▶ Arranging other external 'experiences' that reward relatively few individuals for spectacular performance or outstanding behaviour.
▶ Promoting fun as an integral part of the normal working day and therefore obviating the need for external activities.

▶ Focusing the 'fun events' on helping charities and the local community.

Fun is like the icing on the company cake. Perhaps this explains why fun is rarely given any prominence on the corporate agenda, as most companies exhaust their resources whilst still scrabbling about trying to find and mix together the basic cake ingredients. There are, however, social and cultural, and potentially even economic, arguments that support promoting fun!

The first argument, about encouraging leaders to emerge and develop throughout the organisation, is a consistent theme throughout this book. With each new leader comes increased potential to innovate, to improve and to encourage others. For leaders to become proficient, however, they have to have their own area of responsibility in which to lead. So, just as you can establish leaders for various aspects within each team (e.g. continuous improvement, quality, people and communication, productivity, and housekeeping), why not do the same with 'fun'.

Secondly, fun events held off-site and outside normal working hours promote informal communication in an environment where hierarchy is irrelevant and where respect for individuals can flourish naturally. These activities also help your people to get to know each other personally rather than as colleagues masked by job titles and structural seniority. They can therefore be excellent catalysts for breaking down any 'us and them' in your organisation.

Thirdly, you should be able to blow away your competitors with ease if you can bring the drive and motivation your people have for activities and interests outside work, and channel this energy into your company. The trick, of course, is to create that same level of enthusiasm from each individual whilst at work, as he or she expresses voluntarily elsewhere. Fun is a good stimulus for generating this enthusiasm, especially as there are so many ways of bringing people together to enjoy themselves.

Fun as a Core Value

In contrast to most companies who appear to exclude fun from work, we will look now at how enlightened firms take the above three arguments and act on them to make work really good fun. Admiral Group Ltd and CMG plc, for example, consider fun to be so important that they have made it a core value rather than a sporadic 'bolt-on'.

Admiral Group Ltd is a car insurance services firm employing approximately 1300 people with an average age around 25, in a call-centre environment. The company expects much from its employees, but it will give plenty back too. The chief executive established the company in the early 1990s with 'work is fun' as one of the core values; creating the 'Ministry of Fun' as the way to achieve this goal. Manned by volunteers, the Ministry's brief is to think of ways of making work fun both during and outside normal working hours.

The results are spectacular! The culture is one of equality without 'sameness'. For example:

▶ Everyone has the same type of chair and call-centre position, but there is freedom to personalise your own workstation.

▶ Each department chooses the colour scheme for their area to identify it as their own space.

▶ Break rooms have the team's choice of sofas, television and so on. One team has even purchased a tropical fish tank, presumably to aid relaxation.

▶ Employees decide the dress code; which leads to wearing pyjamas on 'pyjama days' and dressing to imitate famous characters like James Bond or Elvis Presley on 'crazy days'.

Any excuse for a celebration is followed up with vigour by each department; whether a religious festival day, saint's day, or any other special day on the calendar. Decorations miraculously appear from nowhere to festoon various areas of the open-plan offices, which of course provides another reason for selecting and celebrating the best display ... and so the party goes on.

The second example is CMG plc, a global information and communication technology company with the majority of its 14,000 employees in four main countries (UK, the Netherlands, Germany and France). The firm is famous for its principles of openness, fairness and equality; values so deep they lead to all personnel files and salaries being open to everyone. CMG tries hard to balance the needs of 'the family' and 'the business' by reinforcing the 'work hard, play hard' philosophy and by fostering an extended family atmosphere. Consequently the firm finds many ways of making work fun. Examples include:

▶ Family involvement through holding children's parties and annual dinner dances.

▶ Events for consultants based on client sites for long periods of time; for example, go-karting, football or visits to a theme park.

▶ Parties held nationally following the announcement of full year results. These normally include a famous compere, cabaret acts, band and disco dancing, together with a four-course meal and plenty to drink.

▶ Anniversary dinners arranged for employees and their partners when they reach ten year's service, and every five years thereafter.

▶ Buffet and drinks after each company's monthly staff meeting. These are normally held in a local hotel or pub, and hosted by that firm's managing director (and occasionally with the country managing director or group board member).

▶ National and international golf societies.

CMG is a particularly good example of a firm deliberately promoting family-friendly fun events, simply because CMG wants their employees' families to be appropriately involved in the CMG community. The above examples foster this aim well.

Four Formats for Fun

Now let us move on to the various formats for making work fun and consider the four examples suggested earlier.

External Fun Events for All Employees and Their Families

Holding external events that deliberately reach out to include all employees and their families has the great benefit of giving family members an insight into the firm, a better understanding of the company's culture, and of course the opportunity to meet other employees.

Although a few companies spend around £100 to £200 per year on each employee by throwing huge parties, having fun does not need to be expensive and the scope is only limited by imagination. For example, company sponsorship might provide awards for the department that delivers the best service to the company, or to the employee who most demonstrates behaviour beyond the call of duty. Although these two activities in themselves may not be great fun for all your employees, the award ceremony certainly can be and there is every opportunity to invite partners to share these celebrations.

Alternatively you might prefer to have a 'fun day' with a range of sporting and social events for your employees and their families. Or you could celebrate birthdays, hold any number of internal competitions and so on!

The key is to get people involved, create as many winners as possible and celebrate their successes.

External Fun Events for a Few Individual Employees (Including 'Experience' Days)

If rewards for excellent performance or outstanding behaviour are your way of saying 'thank you', then 'experience days' can be a very powerful way of making sure the recognition is remembered and talked about. Many organisations around the world arrange these experience days, so depending on where you are based the following examples will be accessible to a greater or lesser extent. The experiences mentioned below range from the sublime to the ridiculous – and so can the prices!

Most experiences are simple fun, although there is normally some added element that makes them special; a city sightseeing tour that includes an amphibious element without changing vehicle, or racing JCB diggers! Even a visit to a football or cricket club can include meeting a particular sports personality, which makes it much more memorable than just a short tour round the grounds.

The range of experiences is tremendous; from aromatherapy massage, or time spent relaxing in a flotation tank, through to gourmet dinners and concerts. There is even an introduction to Feng Shui (the Chinese art of placement).Those requiring an adrenaline rush have a huge selection of racing cars, boats, planes and military tanks to choose from. However, your corporate golf days just will not seem the same any more when pitched against the outlandish Great White Shark experience, where you apparently have the dubious pleasure of coming face to face with one of these wonderful creatures; or the weightlessness experience where you can spend some time floating around at zero gravity in an aeroplane as it plummets towards the earth. Prices for these latter experiences are available 'on application'!

Then there are the experiences that border on, or shamelessly indulge in, the 'holiday' classification. Your employees will presumably have had to perform true wonders to receive one of these. A few examples include the dolphin experience, where you can swim and snorkel with the dolphins ... in the Bahamas; or the Krakatau Experience Tour as part of discovering Indonesia.

Although all these 'experiences' may in themselves be great fun, most are away from work and probably outside normal working hours too. Let us look at how fun and work can be brought together.

Fun as an Integral Part of the Normal Working Day

As we mentioned with the call-centre example earlier, Admiral Group Ltd goes out of their way to give each individual and department freedom of choice to personalise their work area, and to occasionally create a party-time atmosphere. The philosophy is to make 'people feel good at work'.

Just as important is the attitude of the people you work with during the normal daily routine. If you and your staff have fun working together, and you have established the right kind of environment for communication so that 'everyone feels involved in the business', much of the 'need' for external experiences to help make work fun will be superfluous.

Launching a new initiative is another great internal excuse for more fun. As you have already seen, Mortgage Express is particularly good at presenting upbeat messages with multimedia accompaniment when launching new initiatives or giving feedback on employee opinion surveys. Certainly it takes time and some resource, but it is a spectacular way of showing each employee that he or she is valued.

Focus the 'Fun Events' on Helping Charities and the Local Community

If you are lucky, you will get a few individuals who are really driven to organise significant fund raising events for charity; like employees at the automotive, travel and insurance service providers, Mondial Assistance (UK) Limited. In just four separate events they raised:

▶ £5000, for the National Association for Colitis and Crohn's disease, by holding an employees' version of the television show 'Stars In Their Eyes' (where employees impersonated internationally famous singers).

▶ £1000 for the Wishing Well Foundation, a charity that grants wishes for sick and underprivileged children. An intrepid team of employees abseiled 50 metres down the side of a civic centre building to earn this sum.

▶ £1000 for Juvenile Diabetes Research, collected by several employees taking part in a sponsored walk.

▶ £1000 for the New Addington Education Action Zone, provided because their finance manager ran the London Marathon.

In each case the company matched the sum raised by the employees, adding a further £8000 to the above figures. It just shows what can be done with the right leaders and company support.

Mondial Assistance employees also help the local community by taking part as e-mail mentors and primary school mentors in a 'School Mentoring Programme'. School children visit Mondial Assistance to learn what skills are required to work in a business environment, and once a month Mondial Assistance gives their volunteer mentors an afternoon to visit 'their children' in the local schools.

It is worth noting that the charity and community input mentioned above at Mondial Assistance is in addition to

▶ a competition for money-saving ideas with a prize of Madonna concert tickets plus dinner for two;
▶ annual best team and individual performance prizes of a night out at a restaurant of the team's choice, and a first class trip to Paris respectively.

Not surprisingly, frequent comments from visitors and new staff indicate Mondial Assistance employees are a happy, welcoming team.

Having looked at four different ways of making work fun, the simple conclusion is that as long as your employees are happy, motivated, having fun, realising self-actualisation, and contributing their very best for your company, *how* you achieve the fun team spirit is unimportant. What is right for one firm will need modifying for another, but the 'Ministry of Fun' concept appears to be a really good one providing it has the support of the top team.

Fun is something that should be firmly on the corporate agenda, rather than merely an annual afterthought, so I challenge you now to finish your corporate cake by putting the 'fun' icing on, and see what feedback you get from your happy employees.

Part 4

Improving Your Success

The next four chapters guide you through the practical implementation of 'continuous improvement', which is sometimes referred to as KAIZEN®.[1] We look at how to establish continuous improvement; how to measure its activity level and effectiveness; how to sustain and encourage employee suggestions, and how to continuously improve your organisation's safety performance.

Chapter 21

Establishing Continuous Improvement

Improvements can only be thought of when there is time to think.

Introduction

Continuous improvement relies on employees frequently requesting small changes to improve their working environment, called 'suggestions', together with 'empowerment' that allows the originators to implement their ideas. This gives the employees 'ownership' of these suggestions and positively encourages further improvements. It also eliminates sources of frustration, makes the job easier, and motivates. The great spin-off is that many of these changes save your organisation some money, so continuous improvement is normally self-funding.

Another positive aspect of continuous improvement is that the ideas put forward for change are normally minor alterations to processes or communication channels. Most of the ideas are virtually free to implement or may simply require a small amount of engineering time. The cost of each change is therefore normally measured in terms of tens or hundreds of pounds or dollars, certainly not in thousands.

This chapter, the first of four about continuous improvement, covers the need for time, encouragement of ideas, and the three-tier structure of the continuous improvement organisation; the Steering Team, Process Ownership Team (POT) and Continuous Improvement Team.

Give your employees time for continuous improvement.

Create Time for Continuous Improvement

I cannot stress enough the importance of giving your employees *time* to think about and implement continuous improvement. Although there is the inevitable drive for improved efficiencies and bottom-line profits this month, solving the current issues, and ensuring the customers are happy today; without time for continuous improvement you will find it hard to make steady progress and the inevitable result will be the need for major capital expenditure to catch up, or loss of business as you have been out-paced by the competition.

The best way to ensure time for continuous improvement is to build it into the structure and daily operation of your organisation. You could, for example, ensure you have enough employees to continue serving the customer needs whilst also undertaking specific continuous improvement projects. You might wish to design a shift structure that deliberately has time for each shift team to spend on training and continuous improvement (in which case there is a good example in the Shell Chemicals case study later). Or you might wish to train other people from a different department to cover for a department or team continuous improvement meeting. How you structure the time depends on the nature of your business, but one thing is certain. If you expect your teams to 'bolt on' continuous improvement as an extra task to their already busy day, rather than replace their normal work with time for continuous improvement, you will have to regularly persuade your managers to divert their attention from their main tasks to hold continuous improvement meetings. I have been there and tried to do this and it does not work unless you have some significant slack in your system; whether this be the number of employees or the amount of time required each week to complete the normal workload.

Build in the time and you will be able to focus on coaching and recognising the results, rewarding your teams, and benefit from the improvements and cost reductions made. Fail to build in the time and prepare to lick your wounds later.

Encourage Continuous Improvement Ideas

It is very important to realise that it does not matter how small the improvement is. The key is that if an employee has come up with an idea that the immediate management considers to be a good idea, then that suggestion needs to be implemented as rapidly as possible. Just as important is to let the employee know why, if the idea is rejected. This too must be communicated quickly:

The key is to encourage ideas, not to kill them.

Let me give you a simple example, one so elementary that you may consider it trivial. It is, however, a real event and it illustrates the point well. I remember one of my middle managers telling me about this when he first started to introduce the concept of continuous improvement in his department. Prior to this he was very sceptical about the whole initiative.

One of our employees needed a pen to be able to do his job. Due to his working environment this pen often went missing because other employees borrowed it, even though there were plenty of pens available generally. The problem revolved around not having a specific place for this pen to be kept. Wasting his time looking for the pen annoyed and frustrated the employee, so he asked if we could provide him with a penholder that fastened the pen to his desk. The supervisor ordered the holder, the employee attached it to his desk and the problem disappeared. What is more, we had a happier employee who could complete his work more quickly.

Although the pen example would not have saved the company any quantifiable money, other employees in the same department also began to make and implement suggestions as they realised they could influence their jobs. We later had a suggestion from that same team of people which led to doubling the output rate of the main production line for certain products and saved the company around £35,000 per year. Had we not introduced the continuous improvement scheme, ideas like that probably would never have surfaced.

Structure the Continuous Improvement Organisation

In my experience it really does not matter whether the number of employees is 10 or 1000, the principles of continuous improvement apply to everyone. After all, if you manage a small business your communication methods and systems requirements will be very different from the large multinational, but large organisations also tend to work in smaller teams, which is a key requirement for successful continuous improvement. Consequently, most of what we are talking about in the whole of this chapter is applicable to partnerships, family-owned and owner-managed businesses, plus the larger limited and PLC companies. It also extends to the public as well as the private sector, service industries in addition to manufacturing, and in certain circumstances even voluntary organisations, charities and social clubs.

Any successful organisation needs true leadership from the top together with a clear strategy, but the continuous improvement scheme can also act as a major driving force in terms of motivation for those employees further down the organisation structure. When you consider that people are the one element of your business that can give your company sustainable competitive advantage, reflect too the potential to increase your profits when everyone pulls in the same direction with the great strength derived from the continuous improvement process. To help everyone co-ordinate their efforts, consider the following.

Most of the continuous improvements are thought of and implemented by the people at the sharp end of what happens hour by hour, but it is also possible and desirable to focus their attention on what is considered important by agreeing with their immediate supervision a regular set of goals, or quarterly objectives. As we mentioned in the planning section, it is these goals that effectively act as the vertical link between the company strategy and the day-to-day actions of each individual. They also help keep the organisation as one cohesive structure rather than two distinct ones. Without these goals the operators and first line supervisors are really only able to improve what they are currently doing. Adding the goals facilitates broader thinking and adds more scope to the improvements that the operator can implement. Progress towards these goals should also be monitored at a departmental and individual level by using the key performance indicators (KPIs) discussed earlier. This really drives the strategy implementation all the way down to become each individual's responsibility.

So far we have discussed some of the theory and principles of continuous improvement but we have yet to touch on *how* to establish an organisational structure that will help promote and act as a catalyst for encouraging and implementing improvement ideas. In my experience there should be three levels in the continuous improvement structure (see Figure 21.1): Steering Team, Process Ownership Team (POT) and Continuous Improvement Team. (*Note:* The Continuous Improvement Team level also includes Problem Solving Teams established temporarily to focus on a specific issue.)

Let us briefly look at the role of each level and then who should be in each team.

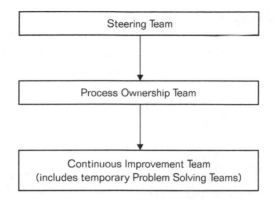

Figure 21.1. Continuous improvement organisation structure

At Steering Team level we will discuss and implement initiatives concerned with:

▶ The kind of recognition or reward to make available to employees for their implemented suggestions.
▶ Ensuring time is made available for continuous improvement by creating the right organisation structure and working day format.
▶ Focusing the attention of the continuous improvement 'facilitator' in areas where major benefits can be achieved. The 'facilitator' concentrates on continuous improvement throughout the organisation. This role is explained in more detail below.
▶ Deciding how to introduce training matrices at different sites, together with support from training co-ordinators at each location, and so on.

At POT level we have the right people involved to implement quarterly objectives, arrange training programmes, make process improvements and so on.

At the lowest level (Continuous Improvement Team) we have our penholder example and of course a myriad of other suggestions raised and implemented by individuals.

Let us look in more detail now at the structure and membership of each type of team within the continuous improvement umbrella.

The Steering Team

Although you must supervise the continuous improvement in all its various forms, you still need to manage the business! The continuous improvement effort and overall business management have to be kept separate (but still remain connected) as they are driven by different needs. To do this you are likely to require two different sets of people. The first is your management team for driving the overall business strategy. The second is the Steering Team.

There is one common link between the two sets and that is the person at the top of the organisation. It is vital to have this person's backing and for him to be part of both the Management Team and the Steering Team (the highest level of the continuous improvement structure) so that the continuous improvement philosophy can permeate all areas of the company. It is, for example, just as important to cover sales and marketing as well as production in a manufacturing company.

Who else apart from the top person should we have in the Steering Team? This will depend on your company, but there needs to be at least one 'facilitator'. To be successful, this facilitator needs to have excellent interpersonal skills. This applies particularly in terms of communicating with the most important people in the continuous improvement structure; the operators, the hourly paid, the office administration staff, drivers, in fact anyone without any direct line management responsibility. The facilitator must also have the credibility to be able to influence the thinking of the senior management. Ideally the facilitator should be comfortable with helping middle management to set up simple systems for collection and analysis of data; for bench-marking purposes and monitoring improvements made. It is the line managers and operators who are responsible for collecting, analysing and implementing improvements based on these systems, not the facilitator. As you can see from these criteria the facilitator is indeed the second key person in this structure. The facilitator role is definitely full time for all but the smallest of organisations, with a second person recommended if the company is greater than around 500 employees. The facilitator should be changed every two years or so for two main reasons; it is an exhausting job if done properly, and a fresh face injects new ways of carrying out this role.

In addition to the managing director and facilitator on the Steering Team, you will need a team of people who manage the areas to be improved. Let us take three examples to illustrate why you will have different team members. First take a manufacturing company where, for example, the cost of materials is around two-thirds of the sales turnover.

The managing director decides a cost reduction is desirable and needs people in charge of production to find ways of reducing material waste throughout the whole process chain. The production managers are tasked to work with their subordinates to measure and quantify potential savings. They will need to be part of the Steering Team to understand the goals, make the changes happen and give regular feedback to the Steering Team about the progress made. They will be helped by the facilitator to establish measurement systems and to train and encourage the operators to put forward their own suggestions on the waste reduction theme.

A second example might look at improving the accident performance throughout the production areas of the same manufacturing company. This time, in addition to the previous Steering Team Members, the Health and Safety Manager would be asked to attend the meetings in order to give feedback on the company safety performance and to discuss and help implement initiatives to drive the accident rate down.

A third example could be the need to increase the effectiveness of the manufacturing company's sales force through improved planning, targets to be achieved at each customer visit, route planning, conversion rate of samples requested to orders received, and so on. Obviously the key people to influence these changes would be the sales director and sales managers and then the sales representatives themselves. It would be the sales director and sales managers who would form the majority of the Steering Team in this circumstance. Should all three of the above objectives be included then a representative sample of production, safety and sales managers would be on the Steering Team.

From these three examples it should be clear that the Steering Team Membership will change with the objectives. How often you modify the Steering Team Members will depend on how quickly the goals are achieved. It will become clear after a few meetings whether the desired waste reduction, accident rate drop, or increased sales effectiveness has not yet started, is progressing quickly, or has almost been completed. If it is the former, please do not be disheartened! The first few meetings can be tough and apparently lack direction simply because you and the rest of the team are actually trying to understand exactly the purpose of the meeting. I am bearing in mind that for many individuals who have 'always done it this way', the concept of continuous improvement and the associated changes can seem somewhat strange at first – hence the need to establish the ground rules and purpose of these continuous improvement meetings, at all three levels in the company. Once this hurdle is cleared, progress will be surprisingly swift. Should the hurdle remain for some time you may need to reconsider the team membership and/or initial goals. As in the pen example mentioned earlier, a few quick wins does wonders for the morale and enthusiasm of the top team as well as the teams further down your structure!

Initially, and certainly until the key objectives have been achieved, holding these meetings at predetermined times once a fortnight is likely to be the right interval. More often than this and the administrative burden outweighs the benefits as each meeting needs to have minutes with action items and target completion dates. Any longer than this and the contents of the previous meeting will have been forgotten so the meetings will lose momentum. You will find out for yourself what works but this would be a reasonable template to start with.

The Process Ownership Team

The next level to consider is that of the POT. The reference to 'process ownership' indicates that the members of this team manage or 'own' a process. This process might be the administration of customer orders, managing a production department, or organising a team of trainers. The purpose of the POT is to manage local departmental continuous improvement issues including the objectives agreed with the Steering Team. As with the Steering Team, the POT meetings are designed to measure, improve and feedback on specific targets, and a fortnightly meeting should prove to be about the right interval. These meetings must also have minutes with action items, so that each meeting moves on from the previous and progress can be monitored. Rotating responsibility for being the chairperson and minute taker in each meeting can avoid an undue burden on one or two individuals.

The members of the POT depend on your organisation size and structure. If the company is small you may actually combine the Steering Team and POT to be one and the same. In most companies, even those with flat organisation structures, the POT will consist of the Department Manager and his first-line Supervisors.

Continuous Improvement Teams

The third level in the continuous improvement structure is that of Continuous Improvement Teams. These teams, of up to approximately 20 people, are made up of the department manager, first-line supervisors and that department's employees. As with the Steering Team and POT, the Continuous Improvement Team also meets once a fortnight. A first-line supervisor runs this meeting, with another employee writing the minutes. The aim of these Continuous Improvement Team meetings is to encourage and facilitate communication in both directions between the middle management and the departmental employees. A typical agenda might consist of:

▶ Review departmental performance since previous meeting, to praise where appropriate and identify areas for improvement too.
▶ Review of continuous improvement suggestions made since the previous meeting (benefits of those implemented and plan for remainder). Where possible, members of the team should be encouraged and empowered to implement their own ideas.
▶ Progress update for departmental quarterly objectives.
▶ Discussion on one specific issue identified as an area needing improvement (e.g. the performance of a particular machine, or elimination of paperwork from a process). The aim is to brainstorm and identify ideas from the team that can be implemented by the next meeting.
▶ Feedback on any health and safety concerns, especially pre-emptive actions required.

The meetings should be held in the workplace and not out of sight in a meeting room, for two key reasons. First, because this is familiar territory for the employees, it will help them feel more relaxed and increase their participation. Second you can ask the employees to point out any new issues, show you their implemented improvements and talk about these with the whole team. This publicises to everyone that change is happening and encourages suggestions from other team members. It also gives the staff a chance to ask questions and make suggestions about the working environment, what is going on in the company and so on.

One word of advice for these meetings is to set out a few simple ground rules at the start. These should cover what is excluded from the meeting (e.g., any questions regarding wages, holidays or other conditions of employment should be discussed elsewhere), and that any contributions to the meeting must be positive (so no moaning or complaining). The aim is to encourage a positive meeting that can help boost morale. For example, if someone has a specific concern, this same concern could be voiced in two ways, one negative and one positive:

▶ 'Why are we wasting my time with this paperwork?'
▶ 'Could we redesign this paperwork to make it less time-consuming?'

The latter approach is the one to encourage!

Problem Solving Team

There is a fourth, temporary type of team called a Problem Solving Team. Membership of this team depends on the objective and will typically consist of a range of people who can contribute their own particular knowledge. Once established, this team holds a series of short, focused meetings to plan, measure/collect data, propose and implement solutions, and check to prove that the implementation has been effective. Membership will typically consist of several operators, perhaps an engineer or two and the departmental manager with a facilitator to complete the group.

Now we have established a structure for managing the continuous improvement, and suggested tentative links with the company strategy through a series of quarterly objectives, we next need to make sure the continuous improvement is implemented and effective.

Chapter 22

Implemented Suggestions Per Employee

Many suggestions may be made by individuals, but all suggestions are worthless unless implemented.

In the last chapter, we established the continuous improvement organisation structure (Steering Team, Process Ownership Team (POT) and Continuous Improvement Team). This chapter takes us through the management support required for continuous improvement until the teams become 'self-managed' and peer pressure takes over. It also suggests a way of measuring the continuous improvement scheme effectiveness by monitoring the implemented suggestions per employee. Finally, we look at the key visual aid called the Continuous Improvement Board.

Support the Continuous Improvement Meetings

So far, we have established who should join the Steering, Process Ownership and Continuous Improvement Teams. You may even have held your first Steering Team meetings and decided a number of key business objectives that the whole organisation can help with and are therefore relevant to the Process Ownership and Continuous Improvement teams.

The Process Ownership meetings may now have started, with minutes and action items, although there is likely to be lack of focus at first. Similarly, the Continuous Improvement Team meetings are beginning to take place. As we said in the previous chapter, moaning and complaining is not desirable in these meetings, but some of the initial meetings may inevitably be awkward to run, either if this is the first time that the employees have had a chance to express their frustrations as a team to their first line management, or if the supervisors are not familiar with running team meetings. Some, if not most, of the initial suggestions are likely to have sarcastic or aggressive overtones. For example, someone may simply ask for a new pair of boots or overalls, or complain that they never get a chance to have hot food from the vending machine (because they work a night shift and the food is eaten by the day shift). Do not be concerned about this, simply let the employees know what you are going to do about the request made, and then make sure you do it quickly. The sarcasm stems from the pent up frustration and the fact that you have in effect simply opened up a new regular channel of communication with your employees. Correcting some of the complaints will soon transform the negative feedback into positive suggestions from your employees. At this point, you will know you are on the road towards a true continuous improvement culture.

So far, novelty is giving the Process Ownership and Continuous Improvement meetings momentum, but what should we do now to make sure the continuous improvement scheme is firmly established and how do we measure success?

In order for the continuous improvement scheme to gain momentum, the *whole* organisation has to realise that the senior management team is serious about encouraging employees to make suggestions, empowering them to implement their ideas and through this helping them to make their jobs quicker and easier.

As we indicated earlier this commitment must come from the top. It is vital that senior management show that they are interested in what the employees are saying and in the changes being implemented at grass roots level. To do this the Steering Team, including the managing director, will need to spend time with front-line employees in the Process Ownership meetings, and at the Continuous Improvement meetings. The Steering Team will also be reviewing the suggestions being put forward with the facilitator and the departmental managers, and saying 'thank you' to individual employees who have made suggestions.

This level of interest will take you away from your strategic review meetings, board meetings, customers and so on, but it is important to demonstrate you are listening and supporting your whole team not just your immediate colleagues. There are many spin-offs from this interface with your whole work force that may not be immediately obvious, but over a period of time will change peoples' opinions and encourage a positive 'can-do' attitude and culture.

The facilitator will also need to spend most of his time with the first tier of employees. Initially, this will be to get some quick successes by finding pockets of people who are ready and willing to make changes and are prepared to put forward suggestions. Once some suggestions are implemented, publicise the recognition to encourage others to follow suit. The facilitator role also involves training employees and middle managers on the techniques for problem solving, how to run meetings, measuring process capability, establishing visual standards and many other skills that will help the whole team develop. At this stage, there is much investment in your employees by your facilitator but this is all part of helping your team to be able to contribute good quality suggestions.

The other major role in establishing the scheme is your middle management team. They need to ensure the suggestions are implemented. They should feel pressure both from their subordinates and their managers to review the suggestions daily and to make and communicate to the originator a decision on whether or not the suggestion will be carried out. If the decision is not to proceed then explain why to prevent demotivation. If the decision is to go ahead, then make the change as quickly as practical and sign it off when complete so that everyone knows. The key is to ensure your middle management team are interested and motivated themselves to ensure this process is completed regularly and on a timely basis. They are likely to do this if you are interested and express this interest regularly, and if there is some sort of incentive other than the simple 'well done' feedback.

Once you have established the continuous improvement ethos, even though management heavily supports it, the responsibility and authority for implementing suggestions can then be moved further down your organisation. This is where the self-managed teams and/or annualised hours can pay real dividends, by realigning employee goals through moving your employees from hourly paid to monthly paid staff status. The peer pressure associated with the self-managed teams should eventually replace management effort.

Measure Success

We have yet to establish some simple measures of success. One key indicator is the number of implemented suggestions. If you have a series of different departments or sites, comparing how well each section is doing in terms of the number of implemented suggestions per employee is an excellent way of injecting a little competition into the middle management. The facilitator is the ideal person to collect and communicate this information.

Table 22.1, headed 'implemented suggestions per employee', indicates how simple but informative this measure is. The overall average year to date figure, of 0.167 implemented suggestions per employee per month, means an average of 16.7 per cent of the work force put forward a suggestion each month. This is a very respectable figure and you should expect to have lower figures than this, certainly to start with. The actual number achieved per employee depends greatly on the importance attributed by the management team, the effort put in to making the changes requested, and the time allowed for the team to think of or brainstorm continuous improvements.

The other measure of success is to receive positive feedback from the Process Ownership and Continuous Improvement meetings to the Steering Team meetings. Regular attendance by, and feedback from, members of the Steering Team at these other meetings is important for two reasons. First, the Steering Team is not acting in a vacuum and it knows what is going on further down the organisation. Second, the signal that it sends to both middle management and the employees about the importance senior management attaches to the continuous improvement scheme. This attendance also acts as an incentive to the middle manager to make sure the Continuous Improvement and Process Ownership meetings take place regardless of the normal pressures of work.

As I mentioned earlier, it is also important to note that you have to structure the organisation so that there is the *time* for these meetings to take place. This point cannot be stressed enough. This might on the surface mean adding more cost into the system, but deeper down it means your people have the facility to drive costs down and improve for long-term benefits. Obviously, your managers and supervisors need to be well organised with the self-discipline to make sure this communication takes place at the allotted time. It is, however, common for the half hour or so spent talking and ironing out any issues together with the positive feedback on achievements made since the previous meeting, to be quickly recovered through efficiency improvements in the department.

Table 22.1. Implemented suggestions per employee

Position	Department	Suggestions implemented	Number of employees	Implemented suggestions per employee
Implemented suggestions per employee for September				
1	Production B	4	5	0.800
2	Site administration	6	11	0.545
3	Production A	23	75	0.307
4	Production C	11	50	0.220
5	Production P	2	16	0.125
6	Production E	6	142	0.042
7	Production T	0	12	0.000
8	Engineering	0	21	0.000
9	Quality control	0	5	0.000
10	Production F	0	16	0.000
11	Head office	0	13	0.000
12	Production S	0	7	0.000
13	Production W	0	62	0.000
14	Production O	0	70	0.000
15	Development	0	4	0.000
16	Warehouse	0	19	0.000
17	Transport	0	39	0.000
Company total for month		52	567	0.092
Average implemented suggestions/month/employee year to date				
1	Development	73	4	2.028
2	Production T	85	12	0.787
3	Site administration	43	11	0.434
4	Production B	20	5	0.400
5	Production F	49	16	0.340
6	Head office	30	13	0.256
7	Production P	33	16	0.229
8	Production A	130	75	0.193
9	Production C	76	50	0.169
10	Production W	69	62	0.124
11	Quality control	5	5	0.111
12	Production E	129	142	0.101
13	Engineering	13	21	0.069
14	Warehouse	10	19	0.058
15	Production S	3	7	0.048
16	Production O	27	70	0.043
17	Transport	6	39	0.017
Company total for year to date		853	567	0.167

The Continuous Improvement Board

There is also one key visual aid called the Continuous Improvement Board. Although you probably have a number of display boards around your firm, it is important to bring to your attention this board because it is helpful for the Continuous Improvement meetings and is also used for displaying graphs and other information relevant to the continuous improvement process. Typically the Continuous Improvement Board is a green felt notice board approximately 2.4 × 1.2 metres mounted on a steel frame so that it can be positioned anywhere in the workplace, or alternatively wall-mounted on its own. Its contents form a great memory jogger to help the less experienced departmental manager who wants to talk with his team about improvements made and targets yet to be achieved.

One format that has proved particularly helpful to use on the Continuous Improvement Board, is the acronym QCDT for the headings quality improvement, cost reduction, distribution performance and training. Under each of these headings you can put a combination of what has been achieved, together with the targets. Taking each in turn, here are some examples of things you may wish to consider.

'Quality improvement', for example, might have the target to bring a particular product dimension within the tolerances allowed in the product specification. A weekly graph of the percentage of measured samples that achieved the desired product dimension, together with the specification limits, shows performance improvements resulting from the team's work. The POT would include this target as one of their action items for the POT meetings.

'Cost reduction' could be a review of waste generated during a process with the aim of reducing at source or recycling. Again display notes or graphs of relevant measures taken.

'Distribution performance' is likely to focus on late deliveries; how many, reasons for, plans for improvement and so on. It might also look at the number of partial deliveries made each week, with the aim of taking steps to produce the right product in time for a complete delivery when the customer wants it.

As discussed earlier, 'training' will normally have the departmental training status in the form of a training matrix.

So far, we have simply indicated that the suggestions are made, discussed and implemented where the middle management agrees with the suggestion. We have not said how or where the employee can communicate his suggestion to the middle management and his colleagues. We have also still to formalise a system for saying 'thank you' to those employees that are making suggestions and to encourage those that have not yet made a suggestion. This is covered next in the suggestion scheme section.

Chapter 23

The 'OEDIPUS' Suggestion Scheme

Empower your employees by listening to their suggestions when they are at work rather than just when you are.

This chapter takes you through the characteristics required of a successful suggestion scheme, using the mnemonic OEDIPUS to help you remember them.

You may be surprised to learn that the most common reason for submitting a suggestion is due to frustration, not to make a job easier or to save the company money. This frustration may be due to a breakdown in the usual communication channels, or a perceived lack of response from the management team to a verbal request. Alternatively it might be a particular difficulty the employee is having in doing his job, a safety concern, or even a system change request. There are potentially many reasons for making a suggestion.

When you start a suggestion scheme there is likely to be an initial burst of enthusiasm from the employees if they consider there is a genuine opportunity to influence the way things are done. This enthusiasm should translate into a significant number of suggestions per employee per month, or put another way, a high 'suggestion rate'. Regardless of the reasons for putting these suggestions forward, however, unless the right feedback is given you are likely to see the number of suggestions reduce. The correct scheme structure will raise the suggestion rate to a level that makes a substantial difference to the way the company operates and also to the morale of employees. This is where the suggestion scheme can really support the continuous improvement culture.

Setting up a suggestion scheme that works is akin to running a successful experiment using the principle of positive reinforcement. Let me give you an example relevant to the suggestion scheme. Consider yourself to be an employee who is stimulated, perhaps for one of the above reasons, to put forward a positive suggestion. You are rewarded first by getting your suggestion completed within days, and second with some form of thanks from the company. You will doubtless be pleased your idea is now in place and, particularly if your suggestion was made out of frustration, also pleasantly surprised that the company management listened and acted. There is a good chance that your motivation level will move up one notch, too. Even more important is what you are likely to do the next time you come to work. Hopefully you will be thinking of further suggestions you can make.

Now put yourself in the same situation but in scenario two. Here you make your suggestion but nothing happens. There is no feedback to say the suggestion is registered and being considered. You do not even know if anyone has bothered to read your important idea. Are you motivated to propose more ideas tomorrow? No. Even if someone eventually gets round to giving you a thank you and a recognition award, you might wish to embarrass them by asking what the recognition is for.

It is clear that with the right structure and operation, a suggestion scheme can help stimulate a myriad of suggestions and be a very positive tool for motivating and even empowering your staff, particularly if they are allowed and encouraged to make the change they have asked for themselves. Great care and preparation is therefore required before launching a suggestion scheme. You need the positive effects to help boost the continuous improvement culture and definitely have to avoid the negative downside otherwise you can very quickly kill your employees' enthusiasm.

There are seven main aspects of a suggestion scheme to get right. Using the mnemonic OEDIPUS, helps define which characteristics should be in a good suggestion scheme. They are as follows:

Open scheme so all can see suggestions made
Easy access to make suggestions
Daily check of suggestions written on flipcharts
Implement suggestions and recognition quickly
Positive reinforcement of behaviour
Uncomplicated recognition system
Supervision responsible for evaluation and implementation.

Make the Scheme Open

The first characteristic is to make the scheme open so that all employees can see a suggestion has been made. One obvious implication of this is that the suggestion must be written and in writing large enough for other people to see even at a casual glance. Avoid the use of complex forms and ballot boxes or equivalent as they are a closed format and generally kill suggestion schemes. I have heard of a ballot box described as a letterbox for suggestions with a paper-shredder on the other side of the wall!

One particularly simple, effective and open channel that works is writing the suggestion on a flipchart using a marker-pen. The written suggestion should include the idea, originator's name and date. Space should then be left for the departmental manager or supervisor to write a response (normally a yes/no decision together with what is going to happen and when) and date. This format has the added bonus that once a suggestion has been implemented it is easy to tick through the writing to make it obvious the actions are complete.

Make it Easy to Put Forward a Suggestion

The second key consideration is to make it easy to put forward a suggestion. Precisely how you do this will depend on the nature of your company and the people within it; for example what is right for a production employee based at one location may not be the optimum for the sales representative spending time with customers. For the first the paper-based flipchart system again scores; for the second the use of e-mail from a laptop could be a real winner, or perhaps through the company intranet. The number of flipcharts required is simply sufficient quantity to make access easy for all employees. This depends on the geographic layout and size of your offices or site, but should be a minimum of one per department. You are also likely to need one in the canteen or other highly populated area for any site concerns. You may also wish to have specific flipcharts for Health and Safety suggestions should you want to focus on this area as part of your cultural change. The aim should be to have the facilities in place to capture any idea from any working employee, 24 hours per day and seven days per week.

Check the Flipcharts Daily

The third is to check the flipcharts daily, acknowledge any new proposals and give some initial feedback indicating whether the suggestion will be implemented or not. It is a little like someone speaking to his supervisor on a mobile telephone when the signal strength is low. You ask a question and just as the answer is expected, the line goes dead. You phone back again but the number is 'not available please try later'. It does not take many tries before you hang up and do something else.

If the suggestion is not going to be implemented, it is very important to explain why not to avoid disappointment and demoralisation. So, if you want to let someone know his suggestion is valued, you must reply fully *and* promptly.

Implement the Suggestion Quickly

The fourth is to implement the suggestion as quickly as practical. If it is going to take some time due to the nature of the suggestion, let the employee know, so that his expectations are in line with what actually happens. Once again the time it takes to implement the suggestion is a brilliant signal of how important this is considered to be by management.

It is also vital to ensure that the recognition (regardless of format) is publicised and given within days of the suggestion being implemented. Ideally a senior member of the management team should give out this recognition, in order to positively confirm to the whole organisation how valued these suggestions are. Even if any one suggestion is relatively trivial, this is a small price to pay for the motivation and the potential big money saver that will appear surprisingly often, sometimes from the least expected source.

Positively Reinforce Behaviour

The fifth aspect is to positively reinforce behaviour. If an employee is already committed to the company cause and wants to make suggestions regardless of any reward other than the satisfaction of getting ideas implemented, then the suggestion scheme will simply reinforce this person's behaviour. As there are normally a relatively small number of people already motivated to this degree, there tends to be a small percentage of the employees who account for by far the majority of the suggestions put forward.

There is a far larger majority who consider they do not have any worthwhile ideas, or cannot be bothered, or make one suggestion and then get switched off when the recognition takes too long to process. It is this larger pool of people that you must also consider and bring into the fold when establishing the structure and operation of your suggestion scheme.

This is where the facilitator can influence the scheme and help those people who are reticent about writing their ideas on flipcharts or those who say they keep having ideas but this is simply part of their job. Obviously you cannot force someone to join in the scheme, but if a low-key recognition or even no public recognition is desired then that wish can be respected. The direct daily contact by the facilitator with the most important people in the suggestion scheme, namely those at the 'coalface', is another key element in getting the continuous improvement culture to work effectively. Encouragement and support of these people is one critical part of the facilitator role.

Keep the Recognition System Uncomplicated

The sixth is to keep the recognition system uncomplicated and easy to understand. Try to avoid different rewards for different numbers of suggestions as although this introduces variety for those employees making several suggestions, it can make the system bureaucratic. Find a recognition that is acceptable to most employees whether they receive one or ten. Ask your employees what they would prefer and be prepared to change the recognition over a period of time to prevent boredom setting in. For example if you set out with T-shirts as the initial form of recognition, which can give rise to some initial pride for the wearer and certainly some publicity for the scheme, you will need to change to something more sustainable in the medium term. Vouchers for the local supermarket is one idea, additional half-day holidays for set numbers of suggestions is another.

Supervision Responsible for Evaluation

The seventh is to keep responsibility for evaluation and implementation with the first-line supervision. Never send suggestions off to some head office clerk who neither understands the implication of the suggestion nor the urgency to get the feedback to the employee. It is the supervisors who understand the value of the suggestion and potentially will gain indirectly from the implementation. The supervisor role is really key as without this person doing the daily flipchart check and ensuring the implementation and recognition takes place, the suggestion scheme momentum will be difficult to increase.

With the seven OEDIPUS characteristics in place, your suggestion scheme has an excellent chance of success. It could be so successful that you might wish to consider if there is a way of making the status of any recognition given to your employees as tax-free. (In the UK, for example, there is the A57 scheme, which allows under certain conditions, for recognition received as part of a suggestion scheme to be tax-free.)

The continuous improvement scheme structure we have looked at so far attempts to capture, implement and stimulate ideas from the workforce during their normal working day. There is, however, the potential to apply similar principles to the area of health and safety, particularly if you wish to focus on reducing accidents at work. This is the topic for the next section.

Chapter 24

Reducing Accidents

A continuously improving Accident Record is not itself an accident; it takes managing, and your people are best placed to suggest how.

Good management practice, not to mention legislation, suggests the need to look after your employees' health and safety. Your strong company culture should reinforce this message by taking positive steps to ensure unsafe situations are eliminated. The question is how best to achieve this objective. This section gives you two potential solutions that complement each other; the Health and Safety Continuous Improvement Team, and the 'observations' system called Zero Accident Potential (ZAP).

Historically I have come across companies where the management has abdicated responsibility for their employee safety to the Health and Safety Manager, and then wondered why their accident record has not improved. There is, however, another approach that fits neatly into the continuous improvement culture and can be a very effective system for reducing accidents at work. Establishing a Health and Safety Continuous Improvement Team facilitates this.

You probably already have a number of safety representatives in your company, hopefully at around one for every 25 or so employees, or one per department. Empowering these safety representatives to be able to change the working environment and practices can be a major stimulation and morale booster throughout the company. Forming a Health and Safety Continuous Improvement Team with the safety representatives as the backbone is a great way to channel suggestions through to those that can action the changes required. Also on this Continuous Improvement Team need to be two people as a minimum; the operations director to give the team weight and the ability to make decisions and spend money if required, and the Health and Safety Manager to provide specialist expertise to the team.

As with the normal Process Ownership and Continuous Improvement meetings, once a fortnight should be about the right time interval between these meetings. During the initial meetings it would probably be a good idea to construct and agree a mission statement, in order to establish the real aims of the team. The statement could be something as simple as follows.

The Aims of The Health and Safety Continuous Improvement Team are:

▶ reduce accidents at this site
▶ increase safety awareness at all levels
▶ promote a 'think safe' attitude.

To channel the health and safety suggestions to this team, establish two paths through the continuous improvement structure. The first is a series of flipcharts specifically for health and safety suggestions. Positioned in prominent locations such as a restaurant, these flipcharts give *any* employee immediate access to the Health and Safety Continuous Improvement Team for pre-emptive or corrective action as required. The second channel is through all the other departmental Continuous Improvement meetings, where any safety concerns can be raised and fed to the safety representatives. At these departmental Continuous Improvement meetings the department manager and his team will iron out most of the concerns raised, but where there are inter-departmental issues or site issues, the Health and Safety Continuous Improvement Team can play a very positive role.

As with any other Continuous Improvement Team meetings, you will need minutes with actions, responsibilities, and timings to make the time effective. Publicise these minutes so that all employees can see action being taken, and also feedback directly to the health and safety flipcharts.

Since the Health and Safety Continuous Improvement meetings are desirable as a regular feature of 'the way we do things around here', occasional attendee changes and new focus initiatives will promote ongoing success.

Another feature that helps raise the profile of the Health and Safety Continuous Improvement Team, and highlights changes in employee attitude towards safety generally, is to publicise safety performance in your canteen or equivalent. One effective method is the use of a Continuous Improvement Board labelled 'health and safety'. This board is used to display the departmental performance as measured by incidence rate for hospital, off-work and RIDDOR (Reporting of Injuries, Diseases and Dangerous Occurrences Regulations 1985) accidents, where

$$\text{Incidence rate} = \frac{\text{Number of accidents} \times 200{,}000}{\text{Total hours worked}}$$

For example, the incidence rate for accidents requiring hospital treatment in a month is the number of hospital accidents × 200,000/total hours worked in that month. Attach the minutes from the Health and Safety Continuous Improvement meetings to this board to show more suggestions have been completed.

This Continuous Improvement Board displays when the department last had a hospital accident, and shows this visually as a cross. Since most departments will not have had a hospital accident, show this with a different symbol to indicate another step has been taken towards recognition for a good safety performance. There are unlimited ways of doing this that all come back to positive reinforcement of behaviour and help promote a 'think safe' attitude. One visual indicator that works well is a slice of cake for each month without a hospital accident. Build up the slices of cake into a whole one to signify when it is time for a safety lunch, which could be your way of saying 'thank you' to your employees for working without an accident (see Figure 24.1). Note that only a hospital or RIDDOR accident prevents progress towards the next safety lunch.

As with the standard suggestion scheme, the safety representatives receive recognition for their implemented suggestions. Since the award for a suggestion is only given once, this stimulates the safety representatives to come up with their own ideas, particularly if they are individually asked to put forward their suggestions at every Continuous Improvement meeting. Each meeting should end up with some ideas completed and fresh ones to consider.

This Health and Safety Continuous Improvement Team, together with the visual impact of the Continuous Improvement Board, works really well to continuously improve the safety of the site by reducing the number of unsafe situations and promoting a positive attitude amongst the employees. The net result should be a reduction in accidents.

The second system for reducing accidents is that of 'observations', a simple safety initiative that tackles the base of the normal accident pyramid called 'at risk behaviour'. This whole concept is described in the

Department..................

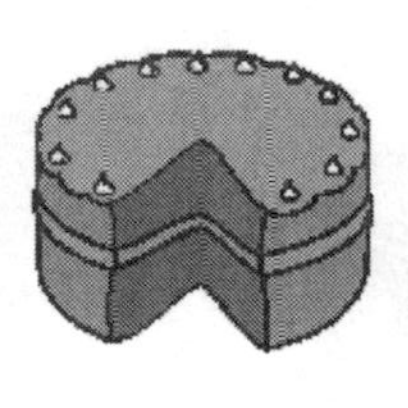

No accidents in January

One first aid accident in February

No accidents in March. Qualify for safety award for working 3 months without a hospital accident

No accidents in April

One Hospital accident in May

No accidents in June

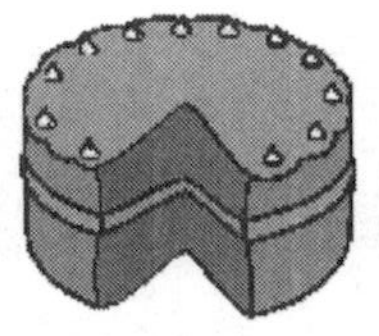

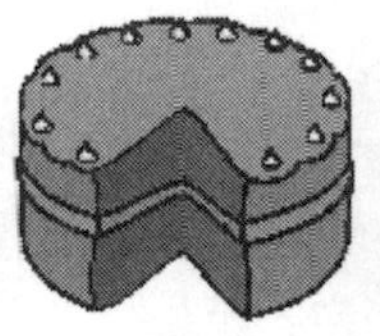

No accidents in July

No accidents in August. Qualify for safety award for working 3 months without a hospital accident

Two first aid accidents in September

No accidents in October

No accidents in November. Qualify for safety award for working 3 months without a hospital accident

One first aid accident in December

Last hospital accident 21st May

Figure 24.1. Departmental accident status

safety section of the Shell Chemicals case study, coming next, where it is applied daily and known locally as ZAP.

So, what follows now is the final case study; one about a cultural revolution at Shell Chemicals. It is a poignant trip down memory lane for me, and a landmark in the history of the site. It is also where this book really began ...

Chapter 25

Shell Chemicals '**Cultural Revolution and Evolution at Carrington**'

In 1985, the Shell Chemicals' Carrington site had a clear choice; become profitable or close. To create a brand-new future, a 'New Carrington', the site experienced Cultural Revolution. Employees agreed radical new working practices, signed a single union agreement, and trained to become multi-skilled technicians. Carrington became a role model for the petrochemical industry. Representatives from over 500 companies worldwide visited the 'New Carrington' to see how this turn-round had been accomplished.

Has the cultural revolution introduced in 1985 survived? If so, how has it evolved since then? Let us find out.

Introduction

In 1985, Shell Chemicals UK senior management announced plans for a 'New Carrington'. In the preface to this book I summarise my recollections of the cultural revolution at Carrington that resulted. This case study expands these memories, revisits the site today, and tells the story of how Carrington regained a profitable future.

The general principles in this case study, for you to consider in your own company, are:

▶ Be prepared for the sheer scale of training you may need for your culture change. Look at the facilities required and number of people employed to train the Technicians in 1985.

▶ Ensure the training is focused on the skills really needed rather than trying to turn everyone into a master of everything. Carrington have revised their training focus. Look at the programme in 1985 and contrast it with 1999.

▶ Build in time for training and continuous improvement into the working day. Carrington has made this compulsory.

▶ Keeping people informed is critical for any culture change. Look at the multiple media utilised, particularly in the 1985 cultural revolution.

▶ If redundancies are on the agenda, keep compassion in mind too and provide the outplacement facilities to help your employees – again look at the 1985 scenario at Carrington and the huge resource employed to establish people in alternative employment.

▶ Employee behaviour can be altered; in this case look at the Zero Accident Potential (ZAP) initiative and the concept of 'observations', to improve your accident performance.

After taking you through the key events of 1985, this case study covers three main themes:

▶ training
▶ communication
▶ safety.

First it takes the promise to train operators and craftsmen to become multi-skilled technicians, a commitment made over 15 years ago, and brings us up to date with the current thinking. Incidentally, this commitment to the training and continuous improvement philosophy is so deeply ingrained that the shift structure design deliberately creates *time* for *mandatory* training and continuous improvement. This is definitely a serious commitment. We will explore how this is done and how there could be parallels in your organisation even if your company does not work shifts.

The second, critical, component is the frank and open communication employed by the current site manager with all employees.

Thirdly we shall explore how the safety record of over 2,000,000 man-hours without a lost time injury, which is the result of a strong safety culture, has been helped by a safety initiative involving 'observations' of people behaviour. More about this later; let us start by setting the scene for Carrington in 1985.

1985: The New Carrington Vision

In 1985 Carrington had a clear choice; become profitable or close. Shell UK's senior management reviewed the site, its petrochemical plants, product portfolio, and people. Similar to a zero-based budget procedure, they started as if with a green-field site, on which they placed only those chemical plants they believed could make the site profitable. Four manufacturing areas would remain. The rest of the site would close.

In terms of the people, less than half would continue their employment at Carrington, but each person affected would receive considerable help to find alternative employment. In the announcement made to all employees in April 1985, Shell indicated: 'We are looking for the best people to run the future Carrington'. The planned restructuring meant shortening lines of communication, removing demarcation, and training the former maintenance craftsmen and the plant operators to become technicians capable of doing both jobs. The aim was to get a flexible, salaried workforce who, when on shift would operate the plant, and when on days would form the maintenance team. Each technician would spend four months on shifts and two months on days in a six-month cycle. The commitment made was to retrain people so that 'Providing the technician is competent, he can do any job he is asked to do'. This meant that technicians would in future maintain, as well as operate, the plants. This was a radical change from historic practice!

The vision was to create a productive culture for the 'New Carrington' that had complementary values and systems (see Figure 25.1).

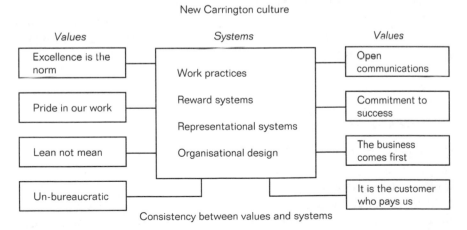

Figure 25.1. The vision – to create a productive culture

Keeping People Informed

The timings for this cultural change meant communications had to be effective, firm, fast and fair:

▶ April heralded the review of all site activities.
▶ June saw the finalised proposals for the site organisation published.
▶ July followed with the proposals endorsed, a new union agreement signed, and individuals advised of their position.
▶ August started individual training programmes.
▶ November witnessed the shutdown of designated plants and full establishment of the new profit-centre organisation structure.

Line managers, specially trained in counselling, asked every employee what he or she wanted and considered their individual wishes in the context of the site's needs. Employees were then told as soon as possible whether or not they had a job in the new set-up. This whole consultation process, for well over 1000 people, took approximately four weeks.

To support this huge effort on site, a senior team took charge of communications. It gave every employee a video to show his or her family what the 'New Carrington' would be like. It produced three clear, step-by-step handbooks on various aspects of the change. It issued a weekly magazine, a site bulletin as required, and at the end of the month a full summary of events.

All discussions about the change programme went down line-management channels rather than personnel, so it was management that owned the programme and management that portrayed it to their teams.

Every person about to be made redundant had access to a manager and a redeployment counsellor, together with the resources of the full-time redeployment unit run by four managers and six employees nominated by the trade unions. This helped both on an emotional and a practical level.

Technician Training

The new organisation began to take shape too, with four layers rather than the previous six, and four production profit centres each with six teams of multi-skilled technicians. Each team had a mix of operator, craftsman and conventional foreman. Four out of the six shift teams operated the plant; the other two performed maintenance tasks, provided holiday cover and allowed the training programme to take place. A small team of day specialist technicians supported the shift teams by performing key equipment diagnosis and other specialist work.

The technicians went through two stages of training, each of six to nine months duration, and an accreditation procedure (City and Guilds level two certificate) to demonstrate competence to do the job. The breadth of training was significant, covering operator and craft skills. To indicate just how broad the training was, craft skills training incorporated instruments, electrical and pipefitting; fabrication, scaffolding and rigging; valves, pumps and heat exchangers. This training, tailored to each individual, took place in the former central workshop with the aim of ending up with around 400 technicians out of a total workforce of 500. No longer would process operators have to hide spanners in their overalls and keep a watchful eye out for craft shop stewards if they needed to do some minor maintenance when operating the plant! Also as a result of this training, Carrington now has a team of technicians with all the core skills needed to cover the major requirements of all production units on site.

In 1991 the flexible, multi-skilling approach went a stage further. The training programme accelerated by providing a fast track route to National Vocational Qualification (NVQ) level three in Engineering Manufacture (craft competencies) maintenance practices. The aim was to have around 80 technicians able to tackle tasks outside the normal routine. This became the new standard for the site around 1995, and now all technicians either have NVQ level two/three in process operations or NVQ level three in engineering maintenance.

1998: A New Vision: 'The Way Ahead'

Let us move forwards chronologically now to 1998, when the current site manager arrived at Carrington. Benchmarking against key competitors showed the site manufacturing performance had slipped, with manning levels, plant reliability and manufacturing costs now only 'average' for the industry. In September 1998 the site manager presented to his people the 'need to change', on the basis that the site was no longer an industry leader.

He launched 'The Way Ahead' in order to define a mission, determine the key priorities, address the issues and achieve the desired manpower reductions. The site management team defined the mission as:

Manufacturing excellence adapting to the needs of individual businesses at Carrington site.

Similarly 'what mattered most' was the 'six cheeses' made up of reliability, people, customer focus, quality, health and safety, and cost effectiveness (see Figure 25.2).

Carrington 'The Way Ahead'

Figure 25.2.   Carrington 'The Way Ahead'

In November 1998, to achieve the mission of excellence, three teams started to look at operations excellence, maintenance excellence and projects and engineering excellence. The aim, publicised at that time to the rest of the site, was to report back with proposals by April 1999. A multidisciplinary team for each defined best practice and proposed *how* to achieve this organisationally.

The reason for requesting this was that if you simply reduce the number of people employed without changing work habits, the remaining people have to work harder. Although this may sound very obvious, many companies looking to drive their efficiencies up in the medium term would do well to heed this advice rather than simply look for short-term benefits. Merely reducing the number of people without changing systems or working practices, ensures the focus will be on today's needs, whether that means production for a manufacturing company, or a service element for the service industry. It takes away any time that previously was available to think about and implement continuous improvement. Manpower reduction without investment, system, or work method changes is a very dangerous trap to fall into.

The site manager's interviews conducted in 1998 showed that although the multi-skilling and profit-centre style of organisation achieved in 1985 was very attractive then, but there were now in effect five sites on site rather than one coherent organisation, so cross-fertilisation of best practice was missing.

More Technician Training – For Excellence

The interviews also uncovered that the multi-skilling training undertaken in 1985/86 was too broad, although at the time the scope of this training had to be completed to break down the demarcation between craftsmen and operators. The non-core skills such as rigging, plumbing and scaffolding had disappeared over the ensuing four to five years. (*Note*: External companies now provide some of these skills, which is more cost-effective.)

The training focus needed to change too. Training operators to be craftsmen, and vice versa, had historically resulted in an *average* level of skill in both functions rather than *excellence* in the one skill group. For example, moving operators to days to do maintenance after four months on shifts, resulted in average quality performance rather than excellence. Also the maintenance team was often depleted to supplement the shift teams.

Consequently when actions to implement 'The Way Ahead' were launched in May 1999, the technicians were asked to decide which of the two core skills they wanted to specialise in; craft or operator. You could of course, say the wheel is now turning full circle, but really it is the drive for excellence that makes this latest change make sense. The training now is aimed at increasing flexibility *within* the core discipline, not across disciplines. People expressed major concerns about returning to the old days of conflict. However, simply by incorporating *common objectives* of *plant reliability*, and *production cost*, into the technicians' individual and team performance measures, allayed these fears.

Building In Time For Training And Continuous Improvement

By April 1999 the operating excellence group had defined a new shift rota, this time with a five-shift system, which includes ten days *compulsory* training, plus a further ten days for continuous improvement built in for each team every year. Thus with five teams this is a total of 100 team days per year to improve the people and plant performance. The training and continuous improvement timing is typically from October to April. The other team days in the summer allow for holidays and holiday cover.

The full five-shift system adds about seven per cent additional people to those required purely to cover shifts, bank holidays, annual leave entitlement, sickness absence, and training time. (To cover one shift position you need about 5.6 people over the whole year; so for a five-shift position plant you need $5 \times 5.6 = 28$ operators. In fact the company has 30 people, which is two extra ($2/28$ = seven per cent).) Efficiency gains and continuous improvement ideas generate savings that largely compensate for this additional cost.

So, I am not advocating simply adding cost. I am asking you to think how much value this could add to your operation; time for training, time for continuous improvement, time to manage situations rather than fire-fight, even time for planning ahead for the future of the business.

> *Consider your employees as a value-adding resource to improve the business, rather than as a cost.*

It is also worth noting that although working 37.5 hours/week, all employees are paid for 39 hours, which means that over a year each employee owes the company 78 hours. Any overtime worked is taken from this 'bank' and no extra payments are required. Any hours not used are not claimed back by the company, and any hours worked in excess of 78 are taken as time off. This incentive to get the job done in normal working hours has reduced what was a very high overtime level site to almost no overtime. One of the other benefits is the impact this has had on short-term sickness absence, which is considerably reduced because it is also taken out of the 78 hours 'bank'. This puts peer pressure on individuals not to be absent because their colleagues have to work extra hours to cover, for no extra pay.

More Communication

In May 1999, having received the operations, maintenance, and projects & engineering excellence proposals, the site manager presented and got approval for these proposals from his senior management. He then spoke again to his people at Carrington. He explained the outcomes of 'The Way Ahead' review, in particular the meaning of each 'excellence' vision and strategy. He also indicated the implications for employment, including further individual consultations and voluntary redundancies. Everything was made clear to all 420 staff in a series of very open and frank presentations.

In June 1999 the team started to implement 'The Way Ahead' and its mission of 'excellence'. Consultants facilitated the process for around nine months from May 1999 to February 2000. The new five-shift system (see Appendix 2) came into operation in January 2000, once the system changes proposed in 'The Way Ahead' had been implemented.

In January 2000 the site manager gave another formal update to all employees in groups of 50 at a time, using the training days for these presentations. For a whole day he reminded people of the progress they had made; efficiency gains, savings achieved, investment in new plant, and the continuous improvement culture. He also outlined the site goals for 2000. These, not surprisingly, were based on the six cheeses mentioned earlier. He asked the shift teams to spend the afternoon devising and agreeing plant and business-based objectives for each plant, team and individual. Through this process, the site manager and his team ensured all employees knew the strategy for the site, and the part they and their team would play in the coming year. It was also a great way to impart a boost to all on site, through encouragement, a genuine interest in their welfare, and simply by saying 'Thank you'.

Carrington still has challenges, and the drive for efficiency and profitability in a difficult global market, makes communication with everyone on site all the more important. The commitment to training is still there, the open culture fostered back in 1985 is still there, and indeed the safety track record is also impressive. Before closing this case study, we will just have a brief look at this simple safety initiative that has helped the site achieve over 2,000,000 man-hours without a lost-time accident. Locally it is called ZAP.

Safety

ZAP stands for Zero Accident Potential. The theory is based on the normal accident pyramid (see Figure 25.3), only this time there is another layer at the bottom called 'at risk behaviour'. The logic for introducing ZAP was to help drive down the number of near misses and first aid accidents. Extrapolating the pyramid statistics indicated that a narrower base (i.e. a smaller number of near misses) would also reduce the number of more serious accidents.

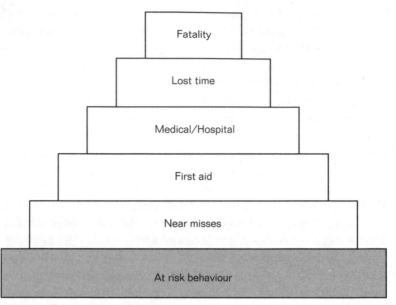

Figure 25.3.   The accident pyramid

ZAP works on the principle of looking at situations, which creates action, to change people's behaviour. The key is the concept of 'observations'. An observation is a dialogue between two people with regard to their behaviour. Observations can be carried out between people at any level in the organisation, but normally it is between work colleagues at the same level. How does this work in practice?

Assuming you are the observer, you ask 'Do you mind if I observe you for the next few minutes? This is a no blame process and I will not be recording your name'. Assuming the other person agrees, you monitor his/her work activity for a few minutes. Then you give verbal feedback, discussing which aspects of the work were carried out safely and which were 'at risk'. Where you identify an 'at risk' behaviour, you discuss the reasons for this. For example, perhaps a job requires goggles to be worn in addition to other personal protective equipment (PPE). The person is actually wearing all the other PPE but has safety glasses on instead of goggles. You would comment positively on the use of the other PPE, but note the 'at risk' behaviour of wearing safety glasses instead of goggles. Then you would ask the reasons why. Perhaps the observed person was not aware of the need to wear goggles, could not be bothered to get them, or maybe there were not any goggles available?

This observations process identifies barriers to safe behaviour that can then be rectified. The main benefit, however, is the interaction between the two people, which increases their safety awareness and promotes a culture of 'looking out for the safety of one's colleagues'. The idea is to change people's behaviour but in a no-blame way.

The observation is written up as a formal event in the observer's behavioural safety pocket book, by ticking whether the PPE, body mechanics, tools and equipment, vehicles, environment, and permits, are perceived as 'safe' or 'at risk'. Each observation is entered into a database on the site intranet to help identify repeat areas of concern, where changes to behaviour could prevent an accident.

The site achieved around 1000 observations in 2000. The target for Carrington in 2001 is to have 3600 observations (one per employee per month) completed in the year. This should do two things. First it should change people's behaviour because they know any one of their colleagues can stop and observe them. Secondly it should influence the potential observer to 'think safety'. The aim is to reduce accidents. This is a very simple, but potentially powerful tool to help reduce accidents before they have even begun to become near misses or first-aid injuries.

Conclusion

Carrington site went through a cultural revolution back in 1985, but it gained a future and established the standards for the rest of the industry to meet. *'We felt as though we were at the forefront of how things were being done.'* It became an acknowledged industry leader. *'People were proud.'* It also made a commitment to multi-skilling training that still stands the site in good stead today. *'We had a sudden injection of new people (on to our plant, so the) training helped build teams.'* The present culture change process is by evolution through continuous improvement, with training goals now focused on flexibility within core trades rather than across craft/operator job types.

The current employees at Carrington, from site manager to technician, are actively living the principles established by Shell, to create an environment and an organisational culture that supports high performance and productivity. In short, the cultural revolution at Carrington in 1985, and the evolution since then, is now supporting 'The Way Ahead' and its mission of 'excellence'.

Summary Action List for Your Business

1. Multi-skill your employees to give flexibility within their core discipline, but don't train employees to be able to do everything. Each person in a team will naturally be stronger at some things, so it is important to get the right mix of people on the team rather than try to train and expect everyone to be able to do everything. Remember the old adage 'Jack of all trades, Master of none.'
2. Design time into the working week for continuous improvement and training activities. Make these activities mandatory.
3. Improve your safety record through modified behaviour (using the technique called 'observations'.)
4. Ensure communication takes place frequently, particularly in times of change, to align expectations.
5. To achieve excellence, first define best practice. Then work out how to achieve this organisationally. You may get a short-term gain, but do not expect long-term success simply by removing people from the company. Remember, people are your most important asset for your business.

Part 5

Reviewing Your Success

Here is your first real chance to think back over the Benchmarking, Planning, Investing, and Improving sections of this book; to think about your own business in this context, and to start formulating your own culture change plans. To help you, there are two elements to Reviewing Your Success.

We will look firstly at the characteristics your company should expect to exhibit when you have achieved your success culture. This should help you recognise where you have already achieved success, and identify target areas for change.

Secondly, there is an one-page model of 'Leading Your People To Success' (Figure 26.1) that brings together the processes, resources and cultural conditions interwoven throughout the book. You might find this model useful as a relatively simple way of communicating your plan to your team, as well as a basis for your own thoughts.

Chapter 26

Reviewing Your Success

Measure achievement against your own initial benchmark;
but measure success only against the best.

Success is the goal; the result of all the process and attitude changes associated with the culture change. To highlight the treasure we are looking for, this is what your company should contain as you approach 'success':

1. Communication – formal and informal – that creates a language unique to your organisation that every employee understands. Communication that is accurate, consistent and timely; that ensures everyone knows what is going on without having to ask.
2. Leaders – from chief executive officer all the way down, that live the company values.
3. Innovation and continuous improvement that cannot be suppressed!
4. Mission, vision and value statements with a named, clear strategy, and systems that support the values. (All are communicated to give each employee a sense of purpose, a meaning and a personal mission rather than just a job). Trust is one of these core values.
5. Business Excellence – setting and driving, not following, the industry standard.
6. Increased efficiency, output and economic performance – a leaner, sharper business with reduced costs and improved profits; by focusing on profitable customers and by becoming an 'e-business' (i.e. using Internet technologies to improve and transform key enterprise processes).
7. Names, not positions, are important. 'Us and them', and 'ego', are history.
8. Goal alignment achieved for company and employees – with staff status for all (via annualised hours if appropriate), plus personal

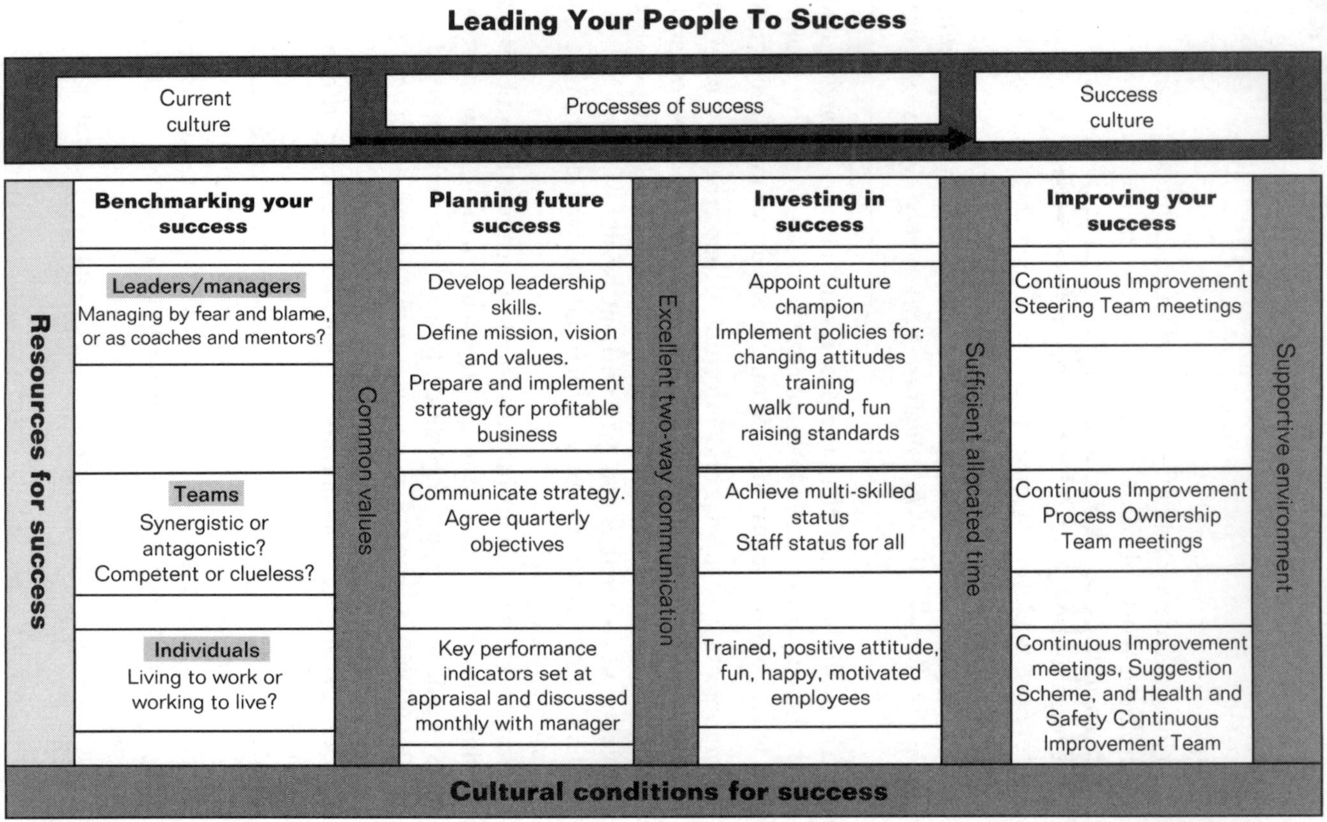

Leading Your People To Success

Current culture		Processes of success	Success culture

Resources for success

Cultural conditions for success

	Supportive environment	Sufficient allocated time	Excellent two-way communication	Common values
	Improving your success	**Investing in success**	**Planning future success**	**Benchmarking your success**

Leaders/managers
Managing by fear and blame, or as coaches and mentors?

- Continuous Improvement Steering Team meetings
- Appoint culture champion. Implement policies for: changing attitudes training, walk round, fun, raising standards
- Develop leadership skills. Define mission, vision and values. Prepare and implement strategy for profitable business

Teams
Synergistic or antagonistic? Competent or clueless?

- Continuous Improvement Process Ownership Team meetings
- Achieve multi-skilled status. Staff status for all
- Communicate strategy. Agree quarterly objectives

Individuals
Living to work or working to live?

- Continuous Improvement meetings, Suggestion Scheme, and Health and Safety Continuous Improvement Team
- Trained, positive attitude, fun, happy, motivated employees
- Key performance indicators set at appraisal and discussed monthly with manager

Figure 26.1. The 'Leading Your People To Success' model

Key performance indicators (KPIs) linked to company annual and quarterly objectives.

9.   Quality of working life improved by recognising the family needs as well as those of the business.

10. Service is our 'raison d'être'.

11. Training and development enabling self-managed teams; where every employee works flexibly within his/her own competence, where responsibility and accountability is accepted at the lowest levels in the organisation, and where reduced absenteeism and improved safety are achieved by peer pressure rather than by management actions. As a result, bureaucracy is slashed.

12. Excellent people, including a customer-focused culture champion, that are motivated, happy, proud, positive, inspired, value adding, passionate about what they do, and have fun too!

Conclusion

This final chapter may be the conclusion to this book, but 'a new future' would be a far more appropriate name. Starting your culture change is akin to a caterpillar shedding its skin and creating its chrysalis in readiness for the metamorphosis into a new being. Your organisation will change internally, sometimes beyond all recognition, until it emerges to spread its wings into new dimensions and territories just like the butterfly beginning its next phase of life.

Before taking that 'leap of faith', by pressing the green button marked 'culture change', consider that your culture change is a journey; one that improves your people's working lives and enhances your company's economic performance. It takes commitment and desire, trust and teamwork. It takes time, and sometimes moments of deep pain and frustration; but it also brings relief, breaths of fresh air and new energy. It aligns each of your people and gives them a genuine sense of purpose, a real meaning and ubiquitous understanding of their role in the overall game plan. It changes the very nature and tone of the language used by employees internally, and naturally inspires your employees to speak in terms that communicate enthusiasm and commitment to your customers; to the extent that your customers will comment and feed back that things have changed.

Culture change is the reward for the millions of new actions founded on your personal beliefs and values, actions that are focused into affecting the feelings and daily behaviour of everyone in your organisation. When those feelings and behaviours translate over time into the 'can do' attitudes associated with innovation, leadership, and motivation, you will know you are on the right track because you will physically see it and your employees will tell you.

Now that you have 'seen the need' for culture change, combine this with a profitable strategy to create a real recipe for success. Take time out to develop those long-term audacious goals we discussed in the vision. Encourage a visionary approach to leadership. Start leading your industry, as well as your company, into new ways of thinking. The principle is the same whether it is James Dyson of Dyson Appliances creating a new market for vacuum cleaners with his dual cyclone bag-less design; or Stelios Haji-Ioannou establishing the low-cost airline easyJet with seat places sold over the Internet instead of retail outlets.

Before lighting the first flare to announce change is on its way, take the first step by visiting other successful firms to benchmark your own company. Formulate the essence of 'why we exist', 'what we wish to be in the future' and 'the principles and beliefs on which the business is founded.' Establish your key small team and share your thoughts. Start planning, then extend your thinking to investing and improving.

Remember that main isolator switch you held in your hand in the introduction, the one that would turn on the firework display for the Sydney Olympic games if you decided to proceed by reading the book? Well, you have read the book and now its time to decide what you are going to tell your children and grandchildren in the years ahead. Are you going to tell them that you cared enough about your employees and your business to press the culture change button, or will you merely relay that you managed your company? Consider this carefully before you announce anything to your employees, because there is no going back. On the other hand you cannot afford to stand still either. So, which is it to be? Will you press that culture change button to transform your company's and your people's future? Will you start to paint pictures for your employees of that butterfly that could emerge in the future?

Go on, start 'Leading Your People To Success'.

List of Useful Contacts

The British Quality Foundation
32–34 Great Peter Street, London, SW1P 2QX, United Kingdom.
Tel.: +44 207 654 5000; Fax: +44 207 654 5001;
E-mail: mail@quality-foundation.co.uk;
Website: www.quality-foundation.co.uk

European Foundation for Quality Management
Brussels Representative Office, Avenue des Pleiades 15,
1200 Brussels, Belgium.
Tel.: +32 2 775 3511; Fax: +32 2 775 3535;
E-mail: info@efqm.org;
Website: www.efqm.org

Investors in People UK
7–10 Chandos Street, London W1M 9DE, United Kingdom.
Tel.: +44 20 7467 1900; Fax: +44 20 7636 2386;
Website: www.investorsinpeople.co.uk

Inside UK Enterprise Ltd
Festival Hall, Petersfield, Hampshire GU31 4JW, United Kingdom.
Tel.: +44 1730 235 015; Fax: +44 1730 268 865;
E-mail: iuke@statusmeetings.co.uk;
Website: www.iuke.co.uk

Kaizen Institute Ltd
Parent Company of the Kaizen Institute Group of Companies,
Poststrasse 15, Zug, 6301 Switzerland.
Tel.: +41 41 729 4242; Fax: +41 41 729 4229;
E-mail: KI@Kaizen.com;
Website: www.Kaizen.com

Leading Your People To Success Ltd
Bretton Barn, Foolow, Nr Eyam, Hope Valley, Derbyshire,
S32 5QR, United Kingdom.
Tel.: +44 1433 631 550; Fax: +44 1433 639 869;
E-mail: nick.kitchin@leadingyourpeopletosuccess.com;
Website: www.leadingyourpeopletosuccess.com

John Spitz Associates
International Training and Business Excellence Consultant,
33 Broadway, Cheadle, Cheshire SK8 1LB, United Kingdom.
Tel.: +44 161 428 7965, +44 161 428 1354; Fax: +44 161 428 8470;
E-mail: john.spitz@virgin.net

Notes

Preface

1. *Competitive Strategy* by Michael E. Porter, Appendix A. Macmillan Publishing Co., Inc. 1980, ISBN 0-02-925360-8.
2. *Leading the Revolution* by Gary Hamel. Harvard Business School Press 2000, ISBN 1-57851-189-5.
3. *In Search of Excellence* by Thomas Peters and Robert Waterman. Harper & Row 1982, ISBN 0-06-015042-4.

Introduction

1. *Who Moved My Cheese?* by Spencer Johnson. G.P. Putnam's Sons 1998, ISBN 0-399-14446-3.

Chapter 2

1. *Corporate Culture and Performance* by John P. Kotter and James L. Heskett, page 24. The Free Press 1992, ISBN 0-02-918467-3.

Chapter 3

1. *Living Strategy* by Lynda Gratton, page 134. Pearson Education Ltd 2000, ISBN 0-273-650157.
2. Building your company's vision by James C. Collins and Jerry I. Porras. *Harvard Business Review*, September–October 1996, page 74.
3. Building your company's vision by James C. Collins and Jerry I. Porras. *Harvard Business Review*, September–October 1996, page 73.

Chapter 4

1. ©EFQM. The EFQM Excellence Model is a registered trademark, where EFQM stands for the European Foundation for Quality Management.

Chapter 6

1. *Sunday Business*, 24th June 2001, page 12.

Chapter 7

1. *Leading the Revolution* by Gary Hamel, page 264. Harvard Business School Press 2000, ISBN 1-57851-189-5.

Chapter 15

1. *Building Capability for the 21st Century* by CREATE (Centre for Research in Employment and Technology in Europe) 1999.
2. *Satisfaction at Work* by Planet Research 1998.

Chapter 16

1. *In Search of Excellence* by Thomas Peters and Robert Waterman, page 235. Harper & Row 1982, ISBN 0-06-015042-4.

Part 4

1. KAIZEN® is the registered trademark owned by Kaizen Institute Ltd, Parent Company of the Kaizen Institute Group of Companies.

Bibliography

1. *Kaizen* by Masaaki Imai. McGraw-Hill Publishing Company, USA 1986, ISBN 0-07-54332-X.
2. *Gemba Kaizen* by Masaaki Imai. McGraw-Hill Publishing Company, USA 1997, ISBN 0-07-031446-2.
3. *All Together Now* by John Harvey-Jones. Mandarin Paperbacks 1994, ISBN 0-7493-1960-7.
4. *Organizational Culture and Leadership* by Edgar H. Schein. Jossey-Bass Inc. 1992, ISBN 1-55542-478-2.
5. *Changing Culture* by Alan Williams, Paul Dobson and Mike Walters, second edition. Institute of Personnel and Development 1993, ISBN 0-85292-533-6.
6. *Corporate Culture for Competitive Edge* by Charles Hampden-Turner. The Economist Publications 1990, ISBN 0-85058-294-6.
7. *Zapp! The Lightning of Empowerment* by The Ballantine Publishing Group 1998, ISBN 0-449-00282-9.
8. *Jack* by Jack Welsh. Headline Book Publishing 2001, ISBN 0-7472-4935-0.
9. *A Great Place to Work* by Robert Levering. Random House, Inc., USA 1988, ISBN 0-394-55725-5.
10. *Leading in a Culture of Change* by Michael Fullan. Jossey-Bass, USA 2001, ISBN 0-7879-5395-4.

Appendix 1

BENCHMARK YOUR CURRENT CULTURE

Poor Performance Culture	1	2	3	4	5	6	7	8	9	Success Culture
Us and them										Equality
Blame/fear culture										Coaching/supportive culture
No leadership										Competent leaders
No vision										Mission, vision and values
No teamwork										Cohesive teams
No time for continuous improvement										Time for continuous improvement is designed into the working day
Focus is on urgent rather than important tasks										Focus is on important rather than urgent tasks
Working to live										Living to work
We have always done it this way. Innovation cannot be started!										Things are always changing and continuously improving. Innovation cannot be suppressed!
Parent/child relationship										Adult to adult trust
'I am not sure we can do that' attitude										'Can-do' attitude
Autocratic control at the top										Responsibility and accountability accepted and thriving at lowest levels in the organisation
Rumours (grapevine) are main communication channel										Excellent, regular, top-down communication with feedback expected/encouraged
Inward focus										Customer focus

Figure 1.1. Benchmark your current culture

'Are you leading your people to success?' **benchmark questionnaire**	Yes	No

The aim of this questionnaire is to help you identify if you are already 'leading your people to success', by assessing key components of the cultural jigsaw. If so, you should be able to honestly answer 'yes' to most of these questions. Any 'no' answers will flag possible areas for improvement through cultural change, which we can mentally note as we go through the following chapters and case studies. You may wish to tick your answers for future reference.

1. External benchmarking
   (a) Do you benchmark your business culture against other firms operating 'best practice'? ❏ ❏
   (b) Have you assessed your organisation against the European Foundation of Quality Management (EFQM®) Excellence Model in the past 12 months? ❏ ❏
   (c) Are you recognised as an Investor in People? ❏ ❏
   (d) Is your absenteeism below two per cent? ❏ ❏
   (e) Is your staff turnover less than your industry average? ❏ ❏

2. Strategy
   (a) Have you identified your mission, vision and values ❏ ❏
   (b) Do you have a written strategic business plan that shows a per cent return on capital employed (ROCE) and per cent profit before interest and tax (PBIT) > per cent cost of capital? ❏ ❏

3. Communication
   (a) Do all your employees know the company strategy and their part in it? ❏ ❏
   (b) Do you ask your employees their opinions in an annual survey, feed back their responses and act on their suggestions? ❏ ❏
   (c) Are you visible to your employees by a daily walk-round and by locating your workplace in the middle of open plan offices rather than a separate office? ❏ ❏
   (d) Do you have volunteers from all levels in the organisation to broadcast the company strategy, mission, vision and values? ❏ ❏
   (e) Do you encourage social interaction during rest periods by providing suitable facilities? ❏ ❏
   (f) Are e-mails used only to pass on important information and to ask vital questions where face-to-face or telephone conversations are impractical?
   (g) Are you able to focus on the important rather than the urgent items in your in-tray? ❏ ❏

4. Physical environment
   (a) Do you have open plan offices? ❏ ❏
   (b) Do you provide single status areas for work, rest, eat and play? ❏ ❏

   (c) Is the site/working environment clean?   ❏ ❏

   (d) Is it easy for visitors to find their way to reception?   ❏ ❏

   (e) Is car parking space on a first come first served basis   ❏ ❏
      rather than designated?

5. Goal alignment

   (a) Do you have quarterly objectives and individual   ❏ ❏
      key performance indicators (KPIs)?

   (b) Are all your employees salaried (and/or working   ❏ ❏
      annualised hours)?

6. Continuous improvement

   (a) Do you have a continuous improvement culture that is   ❏ ❏
      alive and well?

   (b) Do you have a suggestion scheme that works?   ❏ ❏

   (c) Have you structured the working week to include   ❏ ❏
      mandatory time for continuous improvement/training
      regardless of other pressures?

   (d) Is your company safety record one you are proud of?   ❏ ❏

7. Employee attitude/behaviour

   (a) Are your employees and any new recruits generally   ❏ ❏
      positive and enthusiastic?

   (b) Do you reward excellent behaviour beyond the call   ❏ ❏
      of duty?

   (c) Is there a general feeling of trust, honesty,   ❏ ❏
      fairness, openness, fun, pride, empowerment, and
      happiness? (Tick no if the answer to any one of
      these is no.)

   (d) Do employees behave properly, respect each other   ❏ ❏
      and company property, and support the team?

   (e) Do your managers and employees actively encourage   ❏ ❏
      safe behaviour?

8. Employee development

   (a) Are your employees trained to be multi-skilled within   ❏ ❏
      their core disciplines, and able to work in different
      departments?

   (b) Is the training status of each employee published on   ❏ ❏
      training matrices?

   (c) Is significant responsibility and authority thriving at   ❏ ❏
      the lowest levels in the organisation?

   (d) Do you have a rigorous recruitment policy?   ❏ ❏

   (e) Do you have 'self-managed' teams?   ❏ ❏

   (f) Is your training budget more than 0.5 per cent   ❏ ❏
      of your annual turnover?

9. Customer focus

   (a) Do you have a customer focused, full-time culture   ❑   ❑
champion?

   (b) Does your organisation focus on excellent customer   ❑   ❑
service and ensuring that each customer contact with your
company is an excellent experience?

   (c) Does each internal department have a customer   ❑   ❑
status with its supplier?

10. Leadership

   (a) Are you a positive role model for the values of   ❑   ❑
the organisation?

   (b) Do you consider yourself to be a good leader?   ❑   ❑

   (c) Do your employees agree?   ❑   ❑

11. Your attitude towards your employees

   (a) Do you consider your employees as an asset   ❑   ❑
(rather than a cost)?

   (b) Is performance based on output (rather than time at   ❑   ❑
work)?

   (c) Do you operate an 'open door' policy to make   ❑   ❑
yourself available to your staff?

   (d) Do you trust your employees and do they trust you?   ❑   ❑

   (e) Do you operate a coaching/supportive culture   ❑   ❑
(rather than a blame or fear culture)?

Supplement to Figure 1.1
Benchmark Your Current Culture:
Examples to Help You Score Your Own Organisation
Against the 'Benchmark Your Current Culture' Scale

The following examples should help rate your organisation along the scale of one to nine on Figure 1.1.

Us and Them vs Equality

(Refer examples given in benchmarking chapter, plus the following.) Is ego a driver in your organisation? Does each conversation revolve around being right or wrong? Are arguments justified and then invalidated? Are decisions made on a win–lose basis rather than win–win? Do you have to try and dominate rather than be dominated? How can you expect your colleagues to share their true feelings and thoughts, let alone ideas for improvements, if they consider they will be rebuked every time they make a suggestion? If this is your company, score one.

Blame/Fear Culture vs Coaching/Supportive Culture

Refer examples given in benchmarking chapter.

No Leadership vs Competent Leaders

If your organisation has leaders that have a vision of where the company is going, the ability to convince others that this is the right way to go, and are role models in living the company values, then score nine. If there is no plan or strategy, and even if there were the rest of the workforce would not buy in to it, then score one.

No Vision vs Mission, Vision and Values

Any organisation needs to know why it exists (mission), where it is going (vision) and what values it holds as core to the way it undertakes business (values). There are good examples of each in the mission, vision and values chapter. Score nine if all three are excellent. Score one if there is none.

No Teamwork vs Cohesive Teams

If everyone is staff, or on an annualised hours scheme so that they benefit if the company does well by not having to work overtime. If there are self-managed teams, and teams with responsibility and authority well down in the organisation, then score nine. If everyone works within his or her own department without a customer–supplier relationship with their neighbouring department, or if there is in-fighting on a win–lose basis, then score one.

No Time for Continuous Improvement vs Time for Continuous Improvement is Designed into the Working Day

If the working day is structured so there is time allocated each week for continuous improvement activities, and this time is mandatory regardless of production pressures, score nine. If the time is not mandatory, score lower. If time is never available due to pressures of production or other time constraints, score one.

Focus is on Urgent Rather Than Important Tasks vs Focus is on Important Rather Than Urgent Tasks

There is a simple matrix with important on the Y-axis and urgent on the X-axis. In well-organised companies where responsibility and authority are well down in the organisation, it is relatively easy for managers to focus on important items. Where administration is a severe workload (often due to lack of trust) it is common for senior managers to have to focus on the urgent items, including answering e-mails, even though they may be of low importance. If your managers regularly focus on the important rather than urgent tasks, score nine. If the reverse applies, score one.

Working to Live vs Living to Work

There is an old saying about leaving the brain behind when you go in to work, as it will not be needed. This reflects a working to live environment where employees literally come into spend time at work in order to do what they want to do outside work. Score one if this applies. If your employees are interested, highly motivated, sometimes come in because they want to help their colleagues even though they do not get paid any more for this, score nine.

We Have Always Done It This Way vs Things Are Always Changing and Continuously Improving

If trying to make change is like pulling teeth, score one. If change is always happening to continuously improve things, then score nine.

Parent–Child Relationship vs Adult to Adult Trust

This applies to the boss–subordinate relationship. If you as boss shout at your subordinates for not doing something correctly, do not trust them, and treat them generally like a child, score one. If you trust them, give them responsibility and let them take on board accountability, score nine.

'I Am Not Sure We Can Do That' vs 'Can-Do' Attitude

Confident employees with positive attitudes and the ability to make decisions will have a can-do attitude. If so, score nine. If employees are scared to make decisions because they are not sure of the consequences, score one.

Autocratic Control at the Top vs Responsibility and Accountability Accepted and Thriving at Lowest Levels in the Organisation

Do significant decisions within pre-defined parameters get made at lowest levels without the need to refer upwards? If so, score nine. If trivial decisions have to be referred upwards, score one.

Rumours (Grapevine) Are Main Communication Channel vs Excellent, Regular, Top-Down Communication with Feedback Expected/Encouraged

If rumours are the main way people find out what is going on, score one. If you can show from an employee survey that over 80 per cent of your employees know all they want to know about what is going on in the company, score nine.

Inward Focus vs Customer Focus

If senior management places higher priority on looking at internal issues in preference to satisfying the customers' needs, score one. If the whole organisation drive is to excellence at customer service, score nine.

Appendix 2

Carrington Site Five-shift Rota

2001	Team	1	2	3	4	5	6	7	8	9	10	11	12	13	14
August															
	2	N	N					D	D	N	N				
	3			D	D	N	N					D	D	N	N
	4					D	D	N	N					D	D
	5	D	D	N	N				D	D	N	N			
	R			D	D	N	N							D	D
September	1														
	2	D	N	N					D	D	N	N			
	3			D	D	N	N						D	D	N
	4	N					D	D	N	N					D
	5		D	D	N	N					D	D	N	N	
	R		D	D	N	N							D	D	N
October	1		D	D	N	N					D	D	N	N	
	2	D	N	N					T	T	T	T	T		
	3				D	D	N	N					D	D	N
	4	T	T	T	T	T	T			D	D	N	N		
	5	N					D	D	N	N					D
November	1		D	D	N	N					D	D	N	N	
	2	N	N					D	D	N	N				
	3					T	T	T	T	T			T	T	T
	4	D	D	N	N					D	D	N	N		
	5	T	T			D	D	N	N					D	D
December	1		D	D	N	N					D	D	N	N	
	2	D	D	N	N					D	D	N	N		
	3					D	D	N	N					D	D
	4		T	T	T	T	T				T	T	T	T	T
	5	N	N					D	D	N	N				
	R														

, Days; N, Nights; T, Training; R, Relief shift; BH, Bank Holidays.

15	16	17	18	19	20	21	22	23	24	25	26	27	28	29	30	31
D	D	N	N					D	D	N	N					D
			D	D	N	N					D	D	N	N		
N	N				D	D	N	N					D	D		N
		D	D	N	N				D	D	N	N				
N	N							D	D	N	N		B			
													H			
								D	D	D	N	N				
	D	D	N	N		D		N	N					D		
N					D	D	N	N					D	D	N	
D	N	N							T	T	T	T	T			
			D	D	N	N					D	D	N	N		
N								D	D	D	N	N				
			D	D	N	N					D	D	N	N		
T	T	T	T	T			D	D	N	N					D	D
N				D	D	N	N						D	D	N	N
	D	D	N	N					D	D	N	N				
D	N	N					T	T	T	T	T			T	T	T
		T	T	T	T	T		T	T	T	T	T				
D	D	N	N					D	D	N	N					
T	T		D	D	N	N						D	D	N	N	
		D	D	N	N					D	D	N	N			
N	N					D	D	N	N					D	D	
			D	D	N	N						D	D	N	N	
		T	T	T	T	T										D
N	N					D	D	N	N					D	D	N
		D	D	N	N					D	D	N	N			
D	D	N	N					D	D	N	N					
										B	B					
										H	H					

Index